The Boy Governor

To Paul

With best

regards!

Don Fahy

To Paul
With best
wishes,
Dorothy

The Boy Governor

Stevens T. Mason and the Birth of Michigan Politics

Don Faber

The University of Michigan Press
Ann Arbor

Published in the United States of America by
The University of Michigan Press
Manufactured in the United States of America
⊚ Printed on acid-free paper

2015   2014   2013   2012   4   3   2   1

A CIP catalog record for this book is available from the British Library.

Faber, Don, 1939–
    The boy governor : Stevens T. Mason and the birth of Michigan politics / Don Faber.
    p.   cm.
    Includes bibliographical references and index.
    ISBN 978-0-472-07158-6 (cloth : alk. paper) — ISBN 978-0-472-05158-8
(pbk. : alk. paper) — ISBN 978-0-472-02878-8 (e-book)
    1. Mason, Stevens Thomson, 1811–1843.   2. Governors—Michigan—Biography.
3. Michigan—History—To 1837.   4. Michigan—Politics and government—To 1837.
5. Michigan—Politics and government—1837–1950.   I. Title.
F566.M42F33   2012
977.4′03092—dc23
    [B]   2012025919

To Jeannette, of course;
to all Michiganians who share my love for this state;
and to history teachers everywhere

Acknowledgments

Every author is indebted to the people who made his or her work easier on a book's journey to publication. I am among those standing in appreciation of the archivists, reference librarians, curators of graphic materials, and other experts who are so knowledgeable. For me, the thank-yous begin and end at home. The William L. Clements Library at the University of Michigan in my hometown is a wonderful source of scholarship; its staff, especially Brian Dunnigan and Clayton Lewis, has been extremely helpful in getting this book off the ground. The assistance provided by the Clements staff is, however, matched by another hometown bibliophile's dream, the Bentley Historical Library, also of the University of Michigan. I am especially grateful to Malgosia Myc, assistant reference archivist, for her help and timely retrieval of vital materials. I also spent considerable research time at the Ann Arbor District Library.

I wish to thank my editors at the University of Michigan Press—Ellen McCarthy, Scott Ham, and Kevin Rennells—for their guidance, patience, and willingness to answer questions. Emily Westlake and Mike Kehoe at the Press helped with promotions. And I bow in the general direction of the staff at the Library of Michigan in Lansing for its unfailing support. At the Archives of Michigan in Lansing, two people in particular need to be thanked: Julie K. Meyerle, processing archivist at the State Archives of Michigan, and Mark E. Harvey, reference archivist at the Michigan Historical Center. Julie arranged for many of the photographs used in this book.

The Burton Historical Collection at the Detroit Public Library is another treasure trove for scholars of Stevens T. Mason and early Michigan history. Dawn Eurich, archivist, was most helpful to me, and I was constantly reminded that people like her are underappreciated, probably underpaid, but most certainly not unloved. Bob Mason of the J.R. Thompson Company offered words of encouragement in writing about his illustrious forebear. I thank David G. Kowalewski, manager of the Harris Funeral Homes in the Detroit area, for allowing me some precious private time with Stevens T. Mason before the Boy Governor's reinterment. Kerry K. Chartkoff, Capitol Historian, provided some insights on Mason's governorship. Jen Luton, my always cooperative photographer, applied her keen shooter's eye to some of the photographs appearing in this book.

I stand on the shoulders of the Boy Governor's previous biographers and on the historians and authors whose writings shed light on Michigan's difficult path to statehood and her turbulent early history. If I have forgotten anyone who is due a nod of thanks, I apologize for my oversight. In the course of researching and writing a book, there are so many people who offer support, kindly words, and valuable criticism. As always, I take full responsibility for factual errors that may have crept into the text and for omissions. And the circle of thanks is complete with an acknowledgment to my wife, Jeannette, for her skills as an editor and critical thinker; she would keep my writing on track and gently but firmly point out when verbosity was taking the place of economy. All authors should have this kind of home support.

Don Faber
July 2012, Ann Arbor, Michigan

Contents

Illustrations following page 110

Prologue

He flared like a comet across the skies of Michigan in the decade 1830–40. The young man who left an enormous imprint on his adopted state was dead already at age thirty-one. As was said at his death, he was "a statesman of enlarged views."

The year 2011 marked the two-hundredth anniversary of the birth of Stevens T. Mason. Born in Virginia and raised in Kentucky, he came to full flower in Michigan, one of the last states to be formed from the Northwest Territory. Here this young man helped to transform a frontier territory to statehood, bucking the federal establishment in the process. He lived in a tumultuous environment of continuous, extremely partisan political drama. Possessing a strong character, Mason thrived in this atmosphere, and his generosity of spirit set him apart from his peers.

There is something compelling about a man so ideally suited to his times and who fits our romantic ideal of one who stands as a unique blend of youth, wisdom, and charisma. When he had right on his side, as he believed he did during the Toledo War, it took a former president of the United States, John Quincy Adams, to come out and say so. And if our romantic heroes often tend to die young, Mason was like his contemporary, the great composer Franz Schubert, who also died at thirty-one.

The "Boy Governor" (a label Stevens T. Mason did not particularly like but learned to live with) received a presidential appointment at the tender age of nineteen—a record that will never be broken. He served as acting governor before he could vote for himself. When he was elected governor at age twenty-four, he set another record, for youngest person ever to be elected chief executive of any state.

In one remarkable year, he successfully led the battle for statehood, prosecuted a war against Ohio for possession of the Toledo Strip, and helped to write Michigan's first constitution. Fired from his job by President Andrew Jackson, Mason won vindication by getting himself elected as the new state's first governor. He had the good sense and grace to accept the Upper Peninsula as compensation for the loss of Toledo, all the while exchanging 470 square miles of swamp and farmland for 9,000 square miles of a mineral-rich region that paid for itself many times over.

He was a man of outstanding vision. He saw clearly a great state university that would be "unexcelled in the land" and that would become "an ornament and honor to the West." He was influential in helping to move the University of Michigan to Ann Arbor, where the first classroom of that great institution bears the name "Mason Hall" today. He requested an appropriation for locks at Sault Ste. Marie to bypass the rapids of the St. Marys River, only to be scoffed at by such an eminent statesman as Henry Clay. Years later, the locks Mason envisioned would be instrumental in making Detroit and Michigan the "arsenal of democracy." Mason ended one of his last speeches with a call for a unified nation: "Why do we permit the value of the Union to be questioned? Cling to Michigan, but live and act for your country, your *whole* country." If he had lived to see his country torn apart in the Civil War, Mason may have recalled those words with a certain amount of satisfaction.

He championed a system of free public education, a superintendency of public instruction that was unprecedented for its time, and a state university whose governance would be shielded from political influence. He lobbied for a state geological survey and then had the wisdom to appoint Douglass Houghton as the state's first geologist. Mason was directly or marginally involved in three wars—the Black Hawk, Toledo, and Patriot—and proved to be decisive in each one, making an able administrator for one so young.

There were mistakes, of course. He was in over his head on questions of banking and negotiating loans. The schemes to lace the state with railroads and canals fostered every form of speculation, ultimately plunging Michigan into disastrous debt. It made no difference that Mason often urged caution in internal improvements; in the end, he yielded to a public opinion that demanded easy money and jobs for all. It was Mason's great misfortune to be a principal victim of the nation's first great economic depression.

Still, he has come down to us in the twenty-first century as a man whose faith in the people and concept of public service are models for aspiring politicians. He is a romantic figure from another century in Michigan history—a lightning rod, prophet, and statesman. One way we moderns pay homage to the heroes of the past is to build statues of them, and while Lewis Cass holds the place of honor in Statuary Hall in Washington, D.C., Michigan has accorded Stevens T. Mason a worthy second place in downtown Detroit.

In life, he knew disgrace and embarrassment, but today, the Boy Governor still resonates with Michiganians. Is it too much of a stretch to compare him with George Washington, in that the first president set the tone for the Republic and the office of the presidency, while Mason was a precedent setter as Michigan's first chief executive? After two hundred years, Mason has defied obscurity to retain a prominent place in his state's history. The story of his life is worth sharing with another generation of Michiganians.

1 ～ The Early Years

When it came to colonial pedigree, the Masons of Virginia stood second to none. Masons served Virginia and the new nation in a variety of ways that brought honor on the family name. By the time Stevens Thomson Mason—or Tom, as he was familiarly called—was born in 1811, the family enjoyed an immense popularity in the Old Dominion. They were, in short, of patrician stock in what was still a frontier society.

George Mason wrote the first constitution of Virginia, and it was to his colonial home of Gunston Hall on the Potomac River that liberty-minded men came to exchange radical ideas. Another Mason served as a member of the first Supreme Court of his state. In later years, Masons served in presidential cabinets and in the highest military positions. Stevens T. Mason's grandfather, for whom he had been named, died in 1803, but not before he had served as a colonel in the Continental Army during the Revolutionary War. He ably assisted General George Washington on his staff and established an atmosphere of learning and culture at Raspberry Plain, the family estate, in Loudoun County, Virginia, near Leesburg. The elder Stevens T. Mason packed a lot into his brief life of forty-two years; he also was a member of the Virginia state legislature and a U.S. senator from Virginia from 1794 until his death. A lawyer, he was a member of the Democratic-Republican Party.

So the younger Stevens T. Mason, the future governor of Michigan, was born on October 27, 1811, into a family of social prominence. The Masons counted Andrew Jackson among their family friends, and that hero of the Battle of New Orleans in the War of 1812 paid a visit to the Mason home when Tom was just a lad. As the fates would have it, Old Hickory was destined to play an outsized role in the life and career of Stevens T. Mason.

John Thomson Mason (1787–1850) was the eldest child of the elder Stevens Thomson Mason and his wife, Mary Elizabeth Armistead. Born at Raspberry Plain, John T. Mason was educated at Charlotte Hall Military Academy in St. Mary's County, Maryland, and at William and Mary College in Williamsburg, Virginia. Episcopalian by religious preference, he married Elizabeth Moir, a native of Williamsburg, on February 9, 1809, in Williamsburg and settled down to practice law.

What John T. Mason lacked in his ancestors' leadership skills and dedication to public service was counterbalanced by his imagination and improvisation. He had a nose for business and a desire to get ahead. Virginia, where he normally would have been a man of influence, couldn't contain him, however, when the West beckoned. Here money was to be made, opportunities might be cashed in, and a solid future could be staked out.

The new country, not yet forty years old, was already looking to expand. Created in 1787, the Northwest Territory, an immense tract of land northwest of the Ohio River, was attracting settlers. The Louisiana Purchase doubled the size of the nation. Native Americans, pushed off their seaboard lands and then across the Appalachians, were forced westward.

But before the West could be settled, another war with Great Britain had to be fought; on the home front, the War of 1812 was turning out disastrously. The British pillaged Washington and put the White House to flames. Only eleventh-hour victories at New Orleans by Andrew Jackson and in western Lake Erie by Oliver Hazard Perry saved the day for the Americans, with the result that the war ended in a kind of stalemate, with neither side able to claim outright victory. Still, the Americans had rallied to defend their new country, and the result was a newfound feeling of confidence.

That spirit of confidence took expression in two significant ways. First, on the Fourth of July in 1817, construction began on the Erie Canal in New York State. One of the greatest engineering projects ever undertaken, the 360-mile artificial waterway linked Albany on the Hudson River with Buffalo on Lake Erie. As one historian notes, "Americans perceived the canal as an expression of faith in the potentials of a free society, a message of hope for a great young nation on the move."[1] The Erie Canal transformed America and greatly facilitated the Industrial Revolution. Goods, supplies, produce, and building materials of every kind were transported on this highway of water. Then, of course, the people came—thousands of them from New York, Yankees from New England, and immigrants, all seeking better lives in whatever lay in those beckoning lands west of Buffalo. The human traffic on the Erie Canal would forever change Stevens T. Mason's Michigan as well, increasing the territory's numbers in such a short period as to accelerate the timetable for statehood.

The second great expression of confidence was President James Monroe's establishment of the Monroe Doctrine. More of a paper pronouncement than anything else, it was probably regarded in European capitals as an outstanding example of American bravado. But Monroe's articulation of a policy in 1823, declaring the Americas off-limits to European interference, showed the post-Napoleonic world that the United States had some swagger, even if it lacked the gunboats to back it up. Manifest Destiny would soon follow, and the westward-looking country never glanced back.

John Thomson Mason was twenty-five years old in 1812, when he decided his fortunes lay in the West. Always a restless soul, Mason moved his wife, Elizabeth, his two-and-a-half-year-old daughter, Mary, and his infant son, Stevens Thomson, to Lexington, Kentucky, a four-hundred-mile trip that took seven weeks. Social relationships were begun with the leading families of the region. With a large home library and a strong inclination to make his way in the world, it wasn't long before Mason made enough money to buy a large estate, which he named Serenity Hall.

But by 1819, serenity for John T. Mason and his growing family was proving elusive. Although he practiced law with some success, his business ventures, apparently of the speculative nature, turned sour. Entries in old family records fail to indicate just why John T. Mason thought he could make still more money with his investments. It wasn't long before he lost most of the family fortune. Still holding his political connections, however, he accepted an appointment by President Monroe as a U.S. marshal.

It is possible that far-off Michigan imprinted itself on Stevens T. Mason at an early age. In Lexington, he may have witnessed the funeral processions of the brave Kentuckians who were killed in the River Raisin Massacre in Frenchtown (now Monroe), Michigan, in the winter of 1813. He may have associated the name Michigan with violent death in a wilderness where there existed only frontier settlements. During the War of 1812, the state he would eventually serve as its first elected governor was a hardship post as far as the territorial capital of Detroit was concerned.

In October 1815, Stevens T. Mason gained a sister, Emily Virginia, who would live into her nineties and establish the closest of relationships with "Thomson." Emily would still be alive in 1905, when Governor Mason's remains were reinterred in Detroit on the site of the territorial capitol. In 1818, Catherine joined the family, followed a year later by yet another daughter, Laura.

Young Tom Mason seems to have been an intellectually curious child, perhaps even precocious. A family friend and educator who took Tom under his wing schooled him in rote learning, but as noted by biographer Kent Sagendorph, parroting what the teacher demanded to hear did the pupil no service: "All his life this habit clung to him and caused him endless trouble. His mind would grapple with a situation by deciding what sort of an answer the teacher wanted and blithely skip to it across a yawning chasm of intermediate details."[2]

In 1819, the occasion of a visit to Lexington by President Monroe, accompanied by Senator Andrew Jackson, made a great impression on the seven-year-old Mason. The Hero of New Orleans, as Jackson was still being called, paid a visit to Serenity Hall, where the future president was quite taken with the boy's powers of argument. For his part, young Tom Mason formed an attachment to the charismatic Jackson resembling that of son to father. In later years, Jackson would remember this chance encounter with John T. Mason's eldest boy.

John Thomson Mason's business schemes caught up with him in 1819. Unscrupulous friends wiped him out in a mining venture; a distillery in which he invested didn't pay off. He carelessly signed off on a short-term note for a large amount of money, and when the cosigner defaulted, Mason was stuck. He was forced to sell Serenity Hall and moved the family a short distance away to Mount Sterling. His Lexington properties lost value, forcing him to return to the practice of law, albeit with fewer clients. By 1827, barely earning enough to keep his family in food and clothing, he was practically penniless. Kentucky didn't seem so hospitable after all. Virginia might have taken him back as a prodigal son, but John T. Mason had too much pride to admit failure back home. He was on the frontier to stay.

In 1827, nearly sixteen, Stevens T. Mason enrolled at Lexington's Transylvania University, the oldest educational institution west of the Alleghenies. There he studied classical languages and philosophy. But as Patricia Baker reports, the family's hard times continued: "The whole family was disrupted by John's financial disasters, particularly so, young Stevens T. Because of his father's financial plight, he was forced to quit his studies at Transylvania, trading his books for a grocer's apron."[3] Tom got a job at a grocery store in Mount Sterling, where he opened up each morning, stocked goods, and waited on customers. It must have been quite a comedown for Tom Mason—born of a well-bred family and possessed of greater than average intellect—to take orders from the locals and to bear up under the strain of manual labor. In his body of writings, Mason never makes mention of his days as a stock clerk.

At sixteen, Mason was tall—about six feet—and slender. He carried himself well and was conscious of himself as a heartthrob to the girls. Not given to slouching, he walked proudly, with a style that suggested culture and good breeding. He dressed the part; later portraits show tight-fitting broadcloth trousers and a high silk hat. With a strong chin and an aristocratic bearing, he would have stood out in any crowd. We have a description of his persona from a Major W. C. Ransom: "He was tall and handsome. His eyes, bright and beaming with intelligence, seemed to mirror the restless spirit that animated his being. Dark, wavy hair fell in rich clusters over his intellectual forehead, while his commanding presence and polished manners at once challenged the admiration of those who were so fortunate as to have his acquaintance."[4]

Mason was versed in the politics of the day and was, of course, well read. Biographer Lawton Hemans reports, "His father had collected a choice and for that day a moderately extensive library of both legal and general literature, and from the latter both Tom and his sister read with keen avidity."[5] Sagendorph confidently says, "This experience left him with a profound reverence for universal free education."[6] So when he became governor, a model school system became one of his primary goals.

He found Transylvania much to his liking. Scholarship at the small college was taken seriously, and Tom Mason felt at home in the classes he attended. He worked hard, with little time left over for frivolity; study came first, because there was no assurance he would be in college long. Letters from his father, when they were forthcoming, didn't give any cause for hope that family finances were improving.

In 1828, Andrew Jackson was elected to the presidency. It was a watershed election by any standard, as the young nation was wrenched from the familiar meritocracy of the East to a representative democracy of the people. Whatever his faults, and some were considerable, Jackson was a man of the people. His was a magnetic personality, capable of the strongest emotions, and his presidency was marked by bitter political conflicts. But he was a strong supporter of the Union, and he promised to die, if need be, to preserve a strong central government. He opposed the "monopolistic" Bank of the United States, squelched the nullification dispute led by John C. Calhoun of South Carolina, and increased presidential powers. "The America of Andrew Jackson," writes Jon Meacham, "was a country that professed a love of democracy but was willing to live with inequality, that aimed for social justice but was prone to racism and intolerance, that believed itself one nation but was narrowly divided and fought close elections, and that occasionally acted arrogantly toward other countries while craving respect from them at the same time."[7] These contradictions were often exacerbated by Jackson's own divide-and-conquer policies.

His election led former president John Quincy Adams to grump that the Republic's days were numbered, or words to that effect. Adams had won the presidency in a highly disputed election in 1825; he served one term before being defeated by Jackson. At Old Hickory's inaugural on the fourth of March 1829, Adams absented himself from any part in the activities. The two would maintain an icy relationship throughout their public lives.

The Jackson White House quickly let it be known that things would be different for appointed officeholders accustomed to the perks of high office. People such as Henry Clay of Kentucky viewed the replacement of federal officials as dangerous to the future of the country, whereas Jackson saw it as his right and privilege to replace the standing guard. As Meacham explains,

> That a president would have wide power to reward loyalists with offices, both to thank them for their steadfastness and to ensure that he had a cadre of people at hand who would presumably execute his policies with energy and enthusiasm, is now a given, but Jackson was the first president to remake the federal establishment on such a large scale. Jackson's vision was elementary yet expansive in the context of the early Republic. He wanted a political culture in which a majority of voters chose a president, and a president chose his administration.[8]

Into this milieu stepped John T. Mason of Kentucky, desirous of recouping his flagging family fortunes. His family was growing, and he wanted to leave behind those associations that reminded him of his failures. These reasons and perhaps others equally as compelling resulted in Mason's name being thrown into the spoils system of politics. He knew President Jackson and, just as important, he had friends who knew the president. When Jackson began cleaning house in Washington, the door swung wide open for those office seekers who espoused Jackson's policies.

William T. Barry, a former congressman from Kentucky and friend of the Mason family, had accepted an appointment to Jackson's cabinet as postmaster general. It may have been Barry who went to bat for John T. Mason and who interceded with Jackson. According to Sagendorph, "Barry began dickering for a job for John T. Mason in June, 1829, and kept at it until the following spring."[9] Hemans says that John T. "either sought or had tendered to him" a political job at that time.[10] It must have come as a great relief to Mason to see his political connections pay off.

Still, the real political plums had already been passed out, and Mason would have to do with a post of secondary importance. Was that acceptable to a Mason of Virginia who harbored grandiose plans of conquering the American West? A Whig, James Witherell of Detroit, held the post of secretary of the Michigan Territory, and as a Whig, he was destined for removal. The job paid twelve hundred dollars a year, in addition to what the individual who took it could earn on his own. That was the plus side; the downside was that the job was in a frontier town, and the territory was ruled by the formidable Lewis Cass, longtime governor and distinguished veteran of the War of 1812.

The duties of territorial secretary were administrative in nature. The secretary served as acting governor in the absence of the governor—a fact that was to have great bearing on Stevens T. Mason's meteoric rise. Cass was frequently out of the office, exploring the interior of Michigan and on lengthy trips of one kind or another. In those cases, his official duties devolved on the secretary.

John T. Mason must have sensed early on that he was swimming in deep waters if he took the Michigan job. To begin with, the Michigan Territory was vast: by the 1830s, it stretched from the Detroit River to the Missouri River, taking in all or part of what today comprises Wisconsin, Iowa, Minnesota, and the Dakotas. The territory embraced numerous tribes of indigenous Americans, and what did John T. Mason know of Indian treaties and Indian warfare? He had no knowledge whatsoever of Detroit and Whig politics. And then there were the lakes—the Great Lakes—awesome repositories of freshwater that promised to become inland waterways of great commerce. Geography on such as scale was not in Mason's scope of experience.

Governance in the Michigan Territory was under the terms of the old Northwest Ordinance of 1787, which prepared new sections of the country for statehood by having them serve first as territories, until such time as they had the requisite population for statehood. Territorial government consisted of a governor appointed by the president of the United States with the consent of Congress, a territorial council (legislative) chosen by vote of the people, and judges appointed by the president. Michigan was to be one of five states created out of the Northwest Territory, the others being Ohio, Indiana, Illinois, and Wisconsin. Ohio (in 1803), Indiana (in 1816), and Illinois (in 1818) had already obtained statehood; by the time John T. Mason arrived, Michigan would soon be knocking on the door for admission.

The prospect of moving to Michigan must have been appealing to young Tom Mason. Here was the president himself, his hero, placing great confidence in his father. For him, it was another echo of the War of 1812, when so many Kentuckians from homes in Lexington had marched north to Michigan, transfixing him for hours with their tales of exploits. The opportunity to put an interrupted education and his days as a grocery clerk behind him and to take up a new life on the frontier would have seemed challenging and attractive. For all Stevens T. Mason knew, Detroit held hope for making his way in the world. The election of 1828 succeeded in steeping young Mason in national politics, and the favor shown to his father marked the beginning of his debt to Andrew Jackson.

John T. Mason accepted his appointment on May 20, 1830. Farewells were said in Kentucky. Mason senior and his son, for whom he had obtained traveling expenses, first went to Washington to receive official orders. Then the two began their slow trip west by way of Philadelphia and New York, where Tom availed himself of some fancy New York tailoring. From New York, the Masons journeyed on the Hudson River to Albany, thence on the Erie Canal to Buffalo, and then by steamer to Detroit. It wasn't the most direct route from Lexington, to be sure, but the alternative was a long slog by horseback through swamp and unfamiliar territory. The rest of the family would follow after the men had secured housing in Detroit.

On July 18, 1830, the two Masons first laid eyes on Detroit. Old by American standards (it was founded in 1701), it was still not much more than a village. Its French beginnings were strongly evident in the place-names and ribbon farms extending inward from the Detroit River, but the habitants were of decidedly humble origin. The term "culture shock" could have been invented for what the Masons experienced when they debarked from the steamer at Detroit.

The Masons must have been an eye-opener to the locals, too. It was clear that John T. Mason, once he assumed his duties, was a minnow swimming among sharks. And Baker writes of Stevens T. that "young Tom was a shock to Detroit. He fancied himself as a bit polished, a cosmopolite who happened to be stranded in a backwoods village. He drew gaping stares as he sallied forth to explore the town, arrayed in his skin-tight black broadcloth trousers and flowing coat with cane in hand."[11] In a short time, however, Tom grew to like the excitement of living in Detroit with its raucous politics and unsophisticated people, and the people in turn took a shine to the tall young man who seemed so eager to learn.

As bad luck would have it, Lewis Cass was not on hand to greet his subordinate on arrival. In his absence, Mason was acting governor, charged with duties he had never exercised and confronting problems he didn't understand. To make matters worse, the news of Mason's appointment was unfavorably received in Michigan, where it was believed by many that the number two post should be held by a native son rather than an outsider. If they had only known how little Mason coveted the job, their voices of opposition would have been even louder. The Whigs were especially indignant.

The Whigs were an interesting political phenomenon. British in origin, the term by which they were called referred to those opposed to monarchy. In the United States of the 1830s, "King Andy," as President Jackson was derisively called, was vigorously opposed by homegrown Whigs, who were led by Clay of Kentucky. Of Jackson, Clay said that only an American Whig party can rescue the nation from "a Chief Magistrate who is endeavoring to concentrate in his own person the whole powers of government."[12] The Whigs tended to be men of property, conservative in outlook and distrustful of the masses, especially concerning voting rights.

In Michigan, the Whig Party coalesced around groups opposed to the policies of Jackson. At the time of the Masons' arrival, the party was led by William Woodbridge, the go-to man in Detroit politics. He was already fifty years old in 1830, but he looked much older. Born in Norwich, Connecticut, Woodbridge took up law and was admitted to the bar in 1805. He moved to Ohio and was elected to the general assembly of that state before accepting an appointment by President James Madison to the secretaryship of the Michigan Territory. In 1819, he was delegate to Congress from the territory; the following year, he resigned to take up the secretaryship again, serving in that capacity until 1828. Before he retired from public life in 1847, he would serve Michigan as chief justice of the territory, delegate to the state's first constitutional convention, governor, and U.S. senator.

As the capital of the Michigan Territory, Detroit was a Whig fiefdom presided over by Woodbridge. Mason's appointment as a Democrat by the arch-enemy himself, Jackson, was calculated to outrage the Whigs; knowing this,

Jackson felt confident that with the respected Democrat Lewis Cass still in Detroit as governor, the president's new appointee would be able to ride out any storm while learning the ropes from Cass. It didn't work out that way. When Cass returned to Detroit after the Masons' arrival, he didn't want to hear details of how Woodbridge was setting traps for Mason, outmaneuvering him at every turn. Cass had more important affairs with which to occupy himself than listening to John T. Mason's excuses for his inadequacies as acting governor. When Cass's ample figure was in the governor's chair and the forty-eight-year-old former general was barking out orders, it was Woodbridge's tendency to pull in his horns and defer to the man who was revered by Michigan citizens. Cass was already regarded as a statesman, whereas Woodbridge would always be a politician, and John T. Mason would simply be a fish out of water. Mason proved to be no match for Detroit's politicians, its frontier politics, or the intrigues that always accompany grasps for power.

Young Tom Mason would often accompany his father on trips to the capitol from their home on Jefferson Avenue. He was a constant companion, doing menial tasks, asking questions, observing the comings and goings of the territory's politicians, and, in short notice, coming to the attention of Cass. The imperious Cass took a liking to Stevens T. Mason, and it was not long before the young man was performing jobs for Cass that required writing skills, thus relieving his father of yet another responsibility he didn't relish.

Not much is known of Cass's relationship with his secretary. Cass was everything John T. Mason was not, which is to say knowledgeable, a commanding presence, intimidating, and authoritarian. Cass was a man of the outdoors, blunt and direct. For him, a desk job in the capitol building was abhorrent; paperwork was a damned nuisance when there were lands to be surveyed and frontiers to be explored. If he developed any kind of rapport with Mason, the record is silent about it. More than likely, Mason did his best to stay out of Cass's line of sight.

It seems likely that Tom Mason, with his sharp powers of observation and youth's facility for perceiving the motives of his elders, protected his father from the anti-Jackson forces. When Tom came to Cass's notice, it was as a young man aware of what was going on and having the social graces to be comfortable with influential people. He was making his way in Detroit and gaining a reputation as one not to be trifled with, if anyone still thought this Kentucky dandy was a pushover. Tom Mason, as we shall see, could be a pugilist and didn't need his father or anyone else to fight his battles. Moreover, he was learning public administration and hands-on political science in the rough-and-tumble of Detroit. He made up his mind to study law.

When he wasn't helping his father or shadowing Cass, Tom Mason enjoyed walking the streets and drawing attention as an eligible bachelor. There is, in the letters of John T. Mason, a reference to his son's appearance among the girls: "What Thomson had written to you all I know not, but he was very shy of the girls in Detroit and would rarely be persuaded to go into company, but I suppose he learnt something on the subject."[13] Tom's sister, Emily, at one time said that "he had little time and never much inclination for affairs of the heart, though so handsome, gay and amiable as to be much admired by the ladies."[14] We know for a certainty that Stevens T. Mason was active in the Detroit social scene, that he caroused with his friends and partook wholeheartedly of the frontier town's pleasures, without any scandal whatsoever attaching to his name or character. One of Mason's biographers would characterize him in this way:

> There were occasions when he put aside his books and sauntered downtown, dropping in at various clubs and taprooms in his easily recognized gleaming silk hat and ruffled opera cloak. He acquired a wide repute throughout Detroit as a *bon vivant* and drawing-room decoration. He was polished and suave; he had a vocabulary richly embellished with long words that sounded dignified and complimentary; he usually looked bored and hard to amuse. Perhaps for that very reason, hostesses eagerly sought him out and surrounded him with people.[15]

It would be nice to say that John T. Mason grew into the job of secretary, but it was his son who flourished as the de facto second in command. Detroit and the Michigan Territory were a dead end for a man not accustomed to routine and taking orders from Cass, and a salary of twelve hundred dollars a year was pocket change when fortunes were to be made in the West. The action was in Texas and on the border with Mexico. From his father, John T. had inherited certain land claims in Texas. So in mid-1831, after a year in Detroit, Mason submitted his resignation as secretary. As for his wife and family, he thought maybe Stevens T. could get a job and look after them. He was hoping his son would succeed him.

John T.'s timing was impeccable. Cass was about to resign as governor to become secretary of war in Jackson's cabinet. Affairs in the West were heat-ing up, and Jackson was eager to acquire Texas as another state in the Union and was using diplomatic pressure, both subtle and overt, to achieve that end. When family friend Mason arrived in Washington in June 1831, he had his son with him. While Mason officially came to resign as secretary, he was, in fact, seeking another presidential favor. For his part, Jackson was looking to kill two birds with one stone.

Since John T. Mason wanted to go to Texas anyway, Jackson assigned him as a secret agent to deal with Mexico. But what was the president to do about his replacement in the Michigan Territory? And who would succeed Cass? At his audience with the president, Tom Mason had again impressed Jackson as a young man of great promise and decided administrative ability. Why not, reasoned Jackson, appoint the son to replace his father and rile the opposition Whigs at the same time? On July 12, 1831, Jackson officially appointed Stevens T. Mason as secretary of the Michigan Territory, with orders to keep the White House informed of all territorial goings-on. The new appointee was nineteen years old.

Mason's reaction to this great honor must have been mixed. Clearly, he was pleased and flattered and perhaps a little surprised that Jackson would take such a chance on him. If, for some reason, he didn't work out in the job, it was still good experience, and having the president as a friend meant there might be another reward later, when more maturity was gained. But even more on Tom Mason's mind was the imminent departure of his father and his own increase in family responsibilities. Who would look after his mother and the girls? John T. waved it all off—he'd be gone only a year or so.

When he arrived back in Detroit on July 24 after a brief stop in New York for some new clothes, Mason learned that the news was not yet made public. The next day, Cass announced Mason's appointment, unrolled his official commission affixed with the territory's great seal, and administered the oath of office in the capitol. Mason accepted his charge with an "I do" and received Cass's congratulations. With that, Cass left the territory in Mason's hands, as the president had not yet appointed a successor to Cass.

Mason's appointment astonished the territory. The anti-Jackson forces railed against the president's poor judgment in naming one so young to so important a post. When Mason was sworn in, many of the leading citizens of Detroit were lining up in violent opposition. Two days earlier, a public meeting was held to express the sentiments of the people of Michigan on this outrage perpetrated by Jackson. In his history of the region, Silas Farmer reports, "A committee of four, consisting of Andrew Mack, Shubael Conant, Oliver New-berry and John E. Schwartz, was appointed to report the facts. On July 25, they reported that the President was aware of his being under twenty-one years of age. At a meeting of July 26, many citizens vigorously remonstrated. On July 28, Mr. Mason responded in a manner that did credit to his ability, coolness and general good sense."[16]

In seeking to disarm his critics, Mason went straight to the top. In a letter to President Jackson, Mason said that "certain persons had gotten up an excitement, which will result in a remonstrance against my continuance in office . . . In this state of things I have been beset with a sort of inquisitorial scrutiny, and finding nothing to rest upon but the fact of my minority, I have been asked to relinquish my office." He went on to thank Jackson for the confidence that was placed in him and expressed "a confidence in maintaining myself against all opposition, if sustained by you, of which I have a perfect assurance."[17] All of the clamor, he said, was designed to strike at Jackson, not someone "so unimportant as myself. No one has dared to impeach my moral character."[18] A few days later, Mason again wrote Jackson to say, "I feel a confidence in being ultimately sustained by the good sense and correct sentiments of the community, and I am assured a large fraction of the people are ready if called on to sign a petition in my favor. I shall be enabled at a proper time to show you that my appointment is not of that obnoxious character which violent partisans represent."[19]

Mason showed mature judgment in neutralizing his opponents. Yes, he was only nineteen, but the president knew that fact when he made his appointment. There were many in the territory who had higher qualifications, conceded Mason, but he said he wouldn't have any difficulty seeking the advice of wiser and abler men. Indeed, there was more than one occasion on which he asked important men of the territory for their opinions and advice. He eased into office with a cautious approach to his duties that won him respect for his restraint.

But now, in the absence of his father (recently departed for Mexico), Mason wanted assurance from Jackson that he wouldn't be abandoned to "the loud brawlers" who were demanding his scalp. His nomination as secretary was yet to be acted on by the U.S. Senate, and it was to this body that Mason directed his attention in a letter noteworthy for its insight and tone of deference.

Forewarned, that an attempt will be made to prejudice me in your estimation, I consider it due myself that you be apprised . . . of the true estimate in which

I am held by the best portion of society in this Territory. Should it be your pleasure to terminate sooner the little brief authority with which I am clothed no one will submit more calmly than myself under your decision. I indulge a hope, however, and I believe a just expectation, that where no crime has been committed, no condemnation will ensue; and that the crime of being a young man will be assuaged by the recollection that once you were young, and must now feel how slender would have been your advancement in life without the protection and support of older men.[20]

Mason's candor played well with the public. The youth's apparent willingness to tap the wisdom of older men in his decision making was the proper note to sound. The musical chairs continued with the appointment of George Bryan Porter of Lancaster, Pennsylvania, as Cass's successor. Porter was tardy in arriving at Detroit that summer, and when he did show up, it was to find a young stripling as acting governor. It requires no stretch of the imagination to conclude that Porter was serving out of a sense of duty and loyalty to his benefactor, as demonstrated by his reluctance to reach his new posting. As time would prove, Porter was often absent from the territory during the next three years, which was his loss and Stevens T. Mason's gain. In one of the great ironies of early Michigan, the absentee governor briefly returned to Detroit in July 1834 only to die in the cholera epidemic of that year. By that time, Tom Mason had gained considerable experience.

Porter's belated arrival didn't seem to bother Mason. An outsider himself, Mason was ingratiating himself with the citizens of Detroit. The newspapers were slowly coming around to his corner. Porter was viewed as yet another outsider, and when he showed little interest in staying long enough to manage territorial affairs, Mason came to be regarded as an able stand-in. The record shows that already by August of 1831, appointments in the militia of the territory were being made by Stevens T. Mason, "Secretary of the Territory and at present Acting Governor." This is either the first reference or among the first references to Mason as man in charge. In the fourth quarter of 1831, Mason was signing accounts with the United States as "Stevens T. Mason, Secretary of the Territory of Michigan and aforesaid Acting Governor thereof."[21] He was now twenty years old.

The Senate took its time with Mason's confirmation proceedings. Early in 1832, territorial delegate Austin E. Wing wrote to William Woodbridge, "The nomination of S. T. Mason has been some time before the Senate, some think he will be confirmed, others that he will not, my own impression is that he will be confirmed."[22] Not until May 22, 1832, was John Norvell, postmaster of Detroit and a friend of Mason, able to write from Washington that Mason's confirmation "is not certain but probable." Two days later, he reported that the confirmation was favorably reported on by the Judiciary Committee. On June 21, Wing informed Mason that the Senate had confirmed his appointment. The man in whom President Jackson "reposed a special trust and confidence in integrity, diligence and ability" was poised to write his name on Michigan history in large letters.

2 ~ The Michigan Frontier

The frontier settlement first seen by Stevens T. Mason in 1830 was the seat of government of the Michigan Territory. Michigan achieved territorial status under legislation signed by President Thomas Jefferson on January 11, 1805. Detroit was founded in 1701 by Antoine de la Mothe Cadillac, a French explorer and colonial administrator. Much farther to the north, Sault Ste. Marie was an even older city, the area around the falls of the St. Marys River having been visited by French explorers and missionaries. Of course, several tribes of indigenous Americans, including the Ojibway (Chippewa), Potawatomie, and Ottawa, long predated the Europeans.

The French era in Michigan essentially ended in 1759, when General Louis Montcalm was defeated by British general James Wolfe on the Plains of Abraham in Quebec. In the next year, the French formally surrendered Detroit, ending roughly 150 years of French rule in Michigan. The British, in turn, were ousted by the victorious Americans in the Revolutionary War, although the British were slow to take their departure. The lucrative fur trade and the strategic location of their forts were highly prized.

Michigan was destined to be one of the "not less than three nor more than five" states to be created out of the Northwest Territory, under the Ordinance of 1787. By the time Stevens T. Mason was born, the first state (Ohio) had been created out of this region. Detroit was designated the capital of the Michigan Territory because it was where most of the people lived. Its French-speaking population was, for the most part, poor and apathetic about both schooling and the democratic institutions later settlers would so enthusiastically embrace.

The French settlers seemed to have acquired the morals and deportment of the Indians, writes James Z. Schwartz, not intending it as a compliment. The

Yankees who streamed into Michigan in the 1820s were horrified at what they found.

> The borrowing of Indian customs had been common among Michigan's French habitants, many of whom seemed to be more barbarous than civilized. The French dressed like Indians, hunted like Indians, spoke the Indian language and in some cases had even married Indians and produced mixed-race children.
>
> Yankees condemned this hybridization, asserting that the blurring of racial and cultural boundaries had transformed even the purebred French into savages. Indeed, New Englanders expressed alarm that their French neighbors seemed to have more in common with Indians than with their fellow whites. In other ways as well, the French seemed to have taken on Indian traits and blurred the boundary between civilization and savagery. Anglo settlers condemned the French for being nearly as economically backward as were the Indians. Rather than creating a vibrant agricultural economy, the French, like Indians, seemed content to earn their living from the fur trade. The French refused to adopt modern farming techniques and relied instead on antiquated methods developed by their ancestors.[1]

Another writer is equally blunt: "Yankee attitudes toward the French *habitants* were more straightforwardly negative than those toward Native Americans and this for several reasons. While the Indians came by their lack of civilization naturally, the French were ostensibly civilized Europeans who had allowed themselves to fall into a state of barbarism and thus culpable for their failings."[2]

Around the time of the great fire of 1805, Detroit may have had seven hundred inhabitants. The city was a garrison town, under first the British and then the Americans, which gave it considerable importance in the far-off federal capital. Ironically, it was a French priest, Father Gabriel Richard, who did much to civilize the frontier post, first in education and later with a printing press: "In 1806, he opened a school for girls. The next year, he established a school at Springwells, three miles south of town, primarily for Native American children. By 1808, he reported that he had eight schools operating in the area and petitioned for a school building. Then he went east and brought back an organ, a piano, a printing press, and a printer to publish bilingual textbooks of his own selection."[3] Richard published the territory's first newspaper and, along with the Reverend John Monteith and Judge Augustus Woodward, was among the founders of the University of Michigan.

The two clerics and Woodward were farsighted. They put purpose into the noble language of the Northwest Ordinance that read, "Religion, morality and knowledge being necessary to good government and the happiness of mankind, schools and the means of education shall forever be encouraged." These three men "had energized the Jeffersonian ideal of education for all to the extent of the individual's capacity, for without an educated citizenry, democracy would fumble and fail. Since society benefited, education was logically a responsibility of the territory or state to be exercised through its taxing power."[4]

It was Judge Woodward, a man of classical bent, who devised a plan for a comprehensive state educational system that included a university-level institution. (Mason, as governor, borrowed freely from Woodward). The Catholepistemiad, unpronounceable to Governor Lewis Cass, called for centralized control under thirteen didactors, each skilled in a field of knowledge. The Catholepistemiad didn't catch on—in fact, it was generally laughed at—but it contained the seeds of something valuable. Years later, the responsibility for schools was placed in a central body, as Michigan was the first state to call for a superintendent of public instruction. The University of Michigan dates its founding to 1817 and to the Catholepistemiad, although the school didn't open its doors to students in Ann Arbor until much later.

As envisioned by the Northwest Ordinance, "the first government that was uniquely Michigan's consisted of an assembly that, in effect, combined the executive, legislative and judicial powers of government in one unit."[5] The territorial government that Stevens T. Mason would eventually lead was first headed by William Hull of Massachusetts, a man whose fall from grace was complete after he surrendered Detroit in the War of 1812 and was sentenced to death. Michigan historian Willis Dunbar describes Hull as "a man of considerable ability" who "was handicapped in his new job by his total lack of acquaintance with frontier life and problems."[6] How prescient that comment is, given later appointees to the job who would exactly fit that description. President Jefferson also appointed Stanley Griswold of New Hampshire as secretary; three men—Frederick Bates of Detroit, Augustus Woodward of Washington, D.C., and Samuel Huntington of Ohio—were named judges.

As a territory and potential state, Michigan was on a three-step path. First, it would be governed as a territory whose officials served at the pleasure of the president and Congress. Second, as soon as the territory should number a population of five thousand free adult males, it would have both the right to elect a legislative assembly (with the power to make laws) and the right to appoint a delegate to Congress. Finally, when the total population reached sixty thousand, the language of the Northwest Ordinance said, "such state shall be admitted, by its delegates, into the Congress of the United States, on an equal footing with the original states in all respects whatever, and shall be at liberty to form a permanent constitution and state government." Stevens T. Mason would have some fun with that provision, when he tried to bull Michigan into statehood as a matter of right, despite the lack of congressional authorization. It is always well to remember that Congress is a political body and not a legal body, that its considerations will follow the ballot box and not legal precedents, and that he who has the votes trumps him who may have right on his side. Mason would vigorously maintain he had right on his side in the 1830s.

If Hull proved to be the wrong man for the times, the choice of Lewis Cass as his successor was inspired. Michigan's most highly regarded statesman would carve out a lengthy career in public service that stretched from the War of 1812 to the Civil War. It is worth iterating the complete inscription that accompanies Cass in Statuary Hall.

> General Lewis Cass, 1782–1866, dedicated to the memory of the foremost of Michigan's pioneers. More than any other man he shaped the development of Michigan and the whole Northwest Territory. He negotiated twenty-two Indian treaties, supervised the movement of numerous tribes to the hinterlands west of the Mississippi, conducted important exploration tours into the wilderness to discover and measure its resources, enforced the edicts of a young nation on one of its most difficult frontiers. As territorial governor, he set up geographic boundaries throughout the state, created judicial districts, organized many of the counties of the state. He served his country in the War of 1812, attaining high rank. After 18 years as Michigan territorial governor he served in two presidential cabinets, 12 years in the U.S. Senate. Appointed minister to France, he published in Paris his celebrated "Inquiry into the Right of Search" which made maritime history. He was nominated for President in 1848. Often ranked first in the second generation of American statesmen— which included Clay, Webster, Calhoun—he is Michigan's permanent representative in the Nation's Hall of Fame.

Grateful Michiganians might add to this that Cass was also a founder of the Historical Society of Michigan in 1828.

A native of Exeter, New Hampshire, Cass was among the restless Yankees lured to the dazzling prospects of the Great West. He came to Ohio, settled down to study law, and was elected to the Ohio House of Representatives at the youthful age of twenty-four. His support for President James Madison got him an appointment as U.S. marshal for the district of Ohio. A military career followed, and Cass was present, as a colonel of the Third Ohio Infantry, when General Hull surrendered Detroit without a shot being fired. Cass then rode his military reputation to a life of politics in Michigan and service to his nation.

After the War of 1812, federal surveyors were commissioned to survey the interior of Michigan and to offer two million acres as a bounty for those who had fought in the war. That looked promising for Michigan's development. But there was a fly in the ointment: "Veterans of the war who had served in the Northwest often reported that Michigan was good for Indians and disease and not much else."[7] Michigan got some bad press back east just when it was look-ing to welcome new settlers. Worse was to come.

Under an official survey ordered by U.S. surveyor General Edward Tiffin, Michigan came off as inhospitable and uninhabitable. In their 1817 report, the Tiffin commissioners concluded that they could not find one tillable acre in the whole territory. Bogs, mosquitoes, swamps, worthless soil, dangerous critters—if you wanted them, Michigan had them. As a result of the Tiffin report, President James Madison shifted the focus away from Michigan as far as those military bounty lands were concerned, and settlement drifted elsewhere, though not for long.

Cass was angered by the Tiffin report and said that Michigan had been badly misrepresented. He quickly arranged for a resurvey of Michigan public lands, with an eye toward undoing the damage left by Tiffin. In 1820, Cass led a major expedition from Detroit to what is now Minnesota to acquire valuable knowledge about the Indians and natural resources. He would use this valu-able experience to promote settlement in Michigan among westward-moving pioneers. But the wily Cass also had a long-range plan: "He did not want the Michigan Territory populated with war veterans and land speculators. Hoping to attract a better class of settlers, he rose to Michigan's defense in criticizing the Tiffin report, but he pulled his punches to some extent. He would take his time promoting Michigan in eastern circles."[8] Until conditions changed, geography conspired against Michigan's hoped-for growth. The Black Swamp, along the territory's border with Ohio, gave substance to reports about noxious fevers and was a formidable obstacle to overland routes. The great lakes that gave Michigan its unique shape were not yet easy of passage for prospective settlers bent on a water route, although the steamboat would soon change that. And, of course, rumors of hostile Indians still played a part in discouraging settlers.

But the Black Swamp would eventually be drained, and the arrival of steamships on Lake Erie in the 1820s worked to Michigan's great gain. Cass's friendly relations with the Indians negated loose talk of nighttime raids and scalping parties. In addition, "the construction, with federal financial assistance, of roads north from the Ohio border to Detroit and west of that city to Fort Dearborn (Chicago), and the opening of land offices in Detroit and Monroe, combined to make Michigan a more attractive place."[9]

The biggest boon to Michigan's development was the Erie Canal. With its completion in 1825, the trickle of settlers became a flood tide. "The advantages of the territory are every day more and more known and appreciated," Cass confidently told the Territorial Council on June 7, 1824, "and the fertility of our soil, and its adaption to the stable agricultural products of the middle states, promise rich rewards to our citizens. Our climate is highly favorable to hardy and vigorous exertion."[10] Already by 1825, the Tiffin report was just another forgotten federal study gathering dust, and "Michigan fever" was taking hold of easterners and others who were seeking to improve their lot. In 1820, Michigan had 8,896 people; ten years later, the population had jumped to nearly 32,000 inhabitants.

In the meantime, growth was occurring rapidly in the southern part of the Northwest Territory. Ohio entered the Union, albeit with its stated northern border not approved by Congress. When Indiana and Illinois became states, both encroached on the southern boundary of Michigan as Michigan defined it, yet nothing was done in the territory about this landgrab. Efforts against it would not have mattered, because Congress readily approved statehood for Indiana and Illinois, and neither state was prepared to give up land claims without a fight where it counted most, that is, in Congress itself.

Cass now stepped up his public relations campaign for Michigan with influential friends back east. A popular song of the day urged "Yankee farmers who'd like to change your lot" to come settle in Michigania, as it was called. Cass told all who would listen of the opportunities in Michigan, how the soil would reward good husbandry and of how that climate was so conducive to honest labor. "To him more than to any other man," said John D. Pierce, father of the Michigan school system, "is the State indebted for its subsequent rapid settlement."[11]

Westward they came, thousands of New Englanders and New York state farmers, on the great waterway that touched the Hudson River at Albany and extended to Buffalo on Lake Erie. These pioneers had varied cultural backgrounds, liberal ideas on education, and a strong work ethic: "They brought with them not only exquisite Governor Winthrop chairs and desks, Copley portraits and Revere silver, but libraries, printing presses and textbooks. They carried to the wilds of Michigan the New England town system, with its public meetings and universal free franchise. They built churches and log schoolhouses as fast as they built settlements."[12]

With respect to the Erie Canal, "other states hastened to copy New York's example for the merchants of rival cities were hardly resigned to the commercial supremacy of Manhattan. A mania for canals briefly gripped politicians and businessmen in Pennsylvania, Ohio, Indiana and elsewhere, leading states and private companies to build over 3,000 miles of canals between 1816 and 1840, at a cost of $125 million."[13] In a few brief years, the face of commerce changed: "The original flow of western commodities down the Mississippi to New Orleans reversed. Wheat and flour shipped east via the Erie Canal alone rose from the equivalent of 268,000 barrels of flour in 1835 to 1,000,000 in 1840, exceeding shipments south via New Orleans after 1838. Flooding west in return, along with northeastern manufactures and imports, were Yankee immigrants and agencies of cultural transformation. Spreading over the Great Lakes plains and prairies, the universal Yankee nation challenged an older population."[14]

Naturally, this challenge did not go unmet. Old-style thinking by the native population often opposed free public education, as requiring taxes they didn't want to pay and taking their children away from farmwork. Older residents of the West tended to see the Yankee newcomer as "a close, miserly, dishonest, selfish getter of money, devoid of generosity, hospitality or any of the kindlier feelings. Yankees in turn tended to view the native as a long, lank, lean, lazy and ignorant animal . . . who was content to squat in a log cabin with a large family of ill-fed and ill-clothed idle, ignorant children."[15] The old-timers were disdainful of wealth for wealth's sake and lovers of social enjoyment, while the enterprising Yankees "built mills, churches, school-houses, towns and cities; and made roads and bridges as if by magic."[16] One writer says, "Yankees vigorously sought to impose their particular ideas of proper behavior and social order wherever they went. Taken collectively, their influence on Michigan was formidable. During the period when Michigan transitioned from territory to state, Yankees, either directly from New England or after a generation in upstate New York (Yankee-Yorkers), immigrated west in such abundance that, for a time, they represented the state's largest ethnic group. The 1850 Federal Census of the United States places the combined numbers of Yankees and Yankee-Yorkers in Michigan at 164,679, roughly 41.3 percent of the state's total population. From the beginnings of statehood, then, Yankees were in a position to stamp Michigan in their own image; given their energy and activism, not to mention their self-righteousness and sense of cultural superiority, they proceeded to do just that."[17]

The pioneers established schools for their children before districts were organized for that purpose, which didn't come until Michigan adopted its first constitution, with its progressive article on education. As I mentioned earlier, the native French-speaking population in Detroit was indifferent on the subject of education, so the influx of new settlers, with their ideas on schooling, must have had the force of a whirlwind on the local mind-set. John Pierce, who was to serve Michigan so capably as its first superintendent of public instruction, was moved to say, "No new state ever started into being with so many warm and devoted friends of education as Michigan."[18]

One need only start at the top to see how Michigan benefited from a bold approach to educational development. Cass took with him to Michigan a New England reverence for the means of advancement, that is, education. Isaac Crary, another New Englander, would settle in Marshall; he chaired the committee that drafted the article on education at Michigan's first constitutional convention. And it was yet another outsider, Stevens T. Mason of Virginia, who provided the political genius to place Michigan in the vanguard of education. In one of his messages to the legislature, Mason would say, "In contemplating the past and dwelling on the future, we are forcibly reminded that if our government is to outline the term heretofore allotted to Republic, it is to be accomplished by the diffusion of knowledge among the people, and that we must depend upon the power of a liberal and enlightened public as the palladium of a free government . . . Guard the education of the rising generation. Teach them in earliest lessons of life the great principles upon which their government was founded."[19]

The influence of settlers from New England and New York State on the history of Michigan is incalculable, and not just in education: "That Michigan was in the forefront of the anti-slavery crusade . . . was due in large measure to this [dominant New England element]. Michigan's leadership in public education is directly attributable to the Puritan zeal for schools, which was part of the New England heritage. The leadership of New Englanders in the early legislatures, schools and churches attest to the influence of the New England-New York element."[20] A plethora of New England-flavored place-names in the Lower Peninsula is further evidence.

Though frontier Michigan lacked in settlers prior to the Erie Canal, it had furs in abundance. Indeed, one of the reasons the British balked at leaving under the terms of the peace treaty was the money they were making from the fur trade. "In the beginning," writes historian Bruce Catton, "Michigan had nothing to ship east except furs, and in 1826, furs worth $200,000 went down the lake [Erie] to Buffalo and Black Rock" (a Niagara River port that competed with Buffalo for westward emigration).[21] With the arrival of steamships and the growth of a national economy, however, Michigan would find plenty of markets for its lumbering resources. In the meantime, the competition for furs was intense, among both the Indians and enterprising white men, such as John Jacob Astor. The American Fur Company (Astor's firm), writes Catton, moved into the Saginaw Valley in 1828 to crush the competition: "In a short time he raised the take of muskrat skins there from 2,500 annually to 28,000, and got nearly 2,000 marten skins in place of 500. Up and down Michigan, the story was very much the same, with the result that long before it became a settled country, the wilderness had lost most of its wild life."[22]

Ever since the River Raisin Massacre and stories of atrocities during the War of 1812, a low opinion was held of the Native American population. In the late 1820s and 1830s, Michigan contained roughly eight thousand Native inhabitants, most of whom spoke Algonquian and belonged to the Ojibwa, Ottawa, or Potawatomie tribes. Animosity toward the Indians stemmed from several factors: "Anglo-Americans hoped to establish an agricultural economy in Michigan, and Indians, who possessed most of the territory's land, represented an obstacle to their plans. Yankees also viewed Indians as backward, because they equated civilization with a boundary that separated agricultural societies from those that relied on hunting . . . Yankees viewed indigenous people as hunters, who represented an earlier, more primitive stage in evolution. Viewing Indians in this way helped to stabilize Yankee identity, enabling New Englanders to define themselves in opposition to Indian barbarism."[23] There were other reasons for distrust between whites and the Native population. The Indians were suspected of disloyalty, given the ease with which local tribes crossed the international boundary and their allegedly close ties with Crown officials in British Canada. The War of 1812 did not come to its conclusion until the British and their Indian allies were subdued in a final battle near London in Upper Canada.

Taming the Michigan frontier of its perceived Indian menace took place against the backdrop of U.S. expansion westward. The goal, as James Schwartz writes, was to pacify Indians and strengthen the boundary between civilization and savagery.

> Yankee leaders viewed local tribes as savages and feared that they threatened white communities in two ways. First, they worried that any drunken and violent behavior of Indians could destabilize the new order they sought to establish on the frontier. The specter of violence not only represented a threat to the safety of settlers, but also could deter easterners from immigration to Michigan and could thus hamper the territory's economic development.
>
> Second, Michigan leaders expressed concern that growing numbers of settlers were violating racial borders by adopting Indian values and customs and maintaining the hybrid culture that their French predecessors established in the seventeenth century.[24]

If the white leadership wanted to rid the territory of the savagery of the Indians, there would have to be a replacement framework. Michigan leaders established formal, legal boundaries and informal, cultural restraints: "Both types of borders would help to establish order and to stabilize group identity by distinguishing between insiders and outsiders."[25]

But law alone wouldn't tame the savagery of the frontier.

> Reformers realized . . . they would also need to win the hearts and minds of their fellow settlers by establishing informal cultural barriers. Religion and education were to be crucial in creating such boundaries. Just as pioneers had used the ax to fell Michigan forests and to transform empty wasteland into productive farms, so reformers would rely on schools and churches to eradicate the territory's borderland culture. These institutions would educate and Christianize Michiganians, permitting the "cheering rays of sun" to fall on the territory's soil, destroying "the darkness of ignorance and the evils of vice and infidelity."
>
> In establishing the boundaries, reformers sought not only to eradicate savagery, but also to replace it with Yankee culture. They hoped . . . to take a "desolate wilderness" and turn it into a land that, "like New England," was filled with "happiness and prosperity" by instilling Yankee values and beliefs in their wild

and uncivilized neighbors. These included a steadfast commitment to a calling or vocation, as well as to sobriety, industriousness, thriftiness and evangelical Protestantism. Yankees also sought to strengthen such character-shaping institutions as churches, schools and families which they viewed as crucial to creating a stable, orderly and godly community.[26]

For their part, the Indians smoked the peace pipe with the Great White Father Lewis Cass without fully comprehending what it was they were doing. The busy Cass negotiated more than twenty treaties with the Indians, who simply did not speak the same language as the white man, in more ways than one. The persuasions of Cass did much to convey to Michigan tribes that it was all in their best interests to betray their ancestors and remove to areas where they would not impede the white man's expansionist hopes. Cass was more sympathetic to the Indians than most, which is perhaps why they were willing to listen to him and to trust his judgment. Thus, via the Treaty of Saginaw in 1819, Cass prevailed on the chiefs of the Chippewa nation to surrender ownership of six million acres in the area around Saginaw Bay. As Catton reports, "Two years later . . . Cass talked the Potawatomis and the Miamis into giving up the southwest quarter of the state; all the rest of the lower peninsula, together with a good half of the upper peninsula, became American soil in 1836. By 1842, Indian title to all lands within the state's boundaries had been relinquished."[27]

It is always wise to judge a person not so much by what he says as by the thoughts he commits to paper. In the 1820s, Cass was regarded as an authority on Native Americans, and his wide travels among them gave him insights into their way of life. When he was given the opportunity to express his views of Native Americans in the prestigious *North American Review,* Cass penned four essays that, taken together, give a rather different view of Cass.

The essays were published in 1826, 1827, 1828, and 1830, at a time when Cass was attempting to defend the government's Indian policies against criticism at home and abroad. Responding to British critics who charged that the United States treated its Indians inhumanely, Cass depicted Native peoples as drunken savages who were addicted not only to liquor but also to violence and cruelty. On January 27, 1825, President James Monroe sent to the U.S. Senate his "Plan for Removing the Several Indian Tribes West of the Mississippi River," and "it was this newly proposed policy that Cass sought in essence to justify by convincing his readers that Indians would not and could not become civilized."[28]

Throughout his essays, Cass "located the moral cause of the decline of Native Americans in their mode of life, their stubborn adherence to super-stitious beliefs, and their passionate savage nature."[29] As further "justification" for elbowing the Indians aside, Cass played on themes showing Americans as victims of Indian attacks and cruelty, while refusing to recognize that the clear cause of the Indians' decline was destruction of their culture and habitat by the white people. In arguing for removal, Cass was motivated by the weakened position of Indians after the War of 1812 and by growing political pressure to open up new lands to which, unfortunately for Cass, the Indians held title.

It took the lawyer in Cass to argue for the right to rule over Indians as an accrued right of civilized nations. This right "rested on the right of discovery; the sounder claims of agricultural settlers over the imperfect possession of the land by those who only hunted on it; and the absurdity of wandering sav-ages being given title to an immense continent designed by Providence to be civilized. Over time Native Americans had lost all attributes of sovereignty and had become dependent on the physically and morally superior United States."[30] By the time Cass yielded the reins as territorial governor, he had come around to support a removal policy, and when he accepted a position as secretary of war in President Jackson's cabinet, he would be the enforcer of removal policies.

As president, Jackson regarded Indian land claims with contempt: "Treaties with Indians he had long regarded as 'an absurdity,' for he believed that the tribes were not sovereign nations but subjects of the United States."[31] When he declared a legal inability to protect the Indians from their aggressive white neighbors, he tried to represent himself as the Indians' rescuer, by supporting the "voluntary" relinquishment of their eastern lands and removing them to the "safety" of lands beyond the Mississippi. Viewed in the context of the times, removal of the Indians to areas west of the Mississippi River was seen as the only way of protecting the Indians from the corrupting influence of the white people, as if firewater and broken promises hadn't already corrupted them. It was a salve to the conscience of white policy makers that removal to the west, on protected reservations, would allow the eastern Indian tribes to preserve their ways and culture. Of course, it didn't work out that way; it was clear from the beginning that Washington knew it had a problem on its hands when the smooth flow of western expansionism brushed up against unyielding Indi-ans. Even though Thomas Jefferson may not have articulated a formal removal policy, he made it clear that there was a place for Native Americans in the new

Republic, but not as sovereign peoples. From Jefferson's policy of nonrecognition to the Trail of Tears under Jackson, the Native peoples were simply an obstacle to expansion, to be shouldered aside "for their own betterment." Cass the administrator took those Jeffersonian ideas as his own, and Cass the essayist articulated them as a defense of removal policies.

Frontier Michigan grew geographically in 1818, when Illinois became a state. The territory lying to the north of Illinois (modern Wisconsin and part of Minnesota) was attached to Michigan. Cass immediately set out to explore the new domains. When the Michigan Territory was created and given a government of its own, the population was estimated to be fewer than four thousand inhabitants. In 1830, when Mason arrived in Detroit, the city numbered about three thousand people.

The addition of lands north of Illinois and subsequent immigration qualified Michigan for step two in the statehood process, that is, to elect a territorial council, or legislature, and to send a delegate to Congress. But when Governor Cass, a strong believer in the right of the people to choose their leaders, submitted the question to voters, they turned him down: "Most of the inhabitants of Michigan were still of French origin; they were satisfied with Cass's administration and were uninterested in elections and democratic processes."[32] The French *habitants* clearly didn't want change, and that was that. In 1823, however, Congress proceeded with this step on the road to statehood. Michigan's first delegate to Congress was William Woodbridge, territorial secretary, who served one year before returning to Michigan.

The structure of politics in frontier Michigan was primitive. Political parties as we know them were as yet unformed. Mason biographer Kent Sagendorph mentions 1820s politics in Detroit in passing, saying Detroit "was only one example of small-town Whig machines which collectively ruled the United States until the election of Andrew Jackson."[33] By the time Stevens T. Mason arrived in Detroit, the Whig machine was in full flower and dominated by Woodbridge. Mason biographer Lawton Hemans is somewhat more expansive about political life in Detroit and within the territory: "Political activities within the Territory had heretofore been largely individual in character; the most potent single influence being centered in the person of Hon. Lewis Cass whose sagacity, broad tolerance and strong personality had done much to win favor for the principles of the Democratic-Republican party; but as yet no strong central organization had arisen to give unity of effort in support of the principles of either party. However, the growth of population and the prospect of enlarged political responsibilities were now making such organizations both desirable and inevitable."[34]

Divisions, then, were along the lines of the old-time Jeffersonians (Democratic-Republicans) and the rising Whigs. "The average citizen of the time," writes Hemans, "rendered a loose alliance to the principles either of the Democratic-Republican or of the Whig party; but the most strongly marked division was between the personal followers of Henry Clay and Andrew Jackson."[35] Jackson had, according to his followers, been robbed of the presidency in the election of 1824, and Clay was nursing presidential ambitions himself. Hemans goes on to say that the condition of the cult of personality around Jackson and Clay "was rendered even more anomalous by the birth and growth of the Anti-Masonic party, which during its short existence exerted a considerable influence in the political affairs of the Territory, being exerted generally against the men and measures of the Democratic-Republican, or Jackson party."[36]

As mentioned already, the leading voice of the Whigs in Detroit was Woodbridge, who was secretary and acting governor on four occasions under Cass. The Whigs were destined to have a short political life in Michigan, but they were a force to be reckoned with when John T. Mason and his son came to Detroit. The Whigs' father figure was Alexander Hamilton, one of the original Federalists, and the party attracted to its ranks men of wealth with conservative views. The Whigs' national spokesman at this time was Clay of Kentucky, whose Ashland estate was put at the Masons' disposal during their years in Lexington. Clay hated Andrew Jackson with every fiber of his being, so when John T. Mason accepted his appointment from Jackson as secretary of the Michigan Territory, the Whig contingent in Detroit seethed in rage.

This would have profound implications for Stevens T. Mason. Woodbridge, already getting along in years, viewed the younger Mason with the disdain that experience reserves for one so callow. Mason speedily ingratiated himself with the leaders of Detroit, so if there was initial hostility to his brand of politics and his Virginia pedigree, it soon wore off as the young man adopted local ways. His ties with Cass also gave him respectability.

Michigan's vigorous two-party politics of today had its antecedents in the politics of the 1820s. Political contests were marked by "a fierce spirit of liberty and individualism. Newspapers were rabidly partisan, asking and giving no quarter. Religion and political partisanship provided emotional outlets."[37] Outstanding battles were waged for the position of delegate to Congress during the 1820s, with attorney Solomon Sibley, Father Gabriel Richard (pastor of St. Anne's Church in Detroit), and Austin E. Wing (another transplanted New Englander) serving in Washington. The territorial delegate had no vote in Congress.

Also in the 1820s, Michigan witnessed the birth of small towns such as Ann Arbor, Ypsilanti, and, farther west (along the old Sauk Indian trail), Coldwater and Niles. Surveys of the interior showed promising futures for those who wanted to homestead there. Catton reports, "In the year before the Erie Canal was opened, fewer than 62,000 acres of Michigan soil had been sold, all of it in the Detroit area. By 1826, nearly one and one-half million acres had been sold in and around Detroit alone, with corresponding increases elsewhere in the state."[38] Land offices were opened in various towns, and they were so busy in transacting sales that "doing a land office business" became part of the lexicon.

Detroit, too, was changing. The rough-and-tumble settlement may have been a step down from Lexington and what the Masons were accustomed to in that gracious Kentucky city, but it wasn't devoid of pleasures. Being a military garrison, Detroit attracted an officer corps who, if not the best elements of society, was a cut above the common farmer and tradesman. As the capital of the territory, Detroit would have attracted persons who considered themselves socially in the upper ranks, such as public officials, high-ranking military officers, and a business class. Add to the mix the newly arriving families from the East, with their more sophisticated ways, and one gets the sense of a fairly lively town. According to George Fuller, "Detroit had come, by the 1830s, to be a bustling center of east-west trade and it had acquired . . . a degree of cosmopolitanism characteristic of a city many times [its population]."[39]

The Frenchman Alexis de Tocqueville, a keen observer of American ways, visited the Michigan Territory in the summer of 1831 in the course of a long fact-finding mission for the French government. He was twenty-five at the time and apparently expected to find a peasant class in frontier Michigan. He found, instead, a "modern society." He commented on "the New England Yankees who . . . were of a practical bent of mind but came from a reasoning and intelligent society."[40]

Here is Emily Mason's take on Detroit a few months after she arrived: "We found Detroit a charming residence. The French element, which still remains, gave a refinement, gaiety and simplicity which few western towns could boast. It was, besides, a military post, which secured us excellent army society, and plenty of nice beaux. The town was a long, straggling street along the beautiful, broad river . . . Schools were rare as were the churches and such was the unanimity of feeling, that though Protestants, we went to St. Anne's, the French Catholic cathedral, and from the priests we had lessons in music and French."[41]

Of course, there was the other side of the coin: muddy streets, an open sewer running through town, the rabble and lowborn a visible part of the social fabric. Detroit could be "a noisy, raucous community with public drunkenness, quarrels and violent altercations common occurrences."[42] It was still a frontier town, but it was one that stood on the threshold of shedding its French and British ways.

3 ⁓ Mason—Boy in Charge

When George Porter of Pennsylvania officially took office as governor of the Michigan Territory on September 22, 1831, he found his chair warmed by an underage acting governor who had successfully weathered the protest meetings against his appointment as secretary. Although he was yet another Jackson appointee and therefore anathema to the Whig faction, Porter appeared to placate many who had opposed Mason as to both his minority and his politics. Porter was twenty years Mason's senior and from a good family in Lancaster.

Porter and Mason got along well. It's not likely the two men were ever close or shared confidences, but Mason was in a position to help Porter in the ways of territorial politics. It is unclear where Porter went or what he did on his frequent absences, but we may infer that he trusted young Mason to guide affairs to his and to President Jackson's satisfaction. Once, in writing to his father, Mason described the governor as "standing as usual distant, reserved, dignified and unapproachable."[1] On another occasion, shortly after the Black Hawk War, Mason wrote his sister to say, "We are all in a great hubbub at present. The Fourth of July, Black Hawk and the President are all close at hand. What we are to do with them I cannot tell, unless Governor Porter should arrive in time to relieve us from our unfortunate dilemma. It will suit the Governor exactly. An opportunity to shake hands with the President or to make a big speech to Black Hawk will be of glorious doings for him."[2] Mason was too conscious of his standing in the territory to come across as flip or disrespectful, but in his letters to family members, he displays a keen sense of humor at times. It would have been in keeping with his youth, to be sure, and one longs to have eavesdropped at his social gatherings, to more fully appreciate the humorous side of his character. He could needle with the best of them.

Mason used the balance of the year 1831 to gain experience. With his confirmation in the Senate still uncertain, he was both acting governor and interim secretary—an unusual combination of jobs. He could have signed himself "secretary designate" or some such appellation in deference to his elders, but he confidently signed papers as "Secretary of the Territory of Michigan." And it was clear that if circumstances allowed him to be acting governor, he would model himself after his mentor, Cass, who had placed such faith in Mason's character and judgment.

He found permanent quarters in a brick dwelling at 303 East Jefferson Street. On Sundays, he attended church with his mother at St. Paul's Episcopal Church on Woodward. He kept a low profile that winter of 1831–32, to enlarge public acceptance of him. Meanwhile, Porter appeared to come right out of central casting for the part of governor, with "long wavy sideburns which framed his thin face and gave it impressive dignity and maturity—advantages that Mason obviously lacked."[3]

So the territory had Porter the veteran politician and Mason the neophyte as its leadership. About the former, Sagendorph observes, "Because he had an atmosphere of solid citizenry about him, Michigan tolerated more breaches of official duty from George Porter than from any public official in the city or territory. He was annoyed at his appointment but could not gracefully refuse it. Thus he stayed away as long as possible, returned for a few weeks and left again. His salary went on—a subject of considerable newspaper speculation in December, 1831, after he had held office five months and not served more than three weeks."[4] Porter seems to have viewed his posting for its potential in real estate speculation.

The year 1832 was a pivotal one for Michigan. A dispute along its southern border with Ohio over a contested strip of land between two survey lines threatened to grow into an affair of some consequence. Agitation for statehood was beginning to be heard in some quarters, as it became clear that the territory's growth warranted a change in status. Mason would stake his entire political career on (1) achieving statehood for Michigan and (2) claiming for Michigan the disputed land along its southern border; all else was secondary. In both endeavors, Mason was to have a substantial portion of the population firmly in his corner.

Mason got the ball rolling on statehood in June, when he persuaded the territorial legislature to provide for taking a vote in October on the question "whether it be expedient for the people of the territory to form a state government," the necessary first step toward statehood. The statehood question barely won approval by voters in October, but the tepid endorsement didn't dampen the enthusiasm of such statehood advocates as Mason. When Congress established a pattern of *not* finding it expedient to act on Michigan's statehood bid, Mason took charge by calling for a territorial census, which would undoubtedly confirm that Michigan had more than the minimum sixty-thousand residents to qualify petitioning Congress for enabling legislation. As the year developed, however, statehood efforts had to take a second seat to other territorial matters. No sooner was Mason's confirmation as secretary secured than his leadership skills would be tested in the Black Hawk War and ensuing cholera epidemic.

In the spring of 1832, it looked as though Michigan might be embroiled in an Indian war. With Porter again out of state, it fell to Mason's lot to make most of the major decision making as far as this threat on its frontiers was concerned. The Black Hawk War was brief in duration, but it engendered considerable hysteria among whites. The popular feeling was that the Indian uprising represented the red man's last attempt to regain lost lands and so was to be taken seriously.

Black Hawk is one of those romantic Indian figures (not unlike Geronimo and Sitting Bull) on whom history has bestowed noble character and fighting prowess. But in fact, Black Hawk was a minor chief, whose cause—retrieval of tribal lands—was "a generation too late."[5] The war that attached to his name grew out of American Indian policy that called for removal of the Indians to lands west of the Mississippi River. A treaty in 1804 had ceded the traditional area of Black Hawk's Sauk tribe to the United States.

Black Hawk was sixty-five years old and a veteran of earlier scrapes with the U.S. government. He collaborated with the British during the War of 1812 and likely saw battle in the River Raisin Massacre; he was with Tecumseh at the decisive Battle of the Thames in Upper Canada at the conclusion of that war. There was a price on his head for his participation with the British, but war's end found him back among his own people. Originally named Maka-taimeshekiakiak, Black Hawk allied the Sauks with the Foxes and, in May 1832, began stirring up trouble near the mouth of the Rock River in northern Illinois.

He took his raiding parties across the Mississippi and began harassing the white settlers. Since this was in contravention of the 1804 treaty, the settlers demanded protection. Black Hawk brought with him several hundred mounted warriors and a like number of women and children, so it may be that his original intention was not to make war but to retake territory and to plant fields. The pleas from the white settlers for help were answered, and troops were dispatched to chase Black Hawk down. As he retreated, Black Hawk's warriors took their revenge for past grievances and killed a number of settlers who happened to be in their path.

Pursuit took Black Hawk into the present state of Wisconsin, which was then part of the Michigan Territory, and acting governor Mason was apprised of the situation. By now, tales of the depredations committed by Black Hawk had spread and received wide credence among the whites. Rumors of alleged atrocities had reached as far east as Detroit, and Mason, responding to orders from Washington, issued a call for volunteers to take up arms and meet this threat to the west. Some rumors had Black Hawk already in Michigan, gathering new allies. Catton writes, "There were people in Michigan who feared the worst . . . for most of the area now being settled was Potawatomi country, and the Potawatomis were not placid Indians; they had performed the massacres at Fort Dearborn and on the River Raisin, they had provided Tecumseh with a good deal of his manpower, and Black Hawk was making overtures to them."[6] There were reports that the Chippewa and the Ottawa had joined Black Hawk and that "the Potawatomi who inhabited the region were sharpening their hatchets to fall upon the settlers."[7]

On May 15, Governor John Reynolds of Illinois called out his state's militia and issued a call for troops. Reynolds was thinking that the Winnebago tribe had joined the Sauks and that, if this were true, it wouldn't be long before the other tribes also rejected neutrality in favor of the warpath. In point of fact, Black Hawk's attempts to rally the other tribes came to nothing, but state and federal forces were taking no chances. General Henry Atkinson moved up from St. Louis with a force of regulars and gave chase to Black Hawk's band.

Meanwhile, the Indian agent at Chicago sent a letter to acting governor Mason on the eighteenth of May, confirming reports of settlers' houses burned and property destroyed and requesting a "force sufficient to . . . defend ourselves in the event of an attack."[8] Public apprehension was rising with each report and rumor from the western settlements. In Washington, President Jackson and his secretary of war, Lewis Cass took note of conditions, and General Winfield Scott was ordered to take command of a force hurrying westward.

The situation was made to order for Mason to test his wings as man in charge. Here was an emergency on his frontiers that had surrounding states and the federals in a mood to fight Indians, just as in the old days. Volunteers were called for, and Mason ordered the territorial militia to active duty. That was easier said than done, because the militia was commanded by Major General John R. Williams, former mayor of Detroit and one of that city's leading citizens. Williams was allied with Woodbridge, no friend of Mason, and was averse to doing the bidding of the stripling in the governor's chair. So Williams dragged his heels on getting the militia in readiness, in direct defiance of what Mason considered his proper authority.

The wording of Mason's order to Williams is unequivocal: "It seems the Indians have assumed an attitude of hostility toward the frontier settlements. I am satisfied that the public safety requires immediate movements on the part of the militia of the Territory. You are authorized to raise such a number of volunteers as in your opinion may be necessary." Mason went on to urge cooperation with Brigadier General Joseph Brown, "who has rendezvoused at Jonesville."[9] When Williams balked, the acting governor issued another order to call out such troops as he may require, concluding by saying, "You cannot but be aware, that delay is only calculated to give rise to false and unfounded reports, which may possibly have an injurious effect upon the emigration to our Territory. It is expected that you will use every exertion to meet General Brown forthwith, and that you will not return to this place until every shadow of danger from hostile Indians on the frontier is removed."[10]

What was Williams thinking when he ignored Mason's call to arms? Surely he would have known that Mason had the backing of the War Department and, by extension, President Jackson. Public opinion in the territory would have supported some kind of response to a perceived threat from the Indians. As acting governor, Mason held the legal authority to call out the militia. When Mason took a copy of his second order to the Detroit newspapers for publication, Williams saw that further challenges to Mason's authority were hopeless.

On May 23, Williams begrudgingly called out a portion of the territorial militia near Detroit, consisting of one regiment of infantry and a battalion of mounted riflemen. About three hundred men responded to the summons and assembled at Ten Eyck's Tavern in what is now Dearborn. This tavern, on the Chicago Road, was one of the more comfortable hostelries in the area. The inn, built around 1820, was run by Conrad Ten Eyck, a U.S. marshal from Michigan.

While Williams was getting ready to march on May 25, General Brown was at Tecumseh, mustering companies of militia from nearby communities and preparing to meet up with Williams at Jonesville, as per Mason's orders. Brown appears to have arrived at the appointed place in time, but Williams was detained at Saline by other volunteers who needed to be organized and furnished with arms. By that time, a mass of confusion occurred, resulting largely from the poor communications of the day.

No sooner had Williams and his forces left Detroit than a messenger arrived from Chicago to inform Mason that the Indian danger had been greatly overblown and that Michigan troops would not be needed. Another source informed Mason that General Scott's troops from the east, who had traveled from Fortress Monroe, Virginia, to Buffalo and thence to Chicago, would soon be hounding Black Hawk and thus would have the situation in hand. Mason then issued an order for the recall of the militia, prompting an uproar among the citizenry, who were spoiling for a good fight.

When he received the same intelligence at Saline, Williams dismissed his infantry but continued along the road to Chicago with a company of mounted men. Though Williams' men weren't needed, the few inhabitants of Chicago expressed their gratitude to the territory of Michigan for its kindly offer of help under the command of Major General Williams. In Williams' mind, this justified the course of action he had taken with respect to Mason. Williams took added enjoyment in knowing there was a crowd in Detroit denouncing Mason for inconsistency. The acting governor could only fume in frustration over the embarrassment of mobilizing the militia, just as quickly recalling the same, and having to listen to the second-guessers who knew all along that the Indian threat was exaggerated.

Mason got his feelings off his chest in a letter to General Williams on the first of June. "Should we have to march again from this quarter," Mason said sarcastically, "The gentlemen who fight the battles of the country at public meetings will have to march, if it can be effected."[11] This comment was aimed at friends of Williams who, taking heart from his defiance of Mason, were charging Mason with giving contradictory orders.

Black Hawk was run down and taken captive. With the war over, the postmortems began in earnest. Williams complained in a letter to Secretary of War Cass that the orders of the acting governor were inconsistent and contradictory. Some people thought Williams had no business going over Mason's head when the governor was his superior. Public meetings in Detroit criticized Mason for needlessly worrying the people when there wasn't the slightest cause for alarm. For his part, Mason was forced to acknowledge that conflicting reports from the west led to confusion in the deployments of militia units. The governor of Illinois, who had first reacted in fear, would soon say that "the danger had been contained and the fears of a general uprising among Indian tribes unfounded."[12] From start to finish, the Black Hawk War was over in three months.

For all its brevity, few events in the history of the old Northwest furnished more interest or aroused more controversy than the Black Hawk War. "The emphasis on it has been entirely out of proportion to its importance as a war," says author R. Carlyle Buley, who explains, "The reasons are fairly obvious. It was the last Indian war in the old Northwest and as such it had to be cultivated and cherished in memory."[13] If that assessment seems a little unkind, consider that after his capture, Black Hawk was put on public display and exhibited, trophy-like, to a variety of eastern audiences. He showed up in Detroit on July 4, 1833, where the whole town crowded down to the wharf to see him: "Wearing a long blue coat, a white high hat, and spectacles, and carrying a cane, he conducted himself with dignity."[14] On the next day, he paid a courtesy call on acting governor Mason. Black Hawk was one of many tragic figures—and certainly not the last—in the unequal relationship of white men and native peoples.

The human cost of the Black Hawk War was the lives of about 250 settlers. The government spent two million dollars enforcing its treaty and tracking down the belligerent chief. The war did not touch present-day Michigan directly, but it had a psychological effect on settlers: "The war scare delayed settlements in northern Indiana, Illinois and Michigan Territory for a year. Renewed anti-Indian feeling led to increased demands for removal of the Potawatomi from Indiana and the Winnebago from Michigan Territory."[15] The war impeded emigration to Michigan's southwest corner, but only for a little while. The perception that the Indian problem was being taken care of was about to be strengthened by the vigorous removal policy espoused by Jackson in the White House. For now, treaties were negotiated with the Winnebagoes, Sauks, and Foxes, in which they yielded title to even more of their ancestral lands.

For Michigan, the war ended with Mason winning high marks for decisive action. The people of Michigan began to see their youthful stand-in as a leader. Forced, by Governor Porter's absence, to make executive decisions in a hurry, Mason was equal to the task. Referencing Mason's use of the militia, Cass would pronounce his blessing on Mason: "Called out by the Territorial authorities upon the occasion of the recent hostilities with the Sauk and Fox

Indians information has been submitted to the President, and he has decided that the circumstances were such as to justify the call."[16] In addition, Mason had stood up to one of the chief men in the territory—Williams—and had come out on top.

Thus, early in his public career and while not yet of voting age, Mason was showing the determination that would mark his years in office. People were calling him governor, and he, in turn, had faith in the people. Writing to his father in 1832, Mason said, "I firmly believe that the intelligence of the people will always in time be found a panacea for every evil affecting their rights."[17] Years later, in his second term as governor, he would use similar language in stressing the value of education: "If our country is ever to fall from her high position before the world, the cause will be found in the ignorance of the people; if she is to remain where she now stands, . . . educate every child in the land."[18]

But Mason was still a "stripling" to some and the "Boy Governor" to others. It didn't matter that he felt he had proved himself during the summer of 1832 and had reached a maturity that comes with heavy responsibility. He came of legal age in October and cast his first ballot, backing the losing candidate (Austin E. Wing) for delegate to Congress. With this vote and without intending to do so, Stevens T. Mason came to national attention.

The *Western Emigrant*, an Ann Arbor newspaper that had taken immediate umbrage at Mason's appointment, had called Wing a front man for Mason. The newspaper had delighted in using its columns to refer to the latter as the Boy Governor. Mason hated the label, but it stuck with him as long as he called Michigan home. When he encountered the editor of the *Western Emigrant* on a Detroit street, Mason's anger got the better of him, and he applied a sound thwacking. It is one of the few instances in Mason's public career where he lost his judgment.

The story of Mason's prowess with his fists was printed with glee by a rival Ann Arbor newspaper, the *Argus*, whose editor declared that "the stripling, the Boy Governor, if you please, was man enough to give him a sound cuffing."[19] Eastern papers in New York and Washington reprinted the story, and Mason came to personify a tough young territory on the move. He was mentioned as a political "comer," and it must have pleased Old Hickory to see his appointee set the Old Guard on its ear.

The Black Hawk War would have unintended consequences of a disastrous nature for Michigan. Recall that General Winfield Scott was dispatched by President Jackson to lead U.S. troops against Black Hawk and that Scott's orders were to head for Fort Dearborn, near the scene of hostilities. Traveling from Buffalo to Chicago by way of Lake Erie and, from thence, taking the long way around the Michigan mitten, one of Scott's ships stopped on July 4 in Detroit. Several of the soldiers aboard the steamship *Henry Clay* came down with Asiatic cholera; taken ashore for treatment, eleven soldiers died before the next dawn. The contagious disease broke out among the townspeople, amid scenes of rising panic.

It was scant comfort that the disease killed quickly. High fever and raging thirst came first, after which the person was overcome with profuse diarrhea, vomiting, and cramping. Severe dehydration was next, by which time death was near. Victims died and were removed for instant burial. As Willis Dunbar reports of this epidemic in Detroit, "There were fifty-eight cases, and twenty-eight deaths took place within two weeks. Seven percent of the city's population died in August."[20] Before the epidemic had run its course, about 10 percent of Detroit's population died. The island of Belle Isle was used for quarantine, and doctors did what they could to treat patients. Mason opened up the capitol as a hospital for victims, but medical knowledge was insufficient to effectively deal with this menace.

Among those who died in Detroit was Father Gabriel Richard, who worked tirelessly to nurse and to comfort the sick. Mason did his best to keep the territory going and the roads open. On July 18, two weeks after the *Henry Clay* had tied up at the wharf, the city clerk apprised the governor about measures to prevent the spread of cholera. In Ypsilanti, the supervisor and justices of the peace of that town issued a proclamation saying, "Whereas it appears that the Asiatic Cholera now exists in the City of Detroit, and that it is expedient and desirable to use every precaution to prevent its introduction into this village, we do order and direct that no person or persons coming directly from Detroit or any city, town or place where the disease is known to prevail, shall enter the township of Ypsilanti, until such person or persons shall have been visited and examined by a Health Officer."[21]

This order was backed up by the local sheriff, and when Ypsilanti was one of the towns to which Mason traveled to assess the situation, he was detained by a deputy sheriff. Eventually released on his own recognizance, Mason gave the local official an earful of colorful language at being stopped in the performance of duties. Within a few days, Governor Porter, now back on the scene, removed the sheriff and several others who had been involved in the events at

Ypsilanti. This, in turn, provoked an indignant editorial response in opposition newspapers, but interest soon waned.

The Black Hawk War and the cholera scare made Michigan appear to be dangerous territory. But with the coming of autumn and the return of Governor Porter, things settled down, and Mason, relieved of his duties, had time to take up the study of law and to enjoy the social scene. He also participated in the politics of the day and honed his literary pen. "The contesting political factions kept discussion of public issues at high heat," says one writer, "and the newspapers published charges and counter-charges as the Whigs attacked the Democrats and in turn were attacked. The Whigs . . . made issue of anything the governor or his territorial secretary would say or do."[22] In the fashion of that time, Mason took on a pen name and used the newspapers to respond to his critics.

Writing under the pseudonym Aristides, Mason had articles published in the *Detroit Courier* that were notable for their sting and sharpness of rebuke. For example, he addressed the "Knight of Black Rock" as a "habitual newspaper calumniator," who had "intrinsically, no one respectable quality" and who exhibited "unmanly and disgraceful conduct." Aristides alluded to himself as "young, and perhaps in your estimation another stripling," leaving readers with little doubt about who Aristides really was.[23] As for the "Knight of Black Rock," Aristides gave readers plenty of hints as to the identity of the individual, who happened to be Augustus S. Porter, a prominent Whig in the territory.

By early 1833, Mason's star clearly was on the rise. With Porter mostly absent, Mason conducted all important territorial business. He initiated legislation with the Territorial Council, made appointments, and kept in touch with Washington. Among persons his own age, he was "Tom" and an agreeable companion. In April, Detroit elected him alderman at large. Other honors followed, including being tapped for the elite Detroit Young Men's Society (whose goal was to "devise means for greater intellectual improvement") and election to the volunteer fire brigade. "Hardly a week passed," wrote Emily Mason, "that did not see our home extending its hospitality to notable men who had come from the east and who had stopped in Detroit to make themselves known to the 'Boy Governor,' as my brother was known."[24] At year's end, Mason was admitted to practice law, and his proud father was moved to inform Emily, who was away at the time, that "Your brother and Isaac Rowland were admitted to the bar . . . and are now licensed lawyers. They gave a tremendous supper and wine party the night after to which all the gentlemen in town were invited."[25] Many years later, Mason would endear himself to students of history by accepting election as a resident member to the Michigan Historical Society, whose object is "to discover, procure and preserve, whatever may relate to the natural, civil, literary, ecclesiastical and aboriginal history of the country, and of Michigan in particular."[26] His Excellency Stevens T. Mason was informed of his honor by Henry R. Schoolcraft, president of the society and a noted scientist.

In 1833, Mason kept up a brisk correspondence with his father, who was on the Texas-Mexico frontier. In one of his chatty letters, he briefed his father on affairs in Detroit. The Territorial Council, he said, was busy organizing the courts in the different counties, and an upcoming election for delegate to Congress was absorbing considerable public interest. A little later, he wrote to say of the election, "We have three candidates but only two regularly organized parties. Our Michigan Democratic party as was anticipated nominated Lucius Lyon. The Anti-Masons have taken up Woodbridge. I am satisfied that parties must exist under our government, and I would be the last to discourage party spirit when properly controlled. Austin E. Wing has not been nominated by a convention, but his friends have held county meetings and are determined to run him." After acknowledging the opening of the Erie Canal and its expected benefits to the territory, his letter closes with the offhand remark "Governor Porter spends the summer at Green Bay . . . [H]e takes with him all his retinue as usual."[27] It does not take much reading between the lines to conclude that out of sight was pretty much out of mind as far as Mason's boss was concerned and that territorial affairs were in capable hands.

In a letter to his sister Catherine, also called Kate, who was then away at school in Troy, New York, Tom Mason's wicked sense of humor is on display. He writes that a family acquaintance is "somewhere in the swamps of Indiana, it isn't known when he returns." Of the Detroit social scene, he says, "I know nothing of the chit-chat of the Metropolis. Our winter parties have commenced with a dancing party at Sibleys . . . where was collect all the beauty of the country." One of the belles at the dance was a Mrs. Russell of Green Bay, who, Mason chuckles, "has become a member of the Presbyterian Church. The only effect it seems to have had upon her is to make her think more of her precious person. Her vanity is intolerable, and her affectation is played off with so bad a grace that she has become disgusting." He concludes with "my best respects to Miss Mullen, and tell her that her pupil, Mr. Norvell, is improving rapidly in Christianity. He has purchased a pew and goes to church once every Sunday."[28]

As 1833 came to a close, Mason's impatience with the absentee governor showed in an unusual way. He petitioned the president for compensation for services as acting governor during the absence of the governor of the territory, specifying "that from the 11th day of June, 1832, to the 14th day of December, 1833, the Governor of the Territory has been absent from the seat of government in all about eight months; that during this period the Secretary . . . was compelled to discharge in addition to his duties as Secretary, the duties of Acting Governor and Superintendent of Indian Affairs, and that he has only received his usual salary of Secretary for all these services, while the Governor has drawn his full pay . . . in addition to his compensation of $8 per day and $8 for every twenty miles traveled."[29]

Was Mason being small-minded in demanding more pay? Keep in mind that with his father gone, he still had a family to support and the expenses of office. The hospitality of the Mason household that Emily mentioned would have stretched any budget, and the mere acquisition of a law degree was no guarantee of clients lining up at the door. Mason doubtless enjoyed being called governor and mixing with the territory's politicians, but his sense of fair play demanded fair pay for services rendered. He was soon to take the preeminent role in taking Michigan to the promised land of statehood.

4 ～ Statehood and the Toledo War

Michigan's campaign for statehood played out against a transformed national landscape. Sweeping changes were abroad in the land, unleashed by the election of Jackson. Conflicting views on liberty and power were accompanied by the growing sense of connectedness that attaches to the role of political parties. Although a frontier territory, Michigan was not immune to public opinion and the passions that motivated the great thinkers of the day. Stevens T. Mason would be caught up in the swirl of national events.

The greatest change was political in nature. The modern form of American party politics, writes Charles Sellers in *The Market Revolution*, was born when the political enemies of DeWitt Clinton, governor of New York from 1817 to 1822, boldly challenged his leadership. The Bucktails, as Clinton's opponents were known, "challenged on democratic grounds the whole system of family and personal factions that Clinton epitomized. A political party, they argued, should be an internally democratic association run by its members and responsible to its constituency. Only through such a party, experience had taught them, could the majority unite to prevail against elites."[1]

Parties, established on a permanent basis, could accomplish what the old, shifting factions could not do. The latter were loose alliances of individuals who still viewed the Republic as the Framers had envisioned, with slight differences. There were Federalists and anti-Federalists, Democratic-Republicans and other factions, as the young Republic began to come to grips with differing opinions on what the country should become as it moved from infancy to preadolescence. The Framers died out, and their successors were left to chart the course of the country.

The forces at work in the 1820s came to full expression with the election of Jackson, one of the great polarizing men of his time. Liberty and power were at issue in 1828. There was a contest involving "the America of technological improvement, economic strength and political power versus an America that understood liberty as implied economic security and independence for the average family. Jackson took office as the friend of liberty and the foe of unwarranted power."[2] To Jackson, such unwarranted power took tangible form in the Bank of the United States.

The scholar Lawrence Kohl attributed to Jackson the traits of combativeness and a fierce independence. Kohl argued that "the era's great political division between Democrats and Whigs largely reflected the division between those Americans who were deeply unsettled by the emergence of an individualistic social order and those whose character structure allowed them to strive more confidently within it."[3] "Politics in the Jacksonian era," Kohl writes, "was fundamentally concerned with sweeping social changes that were altering the character of the American people."[4]

Those changes included new developments in transportation and communication; reawakened religious fervor, especially in the northeast; "a quickening of business enterprise, the almost universal ambition to get ahead, the impression that the pursuit of money was an end in itself";[5] and, of course, the growth of the political party system. Politics came to be seen as "a struggle between good and evil, expressed as the eternal warfare between liberty and power, virtue and corruption."[6] Although there was considerable hostility toward and suspicion of political parties by many people, "Americans would eventually come to see their government as an arena for routine competition and compromise of contending interests, a political model that scholars call the 'liberal state.' In this view political parties would be accepted as normal."[7] As we saw in the previous chapter, Stevens T. Mason viewed parties as a necessary thing in 1833, and we may conclude that his opinion represented popular feeling in Michigan at the time.

In the 1830s and 1840s, the sharp divisions between Whigs and Jacksonians drove the debates over liberty and power. At issue was the role of the state in promoting development and virtue versus vice. Jackson saw himself as a champion of virtue and rugged individualist pitted against a corrupt and exploitative business or market economy. His successor, Martin Van Buren, echoed Jackson's fear of concentrated power by praising "the democratic spirit that sought to resist the encroachments and limit the extent of executive authority."[8] Van Buren, moreover, argued for political parties as necessary to parry the designs of their partisan foes and, by implication, to foster discipline (within the party) as a means of promoting awareness of common goals. To the Whig, "the state was an indispensable ally in the attempt to promote national development. It could draw people together for constructive endeavors and give their efforts an expansive force they could never have on their own. Jacksonians, for their part, feared to see numerous self-interests brought together into powerful combinations. They denied that government efforts to order and harmonize economic strivings would have the desired effect."[9]

Similarly, the parties differed markedly on the ability of government to avoid corruption and to remain pure: "The suspicious Jacksonians believed only a small, simple government, one incapable of acting on private interests, could be trusted. He had faith only in the representative who was tightly shackled to the will of those he represented. The more trusting Whig put his faith in a large government capable of promoting broad, comprehensive programs serving diverse private interests and in the men of great capacities and elevated views who were required to administer such a government."[10] Historian Martin Hershock put it this way: "Those individuals who embraced the modern world market . . . tended to become Whigs. By contrast, those who believed that modernity had unleashed an impersonal and aggressive predatory tide upon innocent Americans . . . chose instead to join the ranks of the Democratic Party." He adds that another crucial difference between the parties was that "the Whigs maintained the old Puritan concern for controlling personal morality, whereas the Democrats embodied a more liberal attitude toward individual behavior. The Whig vision of American society was more communalistic and hierarchical, while the Democratic vision was more individualistic and egalitarian."[11]

The Whig world-and-life view, as expressed in the legislation they advanced, "was designed to promote the development of the institutions and values of modernity. It sought to stimulate, facilitate and bring order to individual striving. It had its roots in the character of Americans who did not fear the aggressive pursuit of self-interest or the impersonal institutions which inner-directed men created to advance those interests."[12] The Whig party platform would have included language expressing "a profound appreciation of diversified economic growth and the wondrous ways it had transformed the lives of Americans."[13] Progress, they believed, "could be achieved only if government stepped in to stimulate, regulate and harmonize the forces which capitalism had set loose in the world."[14]

Jacksonians and Whigs found other points of disagreement. They differed sharply "over the propriety of enlarging the public sphere. They debated whether energetic government enhanced or diminished the well-being of Americans. They disagreed on whether men could exercise power over others without becoming corrupt or tyrannical. They argued about the degree of unity that was necessary for the nation and about what effect geographic expansion would have on the ties which united Americans."[15] Neither were Whigs and Jacksonians above taking their animosities to a personal level: "The oft-repeated Whig allegations of Jacksonian inferiority was particularly galling because the Jacksonians suspected its truth. Democrats were prone to represent themselves as something less than they should be: they saw themselves as poor, weak, downtrodden, oppressed, injured and outcasts. The Whigs were frequently represented as something more than they should be: swelled, inflated, fat, fortunate, privileged. No evidence of the outsider mentality is more telling than the willingness of Jacksonians to concede Whig superiority in wealth, in power and in the ability of their leaders."[16]

The role of political parties as not only useful but necessary to the growth and development of the American state has been analyzed by many scholars. Would the Framers—particularly Washington, who abhorred factionalism—be horrified by the rise of parties? Perhaps the words of Clinton Rossiter are applicable: "Our modern grasp of the functions of political parties, instruments that the Revolutionists should not be ridiculed for failing to understand, is simply a realistic extension of their belief in free cooperation and majority rule."[17]

Alongside the political transformation of America at this time came sweeping economic change. When President Jackson took on the Bank of the United States, all traditional banking practices and attitudes toward currency were turned upside down. The great economic depression of 1837 and the bank failures that followed only focused the debate on the uses of economic power and the role of government in managing the economy. A new generation of Americans, which saw a frontier waiting to be exploited and potential wealth and opportunity around every corner, would not waste time in pushing ahead, with the mindset of letting the devil take the hindmost. Economic issues, then, occupied men's minds fully as much as the political changes: "Economic issues were of great significance to the Jacksonian generation because, as Tocqueville noted, in an individualistic society the uses of money are infinitely multiplied. It becomes the chief means not only to bind people together but also to allow them to stand above or apart from one another. Thus, the means for obtaining wealth, the tenure of its possession and the uses to which it is put become intimately involved with questions concerning how individuals are to relate to each other."[18]

Although it was Mason who took the lead in pushing for statehood, not all in the territory rallied to his banner. One reason was economic. Michigan's expenses were covered by federal appropriation as long as it remained a territory. As a state, Michigan would have to assess far more in taxes than Congress's annual appropriation. Tax levies would come from hard-pressed settlers, which is one reason the Whig Party opposed efforts toward statehood. Many settlers did not see the fact of statehood as holding any particular advantage to them.

Mason was ready to argue that the Northwest Ordinance was intended to prepare these territories for statehood. In addition, there is always sentiment among a free people to control their own destinies. Statehood conferred prestige, an equal voice with neighboring states in the corridors of power, and access to the institutions of federal government, as well as opportunities to make money by competing in a national economy with other states. Michigan was poised for growth when Mason arrived on the scene, and he clearly saw a new major role for the territory. Michigan's population had risen steadily from 4,762 in 1810 to 8,896 in 1820 and to 31,640 in 1830. But then numbers climbed dramatically, so that by the time Stevens T. Mason was serving as acting governor, it was certain that Michigan's population had reached the minimum number needed to initiate the statehood process.

At this time of his life, Mason presents an almost comic picture of opposites. He was mature enough to be a budding statesman, "leading his people out of the wilderness toward the promised land of statehood and prosperity. He was the boy who aroused all sorts of hopes in the hearts of impressionable girls and their mothers; the frustrated, overgrown kid who, the preceding winter, had gone down to the Detroit River incognito and stayed up late sliding down the steep banks onto the ice in a child's sled."[19] We have this description of him from biographer Kent Sagendorph:

> He . . . had filled out very satisfactorily. His dark-brown hair, almost black, waved from front to back. He had the clean, regular features of a romantic actor, that impression being heightened by a pair of black, neatly arched eyebrows. His nose was straight, his strong chin cleft with a dimple . . . He was

a figure to set many a girl's pulse pounding, and young swains' tongues to sarcasm. He knew it, and often purposely appeared with his wavy hair in great disarray and wrinkles in his satin vest. He thought that the men who came to see him would resent it if he were too well-groomed. There are sketches of him which show his hair pulled forward in awkward blobs around his ears.[20]

These appearances sometimes had the unfortunate effect of making him look disheveled, which his critics credited to debauchery and a social life befitting the life of a bachelor.

It is hard to determine just when the great project of Stevens T. Mason's short political life, that of leading the robust territory into statehood, first took hold. That the bid for statehood would become inextricably intertwined with the Toledo War of 1835 was unforeseen at the time of the first stirrings toward statehood. The endorsement of statehood by voters in October 1832, was the first arrow in Mason's statehood quiver. But when Congress found one excuse after another to find it inexpedient to consider Michigan's application, a subtle change in attitude took place. To keep the pot boiling, Mason began a letter-writing campaign, asking governors of the surrounding states to help in the cause for statehood. In one instance, he wrote to Governor Littleton W. Tazewell of Virginia saying, "Michigan feels justified in making an appeal to Virginia in the fact that she is, in effect, her offspring." Mason here refers to Virginia's former claim to lands in the Northwest Territory, which Virginia later ceded. Michigan, he continued, "looks up to her as a parent, . . . and I might allude to my own feelings as a native of Virginia."[21] In reply, Tazewell gave a practiced politician's response: "When Virginia forgets a Mason worthy of his name, she will dishonor herself, and when a native Mason of that class forgets Virginia, he will do no less."[22] In other words, Virginia wasn't going to fight Michigan's battles, and the matter was dropped.

The cause of statehood was bookended in 1833 by twin rejections. On January 8, the territorial legislature adopted a memorial, or resolution, to Congress, requesting an act that would give the people of the Michigan Territory the privilege of drafting a constitution for a state that would have for its southern boundary the line set down in the Northwest Ordinance of 1787 and in the 1805 act establishing the Michigan Territory. Ohio, by now vigorously disputing the Michigan Territory's claims to the Toledo Strip, contested Michigan's claim as stated in the memorial, and although Congress took the matter under advisement, inaction seemed to be the preferable course.

Then, on December 11, Lucius Lyon, who was Michigan's delegate to Congress, presented the first formal petition for admission of Michigan as a state. His request for enabling legislation was to no avail. Both the House and the Senate found reasons to stall Michigan, with the chief bone of contention now centering around Michigan's southern (and Ohio's northern) boundary. Congress, while it may be a deliberative body, is also a political body, and this latter aspect carried the day. It would not do to offend an established state (Ohio) in matters of politics and votes, and so Congress opted to do nothing about the Michigan Territory's petition.

The new year of 1834 opened with unimproved prospects for Michigan. In the U.S. House of Representatives, the Committee on Territories decided in March that it was inexpedient to admit Michigan "at the present time." In the U.S. Senate, an enabling bill authorizing the people of Michigan to form a state government was debated in May and then tabled, which effectively killed the bill. Then, when the Senate Judiciary Committee reported a bill that upheld Ohio's claim to the Harris line as its rightful northern boundary, the Senate voted to approve the legislation. Lyon could only stand by and fume.

Back on the home front, the summer of 1834 saw a return of Asiatic cholera to the territory. Detroit was again hit hard by the disease, and this time, not even the governor was spared. George Porter, who was so seldom present in the territory he governed, picked the occasion of a rare return to die at home. That was in July; in August, the full fury of cholera was loosed on the city and territory, and some records state that Detroit lost as much as 10 percent of its population.

Now Mason was no longer "secretary and acting governor" but chief executive in full right. Porter's death liberated Mason in the sense that he didn't have to be looking over his shoulder any more for approval of his actions. When President Jackson took his time naming a successor to Porter, he seemed to be saying that young Tom Mason had his approval to govern the territory. When Old Hickory did get around to nominating Henry D. Gilpin of Pennsylvania to the office of governor, the Senate rejected the nomination. After the Gilpin rejection, Jackson was content to leave Mason in charge until he overplayed his hand in the dispute with Ohio.

When the cholera epidemic finally played out, Mason could devote his energies to the statehood issue. Furious at developments in Washington, Mason, his youthful impatience rising, devised a plan that would put Michigan on the fast track to statehood. First, a census was needed to determine beyond doubt that the territory met the requisite population standard. With that out of the way, a constitutional convention would be called to draft a constitution and to institute state government. Finally, this new state would elect a representative and two senators, who would be dispatched to Washington to demand admission as a matter of right.

To build his case, Mason cited the "Tennessee precedent." In 1796, Tennessee hadn't waited for enabling legislation from Congress before it framed a constitution and demanded statehood as its right. Not surprisingly, even in those infant years of the Republic, politics played a hand in the ensuing imbroglio, and Tennessee was voted into statehood. It was an untidy piece of business, but nearly forty years later, it suited Mason's purposes.

As a lawyer, Mason should have known he was on shaky legal ground in building on the Tennessee precedent. To many of Washington's seasoned political veterans, Michigan was trying to barge into the Union, all flags flying, with bells and confetti. What Michigan had yet to learn was that proper procedures were part of the rule of law, and besides, there were political dues to be paid, on which young Mason had yet to make a down payment. For all his popularity—he was portrayed in some eastern newspapers as the brave, bright political light on the western frontier—Mason was setting himself up as an easy target for the powerful men on Capitol Hill. He didn't understand why Michigan's case could not be considered on its merits, and he was probably heartened by a letter from his sister, Emily, away at school in New York State, who wrote, "The ignorance of these people, New Yorkers, of Michigan and our affairs is certainly most astonishing."[23]

In September, Mason informed his Territorial Council that it was time for Michigan to act for itself. Since Congress was not of a mind to act, he would supply the heavy lifting. His request for a population count was readily agreed to by the council. The census Mason demanded in 1834 vindicated him in one respect; returns indicated a total population of 87,278. In fact, Michigan had the largest percentage increase in population during the 1830s of any state in the Union. The state census of 1837 revealed 174,543 inhabitants, and the federal census of 1840 gave Michigan a population of 212,267. In a single decade, the increase had been almost sevenfold.

In a message to the Territorial Council in November, Mason told lawmakers there were two choices: either they could call a convention to form a constitution and institute state government, or they could "petition Congress to admit us into the Union as a sovereign and independent state." "Under ordinary circumstances," he argued, "the latter course would be most preferable. But when the dispute with Ohio is called in question, we have but one course to pursue. We need to prevent all legislation whatever on the part of Congress. If brought to the test, Congress will decide against us."[24] Mason's strategy all along was a delaying action. "An already too powerful neighbor," said Mason, "would rob us of one of the fairest portions of our country" as the price of admission for Michigan. This was unacceptable. Mason recommended that Michigan stall any action by the general government regarding the Toledo Strip until it became a state: "We can then appeal for justice to the supreme judicial tribunal of the country, and maintain the rights that are secured to us by the Ordinance of July 13, 1787."[25]

Early in 1835, the Territorial Council reconvened and ordered an election to be held in April to choose delegates to a constitutional convention. This historic gathering of ninety delegates would meet at Detroit on the second Monday of May. When Mason signed the bill authorizing an election to a convention of delegates charged with drafting a constitution, he did so without the consent of Congress. He also signaled to the governor of Ohio that Michigan was prepared to back up its claim to its southern boundary.

While Ohio opposed Michigan's entry into the Union on the basis of the former's claim to the Toledo Strip, President Jackson, a Tennessean, did not want to deal with slavery, and he did not want his Democratic Party to be split on that issue. The Missouri Compromise preserved a kind of equilibrium, but everybody knew that the Union was a fragile entity as long as the slavery issue festered. The conditions under which Michigan would enter the Union would be debated, off and on, for years, but the fact remained that Michigan would have to be paired with a slave state. Southern opposition to Michigan then turned to support, since pairing Michigan with Arkansas would mean that the Missouri Compromise was still working, and a showdown over slavery would be postponed. Thus, on June 15, 1836, "in air perfumed with the thirty-five electoral votes of Ohio, Indiana and Illinois" (to quote John Quincy Adams),[26] Jackson signed enabling legislation for Michigan. But whereas Arkansas was admitted to the Union free and clear, Michigan had conditions attached, and that seemed unacceptable to many Michigan politicians.

All these conditions were still in the future when the delegates met on the appointed date. Dunbar writes, "Within the surprisingly short time of forty-five days they had completed their assigned task of drafting a constitution for the proposed new state. The speed with which they acted is especially remarkable because few of the delegates had had any previous parliamentary experience. Most of them were men of small or moderate means."[27] Fully half of the delegates were farmers. Most were Democrats, with a scattering of Whigs, and debates were mostly neither quarrelsome nor divisive. In that regard at least, Michigan got off to a good start. On the vote to adopt the constitution, there were seventy-five yeas and two nays, with William Woodbridge of Detroit and Townsend Gidley of Jackson voting no. A salute of twenty-five guns was ordered, "in honor of the new sister being born into the Union."[28]

The document the delegates produced was noteworthy for its progressive nature. The state was authorized to begin works of internal improvements, meaning roads, canals, and railroads. Delegates limited the number of officials to be elected, thus pleasing the advocates of a short ballot. Mason followed the proceedings with intense interest, of course, and no doubt lobbied for language he wanted included in the charter. The education article in particular bears the imprint of the state's first governor. Already in 1832, Mason, addressing the Territorial Council in Governor Porter's absence, had said, "To no object can the public funds raised by taxation or otherwise, be more judiciously or advantageously applied than to the establishment and support of common free schools, with a view to the extension of the blessings of education to all classes of the community."[29] In a message in February 1836, Mason told legislators "to secure to the State a general diffusion of knowledge. This can in no wise be so certainly effected as by the perfect organization of a uniform and liberal system of common schools . . . open to all the classes of people as the surest basis of public happiness and prosperity."[30] With respect to the great state university that he envisioned, Mason predicted that "with the careful husbanding of resources, the University of Michigan would become an ornament and honor to the West."[31]

Mason had his hands full that summer of 1835, as the Toledo War erupted despite pleas for forbearance from President Jackson and federal "peace commissioners" who were dispatched to the scene. Once again, Mason came to national attention as the perceived underdog, this time against the veteran politician Robert Lucas, governor of Ohio. It was youth against age, perceived legal right against political might. Mason's refusal to yield on the boundary question would cost him his job that summer.

When Ohio became a state, its constitution provided for an angled boundary that put Ohio in conflict with Michigan. Two surveys, one ordered by Ohio (Harris) and the other ordered by Michigan (Fulton), produced a variance of 470 square miles of contested territory. The wedge-shaped chunk of land between the two survey lines would become known as the Toledo Strip. The strip contained the promising port city of Toledo, which was then only a collection of villages. Michigan had claimed legal title by moving settlers there, collecting taxes, and organizing township government—all without protest from the state of Ohio or remonstrance from Congress.

In the early 1830s, Ohio began to take renewed interest in the contested tract. The Buckeye State was building a costly series of canals linking the Ohio River on the south and the Wabash River on the west with the Great Lakes. The expected eastern terminus of one of the canals was the port of Toledo. To keep Toledo safely in the state of Ohio, the boundary line delineated by the Ohio survey had to be upheld, which was a job for Congress. That was why, after Ohio's constitution was accepted by Congress, Ohio made repeated efforts to have the national body approve the boundary change as well. As one historian sums up the situation, "Here was a territory, refused admission into the Union, preparing to form a state government by and of itself, and here was a state asking Congress to fix one of its boundaries, declaring that boundary already fixed while the opposing territory was declaring that only the federal authorities had power in the case, and was preparing to defend its claim against all comers."[32] Is it any wonder that President Jackson was nonplussed in the summer of 1835 and looked to his attorney general for help?

The battle lines and strategies for the Toledo War were drawn. Michigan would seek statehood as soon as possible but ask Congress to delay resolution of the boundary question until Michigan could take the matter to the Supreme Court. Ohio, meanwhile, realized it had a potential trump card in blocking Michigan statehood until the boundary matter could be settled—in Ohio's favor, of course. Ohio would treat Michigan as a lesser political entity and maintain that the boundary matter was Congress's to settle.

Technicalities were found in the Fulton survey line, so in 1832, Congress provided for yet another survey. This time, the job was given to Captain Andrew Talcott of the U.S. Army, who was aided in the project by a young graduate from West Point by the name of Robert E. Lee. The future military genius of the Confederacy in the Civil War spiced his field notes with descriptions of "bilious fevers, mosquitoes and snakes" in the surrounding country. The survey was completed despite such conditions, and a report was made to Congress. The Talcott survey was almost identical in outcome to the Fulton survey, but that didn't matter, because Congress ignored it. Meanwhile, a caveat sounded years earlier by Governor Cass—"A disputed jurisdiction is one of the greatest evils which can happen to a country"[33]—was taking a life of its own.

When Michigan voters endorsed the concept of statehood in October 1832, it was time for Ohio to sit up and take notice. In a message to the Territorial Council on November 19, 1834, Governor Mason said it was pointless to hope that Congress would rule in Michigan's favor in the dispute with Ohio: "He had observed enough of politics to know that the simple consciousness of standing for the right is a very unattractive reward in a contest of politics and expediency; and as Michigan was a Territory without electoral votes or political prestige, she had but little more than this reward of conscience to offer."[34] Was Mason reckless, hoping to bulldoze Michigan into the Union without regard for proper procedures? Or is their evidence of a deliberate, calculated policy—one of making haste slowly and appealing to favorable public opinion? Mason had a strategy, to be sure, of seeking statehood as soon as possible while delaying resolution of the boundary question. As for the record of his conduct in the Toledo War, one would have to say it was mixed. At times, he could be either self-pitying or brimming with confidence. He could show sound judgment at one moment and appear impulsive at another.

Mason's opening salvo in the Toledo War was his support of a bill authorizing the people of Michigan to hold a constitutional convention. There was no congressional authorization for such a move, but it got immediate attention elsewhere: "This preparation on the part of the people of Michigan territory to establish a state government aroused the people of Ohio to take more active steps to protect what they conceived to be their rights."[35] When Ohio then made noises of seizing jurisdiction, the response from Michigan was both prompt and, in Ohio's view, insolent.

On February 12, 1835, the Territorial Council approved the Pains and Penalties Act, which made it unlawful for any person to exercise official functions within the territory other than from the authority of the territory of Michigan or the United States. The penalty for violation was either a fine, not to exceed one thousand dollars, or imprisonment for up to five years. News of this act of boldness by a mere territory galvanized the Ohio legislature on February 23 into extending the boundaries of its three northern counties to the Harris line and creating the townships of Sylvania and Port Lawrence in the disputed strip. Five days later, General Joseph Brown was commissioned as a brigadier general of the territorial militia, with instructions as to what actions to take if the Pains and Penalties Act was violated.

In retaliation, Ohio's legislature made provision for a group of survey commissioners to remark the Harris line, stating, "It ill becomes a million of freemen to humbly petition, year after year, for what justly belongs to them, and is
completely within their control." Throughout the summer of 1835, that term
"million of freemen" would be the object of much derision in the territory.
Michigan promised "hospitable graves" to any invaders of its southern border.[36]

By now, the dispute on the western frontier had come to national attention.
Mason had written to Secretary of State John Forsyth to warn of the "serious
consequences" of Governor Lucas's actions. Ohio, said Mason, was "governed
by no fixed rules of justice, but rather by an eager and greedy disposition to
grasp after territory."[37] If this wasn't exactly the language of politesse, neither
was Lucas's condescension in rejecting "any question of boundary existing
between the state of Ohio and *that* Territory."[38] Lucas vowed to disregard the
Pains and Penalties Act.

There were other things on President Jackson's mind than the danger of
an armed conflict involving two of his fellow Democrats. He asked Cass if he
couldn't bring Mr. Mason in line. Jackson wanted his policies to continue under
an administration led by his then vice president, Martin Van Buren, but that
was in jeopardy if the Democratic Party was split. If current actions alienated
Ohio and its allies by coming out too strongly in favor of Michigan, the Whigs
could win the election of 1836. Exercise of the spoils system by victorious
Whigs would broom out of office all those loyalists Jackson had appointed and
would taint his legacy.

The president also had worries stemming from a prior dispute. He had put
down the doctrine of nullification, which held that no state could be bound
by a federal law it believed to be unconstitutional. But in striking a powerful
blow for a strong federal Union, Jackson had angered such ardent advocates of
states' rights as his own vice president, John Calhoun. Nullification was still a
lively topic in 1835, and Jackson had no wish to reopen that issue. When Ohio
governor Lucas altered his state's northern boundary and demanded territory
to which it had no legal claim, Ohio was essentially seeking to nullify the 1805
act creating the Michigan Territory. Lucas was linked with the discredited Calhoun as standing for nullification.

Hoping for a quick resolution of the problem, Jackson called in his attorney general, Benjamin F. Butler, for an opinion. It didn't take Butler long to rule
that the tract in dispute legally formed a part of the Michigan Territory and
that the Pains and Penalties Act was a valid law. Divisions within his own cabi-

net only added to Jackson's worries. Despairing of a solution, Jackson decided to send two special commissioners to sort it all out and broker an agreement between Mason and Lucas.

Richard Rush of Pennsylvania and Benjamin Howard of Maryland were well qualified to attempt a settlement. Howard was a congressman who would serve until 1839; Rush had been minister to Great Britain in 1817–25 and was secretary of the U.S. Treasury for three years after that. The two men headed west with orders from the president that he did not want the Pains and Penalties Act enforced. This only served to anger Mason and strengthen recruitment efforts for a war with Ohio. The federal commissioners arrived on the scene with all good intentions, and letters from the president to both governors arrived, urging forbearance. But neither governor was in the mood for conciliation. Lucas had been goaded by the "stripling Governor," as Mason was called in Ohio, to request more military assistance. Mason was moved to write to Forsyth, "I cannot obey his directions," meaning Jackson. Old Hickory, in turn, denounced that "Young Hotspur" for his stubbornness.[39] Cass, trying to maintain a neutral position but clearly in Mason's corner, received a remarkable letter from Mason that starts out by saying, "It pains me to think I may be pursuing a course of policy contrary to President Jackson's wishes. The feelings of Forsyth are so decidedly against me individually and the proceedings of the government commissioners are so directly opposed to the rights and honor of Michigan that I am induced to look forward to my removal from office. I shall surrender my charge without one sigh of regret, save that bloom produced by the wounded feelings which bind me to the President."[40]

Mason was prophetic, but what he predicted was still four months in the future. Rush and Howard proposed that Ohio be allowed to remark the boundary line unmolested. That was unacceptable to Governor Mason, which, in hindsight, was a mistake on his part, because he ignored Cass's advice on the matter. Cass said, "The remarking of the line claimed by Ohio does not seem to me such an exercise of jurisdiction as necessarily to require resistance on the part of Michigan."[41]

The Rush-Howard team failed in its mission, and the two mediators returned to Washington empty-handed. They cautioned against the use of force in running the line. But hostilities between the Michigan militia and the survey team broke out on April 26 at Phillips Corners, fourteen miles south of Adrian. No blood was shed, but this first thrilling exchange of gunfire and the prospect of bloodshed opened the gates of exaggeration and hyperbole in the communications that followed. The newspapers of state and territory did their part to inflame passions. The *Cleveland Whig* said that Ohio women had been treated with violence and that Ohio men had been taken prisoners, "just as if it were war." "We can destroy this band of ruffians," the paper claimed. The *Detroit Journal* said of Governor Lucas, "His accounts are filled with exaggerations and false conclusions. With such an opponent our governor can well measure skill and wisdom."[42]

Cass asked Mason to understand that as a member of Jackson's cabinet, he couldn't express his true sentiments as freely as he would like in regard to the dispute between Ohio and his own state of Michigan. He told Mason to rely on public opinion and that he wanted the territory to "keep right on its side."[43] Cass could see which way the wind was blowing. On August 11, he warned Mason that his failure to coincide with Jackson's policies might bring about his removal. But Mason persisted: "The authorities of Ohio are now collecting a force to sustain and protect the court about to be held by them on the disputed territory. This attempt to exercise jurisdiction will be resisted by Michigan."[44]

Mason's hand was strengthened on August 24, when he was informed that Michigan Democrats had nominated him as their gubernatorial candidate in the putative state's first election, to be held in October. Mason was thrilled with the honor, even as he must have known from Cass's warnings that his head was on the chopping block. When the blow came on August 29, Mason was mustering his forces near Toledo to prevent the appointed session of the Ohio court.

Mason's firing was all in the timing. It was certain he would have to go, but when? Knowing that Mason was immensely popular in Michigan and that he would likely be elected governor, Jackson concluded that it was better to get him out now and hope the affair would have blown over by the time the presidential election came around. Mason, meanwhile, had been conveying to Jackson his opinion that there wouldn't be twenty Van Buren men in Michigan to support the vice president with their votes.

The date for the opening of a court Lucas had ordered to establish title to the Toledo Strip for Ohio was September 7. A dramatic confrontation seemed at hand. Governor Mason may have had as many as one thousand militiamen ready to move on Toledo; the feeling among the Wolverines was that "old Lucas" needed to be taught a lesson and that they were just the ones to do it. Governor Lucas and his aides knew they were outnumbered, so they cleverly arranged to have the court meet under cover of night. The Michigan forces were badly outwitted, and the Ohioans celebrated a bloodless victory. For all intents and purposes, this "Battle of Toledo" ended the war.

As if the humiliation of the midnight court wasn't enough, Mason then learned that he had been fired. An early historian of the events recounts, "The whole army was ordered back to Monroe, and there on a beautiful September day, Mason rode in and eloquently commended the troops for their soldierly bearing and most emphatically expressed his unalterable determination to spill the last drop of blood in his veins in defending the rights of Michigan in the boundary question."[45] After President Jackson sacked Mason, he named Charles Shaler, a judge in Pennsylvania, as secretary and acting governor. Shaler's political instincts must have been acute, because he declined the opportunity to administer such a hornet's nest. Jackson then named John S. Horner of Virginia as Mason's replacement.

Mason took his removal from office very calmly and simply told his people he was no longer their leader. In the meantime, political life in the territory proceeded on two assumptions: that Michigan voters would approve the constitution at a vote in October and that a state government would be needed to implement the provisions of that document. To accomplish the latter, an election would need to be held to elect state officials. The date set was October 5. Mason, as the darling of the territory, was paired on the ballot with Edmund Mundy of Ann Arbor as lieutenant governor. Writing to a committee of citizens accepting the nomination, Mason said, "The history of my brief career on the theatre of public life has been one calculated to render me peculiarly alive to any manifestation of kindness by my friends. By a determined adherence to the interests of the public whenever committed to my charge, I should in time remove all preconceived prejudices, and ultimately obtain the confidence of my fellow citizens. To accomplish this has been the highest object of my ambition. If elected, I will endeavor to discharge its duties, with fidelity to the public."[46]

The Whigs chose not to run anybody in the election, since they viewed the whole business as a sham. They opposed not only the constitution but also statehood efforts led by Mason. The Whigs contended all along that the territory should wait for congressional authorization to apply for admission into the Union. Some Whigs even took the position that not being a state carried the advantages of no federal taxes, no military service, and no forced return of fugitive slaves. However, most of the Whigs ended up supporting John Biddle of Detroit as their informal candidate for governor. Biddle had served as president of the constitutional convention—quite a feat in itself, as Biddle was a Whig at a convention top-heavy with Democrats. With the Whigs virtually sitting this one out, the election of Mason was assured. He topped Biddle, in a vote of 7,508 to 814. The voters approved the proposed constitution, with 6,299 votes in favor and 1,359 against. A full slate of state officials was approved, and on November 1, 1835, Michigan state government was up and running.

Or was it? The official seal of the state of Michigan gives 1835 as the date Michigan became a state, despite the fact that it officially wasn't admitted to the Union until January 1837, under legislation signed by President Jackson. In the eyes of its people, Michigan was a state, and in his inaugural address, the new governor strongly upheld Michigan's course of action. If Congress would not make Michigan a state, its own people would do it themselves.

Mason was thrilled with his triumph at the polls. So was Emily, who wrote, "My brother was deposed from office for one month, and then elected governor of the state."[47] Now Mason could put aside snide remarks about "the Boy Governor" and how "an illiterate vulgar youth" had been appointed to the office of secretary. He had won the hearts of his people with his staunch defense of Michigan's rights in the Toledo War and in his "damn the torpedoes" fight for statehood.

But bitter disappointment showed in his voice in his first address to the legislature on February 1, 1836. He said then, "It would have afforded me the highest satisfaction, fellow citizens, to have been able to communicate to you at this time the favorable result of our application for admission into the Union." "The people of Michigan," he continued, "have been deceived. Their application remains without the final action of Congress. The position which Michigan now occupies with the nation is a peculiar although not a new one in the history of our government. It is that of a people claiming and exercising all the reserved rights and privileges of an American state, and yet excluded from the bonds of the federal union."[48]

Mason was certainly right about Michigan's "peculiar" position. He was the head of a duly elected state government, but John Horner was Washington's man. Michigan was a state without the rights enjoyed by other states, until Congress and the president chose to act. Moreover, for all its bravado in going it alone, Michigan was still a supplicant, passing resolutions asking Congress for appropriations for internal improvements. The state's first representative in Congress was Isaac E. Crary (chosen in October), and the legislature elected Lucius Lyon and John Norvell as the state's first two U.S. senators, but none of the three was allowed to take his seat as a voting member until Michigan was formally recognized by Congress.

Not until June 1836 did Congress broker its famous compromise whereby Michigan enlarged its borders on one end and saw them diminished on the other. On June 15, Congress passed an act to establish the northern boundary of the state of Ohio and to provide for the admission of Michigan into the Union. If Michigan surrendered its claim to the Toledo Strip, it would receive, as compensation, a large tract of land north and west of the Straits of Mackinac.

Now there were more howls of outrage from Michigan over the apparent worthlessness of the Upper Peninsula. But serendipity soon reared its head, with the discovery of rich veins of copper and iron ore. In time, Michigan would congratulate itself for having pulled off a land scam worthy of Seward's fire-sale purchase of Alaska, thirty years in the future: "Mr. Lucius Lyon, with General Cass behind the scenes . . . secured for Michigan that rich region beyond the straits, which Michigan would not part with today for several Toledo seven mile strips."[49] Many years later, Michigan's foremost jurist of the time, the Honorable Thomas M. Cooley, would say of the Toledo War, "We may rejoice that Michigan stood fearlessly by the right and defied the power until a compromise was offered which gave her far more than she was asked to surrender."[50] Cooley would be echoed by Clarence M. Burton, president of the Michigan Pioneer and Historical Society: "We traded that little strip for the U.P. and acquired hundreds of thousands of dollars for a piece of poverty-stricken mud land. The Toledo War was a war without bloodshed and one that is frequently referred to with a smile of derision, but it resulted in greater gains to the State of Michigan than the wisest statesman of that day could foretell."[51] It was only with twenty-twenty hindsight that Michigan accepted the "gift" of the Upper Peninsula. In 1836, the place was still considered frozen tundra and unacceptable to the people in the Lower Peninsula.

The Toledo War was over, but its immediate legacy was one of continuing bitterness. Governor Lucas accused Cass of wielding his position as secretary of war to secure munitions from the arsenal in Detroit for use by Governor Mason and his militia, but Cass stoutly denied the charge, ending that matter. After the final Battle of Toledo, the Ohio survey commissioners marked the boundary without further interruption. The Harris line of 1817 stood, but politicians in Michigan did not let the matter rest. In his message to both houses of the legislature on January 2, 1837, Governor Mason was still protesting against "the constitutionality of an act of Congress prescribing any condition to the admission of a state. We are compelled to view things as they are, and not as they should be."[52] Litigation followed, by farmers living along the line who were unsure in which state they resided. There were further surveys, and contentiousness over bottomlands in Lake Erie continued as late as the 1970s, in a dispute that went all the way to the U.S. Supreme Court. Today, monuments on the boundary line proclaim friendship between the two states but are not taken seriously.

Mason's worst fears were realized when the last scenes of the statehood drama played out far away from Detroit. As I have reported elsewhere, when the Twenty-Fourth Congress opened in December 1835, Senator Thomas Hart Benton of Missouri "presented the credentials of Senators-elect Lyon and Norvell and moved that seats be given to them until Congress acted on admission. After considerable debate, the motion failed. Six days later, the motion again failed, with the opposition led by Henry Clay of Kentucky. The duly elected trio from Michigan, which included Crary in the House, was relegated to spectator status."[53] Lyon was still optimistic enough to believe that the state would be recognized as early as February. John Quincy Adams, the former president who was now serving in the House of Representatives, would take charge of the matter, Lyon promised, and things looked favorable for Michigan. He soon changed his tune.

Ohio upheld its claims to the Toledo Strip, and its claims were joined by those of Indiana and Illinois, both of whom had been allowed into the Union with northern boundaries at variance with the line established by the Northwest Ordinance. The three states had voting strength and, more important, thirty-five electoral votes that were up for grabs in the presidential election that year. The admission bill was before the judiciary committees of both houses of Congress. On February 11, Lyon predicted that the House Judiciary Committee would report against Michigan and in favor of Ohio on the boundary question. Meanwhile, the Capitol Hill grapevine was alive with rumors that Michigan might be forced to exchange the Toledo Strip for lands north of the Straits of Mackinac. Lyon, who was learning to read the tea leaves with some skill, opted to write off Toledo in favor of "all Congress is willing to give us elsewhere."[54] He was vilified for "selling out" Michigan's interests, but his view proved to be the correct one.

By March, the respective committees had completed their task. On March 1, the Senate Judiciary Committee reported in favor of Ohio, taking a position similar to the House committee. All the "evidence" was stacked in favor of Ohio, and the Michigan delegation was, of course, literally speechless. From March to June, Congress debated Michigan's admission. In the House, Adams was moved to say, "Never in the course of my life have I known a controversy in which all the right was so clear on one side and all the power so overwhelmingly on the other."[55] It didn't matter that most of Washington's politicians probably agreed with Adams.

Michigan had other strong defenders besides Adams. Senator Benton of Missouri said Michigan had been debarred of its rights and had a right to be admitted. Another senator, John M. Niles of Connecticut, warned, "There is a point beyond which a free people cannot be driven. Why are the people of Michigan to be vexed and harassed in this way? They have been opposed and resisted in every course they have pursued to obtain admission into the Union; and you have now divided their territory . . . Do you wish to drive that people . . . into acts of violence?"[56] Niles's statement may be somewhat melodramatic, but it typified the passionate debate over the issue.

A compromise of sorts was reached when Michigan received, as compensation for the loss of the Toledo Strip, the western two-thirds of the Upper Peninsula, a land so remote from the territorial capital that a Detroit newspaper called it "a region of perpetual snows." In terms of real estate, Michigan gave up 468 square miles of farmland and swamp along its southern border for about 9,000 square miles of poor country north of nowhere. The exchange of the Upper Peninsula for the Toledo Strip may not rank among such great land steals as the Louisiana Purchase, but the Upper Peninsula would soon prove its value many times over. Perhaps the last word belongs to an Ohio historian, W. V. Way, who perceptively wrote, "Congress gave Michigan the valuable mineral lands adjoining Lake Superior to make up the loss of the Territory given to Ohio; both parties thereby acquiring lands that neither had any legal right to."[57]

An amended statehood bill passed the Senate on April 2 by a vote of 24–17 and was sent to the House. That body approved the bill by a vote of 143–50, and on June 15, 1836, President Jackson signed it. Ohio got its way, but it also demanded its pound of flesh. Written into the statehood bill was a proviso requiring Michigan to hold a special convention of delegates to assent to the terms of the bill. There would be only one item on the agenda, and Ohio would get it in writing that Michigan was signing off on Toledo for time and eternity.

The news from Congress was greeted with outrage in Michigan. Was that war with Ohio fought for nothing? What about those people living in the Toledo Strip—were they to be left high and dry? As for the Upper Peninsula, it was wilderness, and the only natives were Indians—or were they Eskimos? The required convention of assent was simply intolerable, a condition attached to statehood that was unprecedented in the American experience.

Even so, forces were at work to ease Michigan's pain. Rumors of mineral wealth in the Upper Peninsula continued to filter downstate, fed by such knowledgeable people as Cass and Henry R. Schoolcraft, both of whom had traveled in that distant region. Lucius Lyon opined that Michigan got the better of the deal and that the Upper Peninsula would be worth forty million dollars in twenty years. Someone else thought the tasty whitefish of Lake Superior would offset the loss of those bullfrog pastures on the Maumee River.

An even greater inducement for Michigan to agree to the terms of Congress was economic. Michigan's share of surplus federal revenue would be about four hundred thousand dollars; the catch was that Michigan had to be a state to qualify for those monies. Michigan had a lot to do with the fact there was a large federal surplus in the first place. The year 1836 saw a great rise in land sales, and Michigan land was hot property. In fact, the boom market in Michigan had been building since completion of the Erie Canal and the arrival of steam transportation on the Great Lakes. "Michigan fever" was taking hold, and the new settlers, mostly from New England and New York, had a profound effect on Michigan and the development of its social and political institutions.

There were two land offices in early Michigan, one in Detroit and one created in 1823 at Monroe. In 1831, the land office in Monroe closed, only to reopen two years later; another office opened in White Pigeon. In 1831, 320,467 acres were sold for $401,342. There followed a dip in land sales, partly due to the Black Hawk War and the cholera scare. But by 1834, sales were up to nearly 500,000 acres. In June 1836, a land office was opened at Genesee, adding to the ones in Detroit, Monroe, and Kalamazoo. Historian Alec Gilpin reports, "A summary report from the General Land Office to the secretary of the treasury showed that, as of September 30, 1835, of the over twelve million acres offered for sale in the lower peninsula, more than three million had been sold for more than four million dollars. In 1835, the Detroit office reported June sales of $467,000; Kalamazoo reported sales for May–July of $1,106,676."[58]

So Michigan, which played a huge role in generating the federal surplus, now stood to miss out unless it agreed to statehood terms. Other inducements were the prospect of getting 5 percent of proceeds from sale of public lands within Michigan's boundaries after it became a state and, of course, patronage for deserving campaign contributors. Economics would drive Michigan's decision to say yes to the terms imposed by Congress.

Governor Mason took the lead in drumming up support for a yes vote. At a special session of the legislature called to consider the bill signed by Jackson, Mason forcefully said that Congress had acted unjustly but that he would abide by the decision of the people. That was a clear indication he favored acceptance, and so the battle lines were drawn, with the opposition Whigs holding out for an eventual appeal to the Supreme Court. An election was set to elect delegates to a convention of assent, which would meet in Ann Arbor on the second Monday in September.

As the election neared, those favoring acceptance played the economics card, stressing the potential value of the Upper Peninsula and arguing that the boundary dispute was a national, not a local, issue. The Democrats felt that there was nothing to be gained by spurning Congress. The Whigs favored rejection on the grounds of the alleged illegality of the constitutional convention and the steal of land to which Michigan had rightful claim. The newspapers of the day were divided, with the *Detroit Advertiser, Pontiac Courier,* and *Monroe Sentinel* standing opposed, while the *Ann Arbor Argus, Tecumseh Democrat,* and *Detroit Free Press* were in favor.

The convention opened with forty-nine delegates from twenty-seven counties. The written record was contained in a "Journal of the Proceedings of the Convention of Delegates, chosen by the electors of the State of Michigan, in pursuance of an Act of Congress of June 15, 1836, for the purpose of taking into consideration The Proposition of Congress relative to the admission of the State of Michigan into the Union, begun and held at the Court House in the village of Ann Arbor on Monday, the 26th day of September, A.D. 1836." On Monday, the convention was called to order by Austin E. Wing, and on Tuesday, September 27, having elected officers and adopted rules, the delegates got down to business.

Citing a "radical alteration by Congress of our southern boundary, a palpable violation of our constitution," a resolution of Robert Clark of Monroe County recommended, "therefore let it be resolved, that this convention cannot give their assent to the proposition . . . and the same is hereby rejected."[59] Despite the one-item agenda, delegates heard resolutions protesting against the right of Congress to attach conditions to statehood, as well as arguments that conflicting claims of states to jurisdiction or sovereignty ought to be properly adjudicated. But the discussion over these items was mainly for show.

On Wednesday, Clark moved that his resolution be adopted. But Ross Wilkins of Wayne County offered a substitute motion, stating that the assent required by Congress be given. Delegates would have none of that; in the vote to assent, there were twenty-one for and twenty-eight against. The delegates had pulled a shocker: they had thumbed their noses at Congress, at President Jackson, and at neighboring states that were in league with Ohio. On a motion of Clark, the convention adjourned on September 30, and a select committee of Andrew Mack, Austin Wing, and Clark was named to travel to Washington to report the results to the president.

What would come to be known as the First Convention of Assent had become a "convention of dissent." Two weeks after the final gavel, a lengthy address from delegates of the state convention "to the People of Michigan" appeared, signed by Edward D. Ellis of Monroe, Clark of Monroe, William H. Welch of Kalamazoo, Seth Markham of Washtenaw, and S. A. L. Warner of Oakland. The letter asked whether Michigan should participate in the national councils, "mutilated, humbled and degraded. Must she sell a portion of her brethren, like Joseph in Egypt, as the price of admission?" It responded, "No! Congress cannot bestow upon Ohio any part of our domain without our consent."[60] Just for good measure, the writers roundly condemned Ohio for its avarice.

The vote of the convention and the letter, which received wide circulation, showed how deep passions still ran over the loss of the Toledo Strip and perceived injustices at the national level. But Michigan was no nearer to statehood for its act of defiance. To receive its four hundred thousand dollars, Michigan needed to be admitted by the first of the year or thereabouts. The territory's financial position was getting worse. Governor Mason now took his lumps not only from the Whigs, for knuckling under to Congress, but also from his own Democrats, for not guaranteeing a favorable result from the convention of assent.

But Mason was not one to take this defeat without further fight. Although it was too late to summon the legislature into special session to call for another election of delegates, Mason had one more bullet in his gun. That was to go to the people themselves and appeal for another convention. Thus we find him writing to Esek Pray of Ypsilanti, who was president of a meeting of citizens in Washtenaw County and friendly to admission with all deliberate speed. "It is asked," Mason said, "if the proceedings of the late Ann Arbor convention are final upon the people of Michigan, and if there is no appeal from their decision. The answer is plain. The remedy is with the people themselves. They are sovereign, and are essentially the source of all state power. They have an inherent and indefeasible right . . . to reverse the acts of their agents if found prejudicial to their interests."[61] He went on to "suggest" that the people elect delegates among themselves to a convention, "for the purposes contemplated by Congress. No one can question their right to do so. No one can impede their proceedings."[62]

The Democrats took the initiative in promoting gatherings to overturn the convention of assent. With Mason providing the marching orders, Democrats in Washtenaw County formed a caucus to name delegates to a second convention. In populous Wayne County, David C. McKinstry, Marshal J. Bacon, Ross Wilkins, John McDonell, and Charles W. Whipple signed a statement that called on the people, "[w]ithout any executive or legislative interposition, to elect and call together a convention, to give their assent to the proferred congressional terms."[63] With more and more of these "spontaneous" gatherings, Democrats felt the situation was well in hand, and an election of delegates was called for December 5 and 6.

But the election did not enjoy the sanction of legislative approval within Michigan. Neither did Congress, acting on behalf of one of its territories, give its authorization. There was no legal mechanism to be found that gave blessing to the second convention, and it was a stretch of the imagination when Mason said the people had spoken. Many scholars and historians have agreed that Mason overstepped his authority in counting these "spontaneous" gatherings as legitimate expressions of the people.

The Whigs boycotted this election, and several counties chose not to participate. The result was a stacked convention with no doubt as to outcome. The Second Convention of Assent met in Ann Arbor on December 14–15, with a single question to be debated—agreeing to the act of June 15. Delegates elected John R. Williams of Wayne president, with Kintzing Pritchette and Jonathan E. Field serving as secretaries. Ross Wilkins from Wayne County offered a resolution providing for the assent of Michigan to the terms of Congress. The brief debate was marked by the usual protestations over Congress's role in dictating statehood terms. The resolution was then adopted unanimously, but the delegates still had the gumption to protest against the constitutional right of Congress to require a preliminary assent.

It was cold in the Ann Arbor courthouse that December 14, and one witness was moved to say, "This sure is a Frostbitten Convention." When the delegates adjourned the next day, the Frostbitten Convention took its place in Michigan annals as a major event in the life of the state. "We bow to the power, but question the right," Williams said. Williams was elected to bring the news of Michigan's assent to Washington. "Highly irregular," harrumphed critics of the Frostbitten Convention, and yet no official challenge was made to its legality. Naturally, Mason insisted all along that the election was the will of the people and that the vote of the convention had their stamp of approval.

The focus now shifted to Washington, where it would appear there would be no further obstacles. But politics and old animosities conspired to prolong Michigan's travail. Technicalities were raised about the legality of the Frostbitten Convention. The boundary issue was raised again, and it was decided that the boundary and the question of admission should be voted on separately. Both houses of Congress chose to refer these questions to separate committees. In the Senate, Senator Benton of Missouri, again a forceful speaker on Michigan's behalf, said, "The admission of a state is a question of that dignity to be entitled, not only to a speedy decision, but to a preference over all other questions."[64]

Senator John C. Calhoun of South Carolina took a different tack: "The admission of Michigan is destined to mark a great change in the history of the admission of new states, a total departure from the old usage . . . Everything thus far has been irregular and monstrous connected with their admission."[65] He called the December convention "a lawless assemblage." A future president, Senator James Buchanan of Pennsylvania, then rose to challenge Calhoun. Referring to Calhoun's contention that approval of the bill accepting the decision of the December convention would make the U.S. government "one of the most odious and despotic governments ever existing on the earth," Buchanan declared, "I presume it is attributable to my colder temperament that I feel none of these terrors. In my opinion, they spring altogether from Mr. Calhoun's ardent imagination."[66]

Back in the territory, it was the feeling of many that this was a peevish Congress's final effort to portray Michigan as some kind of backwoods pariah. Mason and Michigan were seen as obtuse in their dealings with Ohio and as less than deferential to Jackson. That Jackson's appointee, Horner, was first vilified and then ignored was taken as proof that Michigan did not respect federal authority. Mason was seen as a man fired from his job, the governor of a de facto state. Not even the respected Lewis Cass could change Washington's low opinion of Mason, a young man who had a lot to learn about the ways of Washington. When Michigan named nine counties in southern Michigan after Jackson and members of his cabinet in an attempt to win over Washington's politicians, it didn't help.

Mason's prosecution of the Toledo War, coming as it did from his alleged "hotspur" nature, did not sit well with official Washington. Even the president's cabinet was divided. The attorney general took Mason's position, and Secretary of State John Forsyth backed Jackson, while Secretary of War Cass stood to the side, cautioning forbearance on Mason's part.

On January 5, 1837, the Senate voted to accept the Michigan statehood bill by a vote of 25–10; among the no votes were Calhoun and Clay. The House passed the statehood bill on January 25 by a vote of 132–43. Two future presidents—James K. Polk, who was then Speaker of the House, and Vice President Martin Van Buren—added their signatures to the statehood bill. Then both houses approved an act on January 26 accepting the Second Convention of Assent as meeting the requirements of admission.

Even for Congress, that bit of hypocrisy was astonishing. The act contained a preamble that the people of the state of Michigan had given their consent to the proposed boundary, when, it can be argued, they did no such thing. They didn't give their consent at the First Convention of Assent or, according to many legal experts, at the illegal, boycotted, unrepresentative Frostbitten Convention. Five years after Michigan first applied for statehood, it was admitted as a state *without its people's consent* but with Congress deluding itself into *thinking* they had given consent.

Michigan accepted the date of statehood as January 26, 1837, and when news of Jackson's signature on the admission bill reached Detroit, it was time to party. On February 9, a major celebration was planned. The Brady Guards, a crack militia group named after General Hugh Brady, fired a twenty-six-gun salute for the twenty-sixth state. Detroit was literally aglow; people placed candles in windows, and there were bonfires on Jefferson Avenue. Governor Mason was guest of honor at a gala dinner at the Woodworth Hotel. Called on to make some remarks, a jubilant chief executive took the high road of statesmanship by expressing the hope that the controversy over the Toledo Strip was over. The most important consideration, he said, was that "Michigan had become a State of the Union and it was the duty of every true citizen, forgetting all past differences, to unite in the endeavor to elevate her standing and advance her prosperity."[67]

This was the zenith of Tom Mason's public life in Michigan. Statehood had been achieved at last. He had fought the good fight in the Toledo War. Big plans were being made to develop the state's interior. Never again would he appear higher in public standing than he did on that memorable night in Detroit—as a "hotspur" triumphant. As that year progressed, Mason would be caught up in momentous events not of his making. The country and its newest state were on the brink of financial catastrophe.

5 ～ Building a State

When Michigan began functioning as a state on November 2, 1835, its timing was good in one respect. Wonder of wonders, the U.S. Treasury would soon be reporting a surplus, and the monies were going to be distributed among the states. The lure of lucre was a powerful stimulus for Michigan politicians to act, so when the First Convention of Assent surprised everybody by rejecting the terms of Congress, Governor Mason went into overdrive.

As soon as Michigan became a state, explains historian John Kern, "she would begin to receive five percent of the proceeds from the sale of public lands within her boundaries, and as a state she would be eligible to share in the distribution of the surplus in the United States Treasury. Estimates which placed the combined benefits of statehood at more than $650,000 provided strong inducements for reconsideration, as did expectations of prestigious and lucrative federal appointments for loyal Michigan politicians."[1] The Frostbitten Convention hurriedly assented to the terms of the act of June 15, 1836, thus qualifying Michigan for revenue sharing, only that's not what they called it in those days.

Stevens T. Mason took the oath of office on November 3, 1835, the bloom of youth still on his visage. Eyewitness reports of the events of that day found their way into the Michigan Pioneer and Historical Collections. Cheering throngs greeted Mason after he left his house on Jefferson and proceeded along Woodward to the Campus Martius, where his open carriage made the turn for the capitol. Bowing to the crowd, he entered the building and shook hands with his secretary of state, Kintzing Pritchette, then with his lieutenant governor, Ed Mundy, followed by Ezra Convis of Calhoun County, speaker of the House, and the Reverend John D. Pierce, superintendent of public instruction.

Finally at the rostrum, Mason launched into a speech that was notable for its length and grasp of four-syllable words. He spoke with an air of confidence and pride, again promising to seek advice from his elders.

But when the bunting came down and the day ended, the fact that his state was broke remained, a bad situation to be in when one is standing, hat in hand, asking to be accepted in the union of states. Michigan was passing resolutions asking Congress for appropriations for roads and other internal improvements. Mason was informed by the secretary of the U.S. Treasury, Levi Woodbury, that money appropriated by Congress for "making roads and canals within the State" was null and void until Michigan was admitted as a state. When the state treasurer reported on July 6, 1836, that the treasury contained only fifty-seven thousand dollars, it was clear that this pittance was inadequate for what needed to be done. The First Convention of Assent, in its lusty stand on principle, didn't concern itself with the sad state of the treasury.

If statehood is accepted as beginning on November 2, 1835, the first several months were times of uncertainty. A judiciary wasn't yet in place. At Governor Mason's request, the legislature limited its functions to routine matters and general discussion, rather than approval of any legislation to which a prickly Congress might take exception. This marking of time when critical problems needed addressing did not suit the state's dynamic governor, but his hands were tied. He moved ahead with plans to develop Michigan and, in so doing, had the unique privilege of laying the foundation for his state's institutions and distinct characteristics.

Mason had a vision of a state interlaced with serviceable roads, canals on which freight and produce would be easily borne, and railroads that would link the state's communities together. Development of three railroads and two major canals was planned. With the state's share of the federal surplus in hand, it was easy to believe that Michigan's growth would continue through the 1830s and that an ambitious program of internal improvements could be funded without onerous taxation. On January 2, 1837, Governor Mason urged the legislature to begin a series of internal improvements and to create a board responsible for overseeing such activities.

In that message, Mason requested of Congress a sum of money to build a ship canal around the rapids of the St. Marys River at Sault Ste. Marie. Mason thought that the cost of the canal was "trifling" compared to the advantages that would derive from it. Mason said that if the federals showed no interest, the cost would be underwritten by the state. The federal government declined to finance a canal connecting Lakes Huron and Superior, and Michigan was forced to take the initiative. One of the most influential opponents of the canal, which was to be the forerunner of the great Soo Locks, was Senator Henry Clay of Kentucky. Clay contemptuously allowed that considering building a canal there "contemplates a work beyond the remotest settlement in the United States, if not the moon."[2]

The canal project, coming so soon after the Toledo War and the disputatious admissions process, was destined to place Mason and the federal government at loggerheads again. During the canal controversy, "Michigan directly blamed the United States government for having thwarted its canal building project illegally and condemned federal intervention as a 'reckless disregard of the rights and honor of the state of Michigan.'"[3] The fight started when the legislature directed the governor to hire an engineer to survey a route for the proposed canal and appropriated twenty-five thousand dollars to aid in construction. The engineer, John Almy, drew up plans for a canal and locks at an estimated cost of $112,500. In his annual message of 1838, Governor Mason recommended an appropriation of that amount, but "before acting, the legislature sent a resolution to Congress requesting a donation of land to aid in building the canal."[4] Because the project was believed to be national in character, lawmakers thought the donation of land would be a routine thing. It was not.

After the contract was let and when work was about to begin, the federal government intervened. The line of the proposed canal crossed a millrace that led to a sawmill on the grounds of Fort Brady, the federal fort at Sault Ste. Marie. When the contractors arrived, with their work crews and implements, they were met by Lieutenant William Root, assistant quartermaster at Fort Brady, who informed them that it was his duty to prevent work on the proposed canal. Root said he was acting under instructions of the War Department.

The millrace was regarded by the War Department as an improvement of the greatest importance to Fort Brady, although one writer says, "The millrace had not been in use for a number of years and the saw mill was a useless and dilapidated affair."[5] Root neglected to say that he had been ordered not to object to the work "being conducted through the military reservation or grounds, provided it can be done without serious injury to the interests of the United States."[6] Meanwhile, Aaron Weeks of Mt. Clemens had assumed a one-third share of the canal contract, and he wrote Root to say that he and his men were bound by the state of Michigan to excavate even if the canal lines intersected with the millrace. Anything less would frustrate the object that the state of Michigan had in mind.

Now the commander of Fort Brady got into the picture. The contractors under Weeks had begun work and were prepared to continue working until prevented by a superior force. Captain A. Johnson informed the men that the army would not permit the canal to bisect the millrace. The men ignored this warning and continued working, whereupon Johnson and a company of armed soldiers drove the workingmen off the line of the canal. Seeing the hopelessness of the situation, the contractors were forced to abandon the project. Governor Mason protested the federal action to Secretary of War Joel R. Poinsett (Cass's successor) as a violation of Michigan's sovereign rights, but Poinsett made it plain that the contractors had caused the difficulty "by their own precipitancy."[7] He assured Mason that the War Department would not stand in the way of internal improvements in Michigan. Mason went over Poinsett's head with a letter to President Martin Van Buren, stating that the millrace was of little importance to the United States and that it was rarely, if ever, used by the garrison. The appeal was to no avail, however, and Michigan was left with nothing to show for its challenge to the federals. It would be 1852 before Congress got around to granting the necessary acreage of public lands for the construction of a canal.

Poinsett's response had angered sensitive state legislators: "Still smarting from a sense of injustice over the settlement of the Ohio boundary question, they felt doubly wronged in being unable to carry on an improvement of the country so ungratefully thrust upon them—a wrong aggravated by the knowledge that the improvement was national in character, and for the doing of which they should have been praised and honored, instead of being met with a humiliating indignity."[8] There was some evidence that the commanding officers at Fort Brady had received instructions from the War Department several weeks before they informed the state.

Federal-state relations during the Mason years were contentious, to be sure, but they must be seen in the context of the times. States' rights, though dealt a heavy blow by President Jackson's putting down of nullification, still had many strong proponents. Although Mason supported Jackson on nullification and was committed to a strong federal union, there was just enough of a states' righter in Mason to challenge Washington from time to time. Recall how it "pained" him to oppose Jackson's course of action in the Toledo War.

Other public works projects were soon under way, including what would be the first steam-powered railroad west of the Alleghenies. The Erie and Kalamazoo Railroad was chartered in 1833 and linked Adrian with Toledo. On November 2, 1836, accompanied by much hurrahs and boom of cannon, the railroad ran its first car from Toledo to Adrian, a trip that took several hours, with horses pulling the coach. In the next year, a steam locomotive was put to use, and iron straps were laid over the oak rails. The line never was completed to Marshall, where it would have connected with the Kalamazoo River, a stream that emptied into Lake Michigan. When Toledo was awarded to Ohio, financial backers had a change of heart, and the railroad that was supposed to promote the economic development of the southern tier of Michigan counties came to be seen as an entity only helping to build the port of Toledo.

In February 1836, Governor Mason, caught up in the spirit of the times, was calling for "liberality" in the development of the state's wealth. As it turned out, this was a grave mistake, because Michigan didn't have the money to see its internal improvement projects through to completion. Mason was talking wealth of a different kind—the state's plenteous waters, a favorable terrain for railroads, and his people's work ethic. He told legislators there was something for every constituent, which was music to the ears of every vote-conscious lawmaker. A year later, he was still optimistic, as Michigan was soon to be admitted as the twenty-sixth state.

His State of the State message of January 2, 1837, painted a rosy picture: "The tide of emigration is rapidly extending its course to the remotest borders of the state; unprecedented health has blessed the habitations of the people; abundant harvests have crowned the exertions of our agriculturist; our cities and villages are thronging with an active and enterprising population; and notwithstanding the embarrassments which have surrounded us in our relations to the federal Union . . . the majesty of the law has been supreme."[9] The state census that year revealed 174,543 inhabitants.

In calling for an ambitious program of internal improvements, Mason was only following orders. The state's constitutional convention of 1835 contained a proviso saying, "Internal improvements shall be encouraged by the government of this state; and it shall be the duty of the legislature, as soon as may be, to make provisions by law for ascertaining the proper objects of improvement, in relation to roads, canals and navigable waters." Mason was a creature of his times, and the times showed "a desire for economic development as part of the democratic movement of Jacksonian America and accurately reflected the material aspirations of a land-holding democracy."[10] It was confidently asserted that an internal improvements system "would pay for itself and yield a net profit of three million dollars to the state in twenty years."[11]

How were internal improvements of a scale contemplated by Mason to be funded? One source was the full faith and credit of the state, as supported by a healthy treasury. Another source was banks, which would extend the credit needed by businessmen to exploit the opportunities that were opened by an expanding transportation network. As we shall see, communities in burgeoning Michigan could not form banks fast enough to extend credit, and it was thought that the potentially booming market of agricultural production would lay the foundation for an industrial economy.

In writing the state's first constitution, delegates found a model in that of New York, adopted in 1821. That document required that all corporation charters had to be approved by a two-thirds majority of both houses of the legislature: "New York's provision was designed to limit the number of banks in the belief that a two-thirds vote would insure the investigation of all bank promoters to see that their banks would supply legitimate credit needs."[12] A provision requiring each bank to make an investment in bonds or mortgages equal to the amount of banknotes it had in circulation as a hedge against insolvency was considered and rejected by the Michigan delegates: "The two-thirds clause was the only restraint the convention imposed on the creation of banknote credit in spite of a determined attempt by a number of delegates to prohibit all incorporations as the only assured way to avoid frauds and banknote inflation."[13] When Michigan launched its program of internal improvements, it was with the understanding that all the projects would be financed by credit, and the two-thirds clause was ignored in the haste to get things under way.

Here's how things were intended to work: "The state would finance its large-scale projects by selling bonds; and local manufacturing businesses and local transportation improvements would be financed by local bank credit."[14] Passage of a free banking statute in 1837 ended up creating a multitude of local banks, charged with generating credit for local use; they were "free" because they did not need an individual charter approved by a two-thirds majority of the legislature. The free banking law permitted any twelve individuals to establish a bank simply by applying to their county officers. With no experience in these matters and with banking expertise in short supply, Michigan was writing a prescription for trouble. The national financial crisis known as the Panic of 1837 was just over the horizon.

Early profits from the pioneer Erie and Kalamazoo Railroad prompted state legislators to indulge their dreams of "vast viaducts of wealth and prosperity."[15] On March 20, 1837, a law providing for state construction and operation of internal improvements authorized Governor Mason to fund the program by selling bonds for five million dollars to eastern banks. Mason had recommended that the state borrow money and subscribe to the stock of private railroad and canal companies. The legislature chose to ignore this recommendation and preferred to proceed by state action. When Mason approved the bill providing for state-built railroads and canals, this decision seemed to be against his better judgment.

The bulk of the plan for three railroads and two canals never came to fruition. A southern railroad was to run from Monroe on Lake Erie across the southern tier of counties to Lake Michigan on the west, a central railroad was to run through the second tier of counties from Detroit to St. Joseph, and a northern line was to run from St. Clair to Grand Haven. The first canal, a gigantic undertaking, was to connect the waters of the Clinton River on the east with those of the Kalamazoo River on the west; a second canal would link the waters of the Saginaw and Grand Rivers; and a separate act called for construction of a third canal to bypass the rapids of the St. Marys River at Sault Ste. Marie. A seven-man board of internal improvements would oversee the construction and operation of the railroads and canals.

Why didn't Michigan construct just one east-west railroad, with branch lines serving major communities? As it was, villages were planned in anticipation of the railroads coming to their towns; when the economy turned sour, ghost towns were often the result. But one must remember Mason's high-flown rhetoric of "something for every constituent." Unfortunately for Michigan, the state's public works projects relied heavily on continued economic good times, and that was not to be. The tea leaves of impending danger were there to be read, but state leaders were not drinking tea.

Mason had used his State of the State message in 1837 to warn about "the wild and reckless spirit of speculation which has overrun the land."[16] In Michigan, the speculation in land values during the 1830s was spiraling out of control. Elsewhere, banks were issuing notes of credit far out of balance with their resources, and states were trying to outdo each other in public works projects they could not afford. In July of 1836, President Jackson issued his famous Specie Circular, which required a metallic currency (gold or silver) as the only allowable payment for the purchase of public lands. Speculation stopped for a time, but the troubles were only beginning.

Earlier, Jackson, whose attitude toward bankers was that they were "soulless monopolists," had conducted a campaign against the Bank of the United States and its autocratic manager, Nicholas Biddle. When the bank's charter was not renewed in 1836, that was the signal to disperse its deposits among various state banks. This, in turn, led to laws permitting any group of citizens to open a bank by fulfilling minimum conditions. In Michigan, "the democratic westerners believed that banking, like the manufacture of cloth, ought to be open to anyone who wanted to get into the business."[17] A vast amount of paper money was printed, confidence in which was undercut by the Specie Circular. In time, the banks did not have enough specie on hand and were forced to sell what they held as collateral, usually land; insolvency followed. Jackson left office with the country in full-blown panic; banks were failing left and right, and people were losing their savings.

A piece of farsighted legislation in 1837 almost escaped notice, but it paid dividends to Michigan many times its original cost. Provision had been made for the appointment of a state geologist, carrying an appropriation of three thousand dollars. The job went to Douglass Houghton, who reported in 1841 that a geological survey of the Upper Peninsula had located mineral wealth in sufficient quantity to warrant commercial development. Before his tragic death by drowning in Lake Superior, Houghton's work and that of his assistants would provide a valuable tool for nearly every important industry based on the natural resources of the state.

Moving ahead with his plans to develop Michigan, Mason saved some of his best eloquence for the cause of schools and higher education. His message to the legislature on February 1, 1836, in regard to education is worth quoting in some detail: "Here the people are the primary source of all power. Public opinion directs the course which our government pursues, and as long as the people are enlightened that direction will never be misgiven. It becomes your imperious duty to secure to the State a general diffusion of knowledge. This can be effected by the perfect organization of a uniform and liberal system of common schools, open to all classes, as the surest basis of public happiness and prosperity."[18] Mason told the legislature that to obtain competent teachers for Michigan's school system, it was necessary to provide for liberal salaries. That advice was not heeded, however; in 1843, the superintendent of public instruction reported the average monthly salary was $12.90 for male teachers and $5 for female teachers. The state's economic plight may have had a lot to do with this situation.

Under the direction of the government, Mason proposed that section 16 in each township be reserved for schools. He further noted that "under the Act of Congress of January 20, 1836, seventy-two sections of land are reserved for the use and support of the University of Michigan. Forty-nine sections of the University lands have been located and consist of some of the most valuable tracts on the peninsula. I would suggest that the proper authority be requested to make the remaining locations. These locations judiciously made will . . . place the University of Michigan among the wealthiest institutions of the country, and under a proper direction, render it an ornament and honor to the West."[19] A year later, he would proudly predict an endowment for the university, "which will enable the state to place that institution upon an elevation of character and standing equal to that of any similar institution in the Union."[20] Mason did not live to see his state university become the leading institution of its kind in the country, but generous support for the school's mission in annual state appropriations has been shown by succeeding state legislatures up to the present day. It would gladden Stevens T. Mason's heart to know that the university he was so instrumental in creating is among the great centers of learning in the world.

Of course, in Mason's time, there were no buildings yet for the university, which was soon to relocate from Detroit to Ann Arbor. When the university requested a loan of state bonds of $150,000 for twenty years, Mason was strong in support: "The University of Michigan is the common property of the people of the State . . . It is highly important to the formation of our state character that the institution should be opened for the reception of students at an early a day as practicable. But the necessary buildings must first be erected. The loan asked will accomplish this end."[21]

With the education system as with so much of Michigan's early development, the influence of New England was considerable. Lewis Cass had left New Hampshire to become Michigan's longtime territorial governor, from which post he had advertised the advantages of the state. Another former New Englander, Isaac Crary, was the chairman of the Committee on Education at the state's 1835 constitutional convention; Crary was instrumental in providing for a state superintendent of public instruction, and through Governor Mason, he secured the appointment of John D. Pierce to that position. Pierce was born at Chesterfield, New Hampshire, and he had come to Michigan as a home missionary. Pierce would famously say, "No new state ever started into being with so many warm and devoted friends of education as Michigan."[22]

Crary, thirty-one at the time, and Pierce, who was thirty-eight years old, lived in the same house in Marshall. The two men took to discussing the condition and prospects of the new state, especially the topic of schools. They had read M. Victor Cousin's study of the Prussian system of education and together believed that the Prussian idea could serve as a model for Michigan. "Paradoxically," notes historian Alan Brown, these two men borrowed educational ideas from an autocratic government to help maintain a free, democratic society."[23]

When Crary was elected to the constitutional convention, the idea took shape, with Pierce responsible for implementing measures to fulfill the proposals adopted by Crary's committee. These proposals included a public school system in which schools in each district would be open at least three months a year; a state superintendent of public instruction who would supervise the public school system; and libraries to be established in each township as soon as possible. In addition, districts that did not remain open would lose proportionately from primary school monies; university lands would be protected, and funds from the sale of these lands would go to the university and its branches; and revenues from public lands in section 16 in each township would be placed in a state fund, with the interest used for school support.

Crary became the state's first congressman after his tour of duty at the convention. He used the delay in Michigan's bid for statehood to word the admissions act "to ensure that the state would control the monies generated from sales of the section sixteen lands. Other states had let the individual townships manage these lands, and the results had been uneven and occasionally detrimental to the advancement of education."[24] The clever Crary also worded the admissions act so that the university lands granted to Michigan by Congress would only go for the support of the University of Michigan, "rather than for all schools of higher learning."

Following the people's adoption of the constitution, Pierce received his appointment and was directed to submit a plan for common schools and for a university. Pierce sold his house in Marshall and spent some time in the East, studying education systems. Upon his return, he would write the report that would gain for him everlasting fame as the father of the Michigan public school system.

Pierce's comprehensive plan for public education was presented to the legislature in January 1837. The state would create, administer, and support a system of primary schools, to give flesh to the idea of education from first grade to university "as a continuous flow of public instruction under public responsibility."[25] Pierce's outline of public instruction defined the roles and duties of primary school districts and their officers and of township officers. The organization and support of the university was explained; control would be vested in a board of regents. Disposition of the public lands was prescribed after a certain fashion. Pierce called for a system of tax-supported schools in which no primary schoolchild would be required to pay tuition, but "almost from the beginning of the statehood era, taxes and income from the primary school fund proved insufficient to keep schools in many districts open the required minimum three months."[26] In fact, this goal was not achieved on a statewide basis until the 1860s.

Crary and Pierce found a strong ally in Governor Mason. He liked placing the schools in the custody of the state, under a superintendent of public instruction who would administer the system. He also expressed approval of a board of regents who would be appointed by the governor and would determine policy for the university. Guarding the land grants from grasping township politicians made all the sense in the world. Pierce confided to Mason that the school plan "is truly a subject of immense magnitude and I cannot but feel the weight of responsibility resting upon me in my present position. What we do is not only to affect the present but coming generations."[27]

The provision that Crary wrote into the admissions act to grant a section of land in each township to the state for educational purposes formed the basis of Michigan's primary school fund. That this unprecedented provision slipped by unnoticed when Congress considered the statehood bill may be attributed to Crary's political genius, especially considering the fact that he was not permitted to take his seat. It had been the practice of Congress, Willis Dunbar writes, "to grant to the states, at the time of their admission to the Union, other public lands, usually seventy-two sections, for the support of a university." In Michigan as elsewhere, some of the finest land around was reserved from sale. So when Michigan became a state, "the story of the disposal of these lands resembles that of the school lands: high hopes, followed by hard times, constant pressure on the legislature to reduce the price per acre (originally set at twenty dollars), and finally the surrender of the lawmakers to this pressure."[28]

In March 1837, the legislature authorized the superintendent to sell a half million dollars' worth of the university lands at public auction, at a minimum price of twenty dollars an acre. For the purpose of holding these lands out of the market until they would rise in value, a price of twenty dollars was fixed for them when other government land could be purchased for $1.25 an acre. But there were schemes to bring down the price of the university lands: "These lands had been selected with unusual care and their superior quality caused certain private interests to scheme for their acquisition on the usual Government terms. Candidates for the legislature were promised the political and financial support of the land-grabbers if they would pledge themselves to vote for a sale of these lands at $1.25 an acre."[29]

On several occasions in 1838, the legislature had resisted any tampering with the price of lands as fixed in 1837. But then it reneged on its pledge that none of the university lands should be sold at less than twenty dollars an acre. The problem was that Michigan's free banking law, enacted before the Panic of 1837 had fully set in, had resulted in far too many banks extending credit with great profligacy. Settlers who had purchased land during the phase of wildcat banking now found their property "rated as much below as in 1836 it had been above its real value, and many of the purchasers were clamoring for relief by a retrospective legislation in lowering the price of lands."[30] There were also squatters, "who had taken possession without form or title both before and after the land had been set apart for another purpose."[31]

In 1839, the legislature caved in to the special interests. In effect, lawmakers were being asked to put all university-earmarked lands up for grabs in the market at nominal prices, no matter what their value. They were asked to disregard that the state had accepted the lands as a trust and that the constitution "enjoined upon the legislature their protection and improvement, as well as the provision of means for the permanent security of the university funds."[32] A bill for the relief of certain settlers on university and state lands, authorizing the sale of these lands at the old federal price of $1.25 an acre, was passed and sent to Governor Mason.

Protests from the Board of Regents got nowhere. The regents appealed to the governor, who was under enormous pressure to allow these settlers their "just rights." But Mason showed the same backbone he displayed in the Toledo War; he vetoed the bill "and saved the University lands from political spoliation."[33] Mason's courageous veto was accompanied by a message in which he demanded to know the object of this temptation to fraud. The legislature came back in 1841 with another bill to relieve squatters and settlers, cutting in half the price they need pay for university lands. This time, Governor Mason wasn't around to veto the pernicious legislation, and his successor, William Woodbridge, signed the bill.

It is a familiar spectacle played out wherever public interest and private interest clash. In Michigan, "on one side was a great public interest with no protector but public spirit; on the other hand were clamorous squatters and land speculators of different degrees of honesty, with their friends, retainers and potential associates; while between them stood the legislature, more or less competent, more or less honest, pushed forward on the one side with far more power than it was held back on the other."[34] The record shows that over the years, the Michigan legislature acquitted itself well in its handling of university lands. In fact, Michigan obtained more from its federal grant of land for university education than most other states. By 1885, "when all the lands belonging to the University had been sold, it appeared that the average price per acre was $11.87—more than twice the price received for educational lands elsewhere in the Northwest."[35]

On March 20, 1837, shortly after approving the act providing for the organization and government of the university, Governor Mason signed an act providing for its location in Ann Arbor. The Board of Regents held their first meeting in Ann Arbor on June 5–7, and Mason was elected president of the board. Today, Ann Arbor and the University of Michigan are synonymous, but back then, the town was known for the Frostbitten Convention and not much else. The first building to be finished on campus was a boys' dormitory, completed in the fall of 1841 and given the name of Mason Hall. Today a bronze tablet on the structure bears the inscription "Mason Hall, this tablet erected by the Sarah Caswell Angell Chapter of the Daughters of the American Revolution."

Other encomia would come later. Mason's university was "the first state university, the first state university to admit women, the first of any university of any kind to unify and crown the work of the public schools, the first to give inspiring effect to 'Religion, morality and knowledge being necessary to good government and the happiness of mankind, schools and the means of education shall forever be encouraged.'"[36] At a gathering in 1905 honoring Emily V. Mason and Mason's daughter, Mrs. Dorothea Mason Wright of Newark, New Jersey, Clarence Burton, president of the Michigan Pioneer and Historical Society, said, "Another thing that Governor Mason instituted was the establishment of our state university, and I believe it has added more glory to our state than any other one thing within its boundaries."[37]

Mason's paramount interest in his university may be contrasted to the opinion of one of his successors, John S. Barry, who inspected the Ann Arbor site in 1841 and announced, "Well, we've got the buildings . . . I don't think they're good for anything else, so we might as well declare the university open."[38] It was part of Crary and Pierce's original plan that a series of branch academies would be opened to prepare students for university work. As specified in the Constitution of 1835, these branches also envisioned coeducation, teacher-training schools, and an agriculture department. As Dunbar writes, "Pierce's plan embodied the establishment of elementary schools in the school districts through local initiative, the state university as the capstone of the system, and the branches as intermediary schools under the control of the University Board of Regents."[39]

Mason stood for reelection in 1837, but it was clear that he was damaged goods. The Whigs had made important gains since the last election, and they had jumped on the Democratic legislature's program of internal improvements as too ambitious and too costly. What was worse for Mason was that the national Panic of 1837 was in full cry. When New York banks suspended specie payments in May, "the Michigan legislature allowed state banks the same relief from paying out coins for bank notes. As a result, forty-nine new banks were organized in the state . . . and they all began issuing paper currency that was not redeemable in cash. With such easy money, speculation was rife."[40] Mason's strong suit never was finances, and now the banking laws Mason had promoted were hurting him. As the banks closed, panic set in, and the dreams of limitless prosperity vanished overnight.

The Whigs were jubilant, the Democrats disheartened. To increase the pressure on the young governor, the Whigs discredited him and vilified him nearly every chance they could. William Woodbridge was telling all and sundry that Mason's election in 1835 was illegal because it had occurred before statehood was granted. In July, at Woodbridge's invitation, the Whigs called in the "mouthpiece of God" himself, Daniel Webster, who spent four days in Detroit issuing prodigious gusts of oratory against Mason and his policies. The presence of that great man, whose piercing eyes would reduce the devil himself to jelly, was played up in the press, with editors saying, "He was full of his hearers and full of himself."[41]

At their nominating convention in the next month, the Democrats supported the team of Mason, Ed Mundy, and Isaac Crary. Resolutions of praise for President Martin Van Buren were dutifully passed. At their convention, the Whigs nominated Charles C. Trowbridge of Detroit for governor, Daniel Bacon of Monroe as lieutenant governor, and Hezekiah Wells of Kalamazoo for member of Congress. Trowbridge was well known to Mason as a member of a prominent Detroit family, and he was popular in Detroit. He portrayed Mason as "selling out" on the Toledo War.

The campaign itself was a free-for-all. Mason was accused by the Whigs of buying votes. The Democrats created a "front" party in the hopes of drawing off votes from the Whigs. Just before the election, Mason was asked to go to New York to negotiate a loan for five million dollars, by means of a bond issue, to pay for the internal improvements the legislature had ordered. Mason pleaded inexperience in these matters, but he went anyway. When he returned, he gave the appearance of having been successful.

Mason was reelected, but only narrowly. Trowbridge tallied 14,800 votes to Mason's 15,314. Only two years earlier, Mason's opponent, John Biddle, received 814 votes. Mundy was reelected, and the Democrats still controlled the legislature. In his last election as a public servant of Michigan, Stevens T. Mason would be remembered as a man who had led his state into deep difficulties. It would get worse before it got better.

6 ∾ The Financial Panic of 1837

The storm that broke over Stevens T. Mason's head in 1837 was national in character, but the great undertow of financial disturbances that swept Michigan out to sea was also one of its own doing. The surge of optimism over hard-purchased statehood was understandable, but the program of public works the state mapped out for itself, although breathtaking in scope, was far beyond the state's ability to pay. Mason was a visionary, to be sure, but in his support for internal improvements, free banking, and state ownership of railroads, sound instincts deserted him.

In the spring of 1837, Mason was a nationally known figure who still had a bright political future. He was idolized in the eastern press. We can only speculate how, with America on the brink of presidential campaigns based on selling tactics and slogans ("Tippecanoe and Tyler Too" and "Log Cabins and Hard Cider"), Mason might have used his youth and good looks to impress a wider electorate. Today, he would be a handler's dream—photogenic, quotable, pedigreed, and a capable, if occasionally inspiring, public speaker.

He accepted the blame for later disastrous events as he should, but the record also shows that Mason's was a voice of caution when there were few who were willing to temper their enthusiasm with sober reason. For example, the free banking act passed by the legislature in the spring of 1837 came with a warning from Mason of the danger of too many banks flooding the state with worthless paper notes.

Mason strongly favored improving transportation, but he added that the state should not oversubscribe to its public works program. The legislature saw an interior of busy little towns linked by roads and canals and railroads that would spur development and bring about a sustainable prosperity. Mason once denounced legislation that would permit a private railroad as "extortion from the public." But the state's own sad experience in the way it ran its canals and railroads soon came to be considered a great mistake, and by the 1840s, the railroads were turned over to private interests and began making money.

If Mason sometimes was the brakes on a runaway locomotive and the offstage voice of Cassandra, conventional wisdom held that the state should play a dominant role in development. When Mason recommended borrowing money to subscribe to the stock of private companies that would build the railroads and canals, he was overruled by a legislature that preferred state action. The bill providing for internal improvements to be built and operated by the state was approved with only one dissenting vote in the entire legislature. Of course, the bill was signed by Governor Mason, and "the newspapers praised the legislators for their wise enactment. Indeed, Michigan was only following the lead of its sister commonwealths of the Old Northwest, which were already engaged in constructing internal improvements at public expense."[1]

As I already noted in chapter 2, other states hoped to replicate New York's success with the Erie Canal. The Empire State's experience had shown how a bold venture in internal improvements could pay huge dividends; that experience was not lost on Michigan's legislators or on Mason, who had seen for himself the success of the Erie Canal. If such a canal would work in New York, wouldn't one work even better in Michigan, with its network of inland streams feeding into the great lakes that defined Michigan's geography? So the thinking went.

But "unfortunately for New York's rivals, the Erie Canal's imitators never matched the revenues of the original. Overextended states were almost bankrupted by the indebtedness incurred in canal building, and others were severely frightened by close brushes with financial calamity."[2] After the Panic of 1837, canal building virtually ground to a halt, and railroads eclipsed the ditches. As the newest technology, railroads attracted much fascination and the attention of speculators, some of whom hoped to make fortunes from the Iron Horse.

The state's involvement in railroad development was similarly vexed: "To Mason more than any other man is to be given the credit of the admirable location of our scheme of railroad transportation. But he and the wisest men of his day everywhere started with the idea of state ownership of these most necessary of the public utilities."[3] Michigan learned from its mistakes, but too late to avoid years of financial dislocation. In its next try at constitution writing, delegates wrote into the 1850 state charter language saying, "The state shall not subscribe to or be interested in the stocks of any company, association or corporation, nor shall it be a party to or interested in any work of internal improvement, nor engage in carrying on any such work."[4]

As far as the statute books were concerned, Michigan didn't wait until 1850 to rectify past mistakes. The free banking statute the legislature so confidently passed in 1837 required specie subscription. When bad times hit, Mason suspended specie payment (metallic currency) in favor of paper notes. As hard currency became scarce, fraudulent activity increased. Mason and the legislature repealed the banking act in 1839, but by that time, the damage had been done in the form of failed farms, bank closures, and panic. One way to get rich quick during the economic growth of the 1830s was to speculate in land: "An army of individuals descended upon Michigan in the middle 1830s convinced that public lands were a lucrative investment. In an age before the widespread sale of stocks, unimproved lands . . . were the chief items of speculation in the United States." Real estate values in the country soared, with land sales by far the greatest in the western portion of the country, and "by 1835, the principal attention of those who had been seized by the land mania was being focused on Michigan."[5]

The Detroit land office had opened in 1818 with sales of public lands at only 37,865 acres; that figure reached 134,946 acres in 1825. After a brief fall-off, sales in the territory took off to astounding heights: "By 1834 sales were up to 498,423; in 1835 they reached 1,817,248, and in 1836 the figure of 4,189,823 acres was recorded. This exceeded the sales in any other state or territory during 1836 and constituted one-fifth of the national total of public land sales in that record-setting year."[6] Despite opening land offices elsewhere in the state—the land office in Kalamazoo was especially busy—officials couldn't keep abreast of sales.

As other historians explain, "How much of the tremendous increase in sales was due to the wholesale purchases of speculators has never been estimated to any exact degree for Michigan. Certainly, the prevailing belief of contemporaries was that a very large percentage of the land went to speculators and not to actual settlers. Much evidence exists to support this contention."[7] What is not in doubt is that a major factor in the Michigan land boom in the early 1830s was easy credit. Until 1833, writes state historian Willis S. Dunbar, "the Bank of the United States had dominated the banks of the nation; conservatively managed by Nicholas Biddle, the bank's notes circulated as money and drove the notes of shaky state banks from circulation."[8]

In 1832, President Jackson trained his populist guns on Biddle's bank: "Believing that the bank was hostile to him, Jackson set about destroying the bank by withdrawing from its custody all Government funds. This immediately destroyed the machinery which had been controlling the distribution of available money without substituting another and an equally efficient machine for the same purpose."[9] Jackson's views of the banking situation were, of course, more complex than his vendetta against Biddle would suggest, but as another writer says, "his struggle with the 'Monster Bank' and its supporters became the centerpiece of his presidency."[10] At a time when the presidential veto was still seen as a tool to be sparingly used, he vetoed an act of Congress to renew the bank's charter, which was due to expire in 1836.

Jackson's reelection in 1832 was considered to be an endorsement of his banking policies, which freed up credit and led to laws across the country, including in Michigan, permitting virtually anyone to open a bank. Here is where Jackson forged links with the common man and the toiler of the soil. Old Hickory saw himself "as champion of a virtuous populace against a corruptive and exploitative market elite. Virtue was to be found amongst the farmers of the country alone, not about courts where courtiers dwell."[11] Put another way, "the President thought of himself as the restorer of traditional American values, but his principles marked a significant departure from those of his predecessor."[12]

With Jackson, though, things were not always as they seemed. For example, the freeing up of credit that sprang from Jackson's banking policies did not match Jacksonian rhetoric. Lawrence Frederick Kohl , in his book on the Jacksonian era, says "modern methods of credit and new means to create money, which Whigs considered agents of liberation, seemed quite the opposite to the Jacksonian—they were attempts to rob him of his freedom."[13] Furthermore, "Jacksonian rhetoric customarily defined freedom as independence from Whiggish financial institutions. Credit was temptation and debt was slavery. The truly independent man was the one who stood apart from the world of banks and corporations. The only free man was, by definition, the outsider."[14] The popular view, all these decades removed from the Jackson era, is that the Whigs were the party of standpattism, destined for oblivion, while the Jacksonians were the radicals who transformed the political and economic landscape.

The Whigs did indeed die out, and the party of Jackson lives today in the Jefferson-Jackson Day dinners that raise funds for Democratic candidates. In the mid-1830s, change was coming to American politics, but the Jacksonians were still preaching the joys of an agrarian society and party-free politics: "Life should retain a natural tempo. Individuals should not be so eager to get ahead that they would destroy the old ties of community. This desire was at once a description of the Jacksonian's ideal world—one that was about to change. Change was coming too rapidly for the Jacksonian to accommodate himself to it. It is ironic that the very Jacksonian policies designed to slow change ultimately accelerated the change of both men and institutions to modern forms."[15] It was the Whigs whose time was expiring on the national scene, but their party did not sound like it was on the way out when its chief spokesman, Henry Clay, proposed "a sweeping plan for economic development. A national bank provided capital for entrepreneurial activity, and a circulating medium to facilitate trade among Americans spread over a vast land. A protective tariff encouraged the development of a manufacturing interest which would complement the existing interests of agriculture and commerce. Federal aid to internal improvements promoted a comprehensive network of transportation and communication. The Whig agenda was broadly nationalistic, geared to drawing together the disparate localities, states and regions of the young Republic."[16]

Was Stevens T. Mason, a strong supporter of internal improvements, a Whig at heart? Wouldn't Mason, trying to draw together the "disparate localities" of his far-flung territory turned state, have been more at home in the Whig camp? We know that while the Whigs favored the use of government authority to promote economic development, the Democrats generally opposed the use of public power for these ends: "Democratic objections to government involvement in economic life were several, but perhaps the most significant was the Jacksonians simply did not believe that such involvement could have the desired effect: the greatest possible economic well-being for all Americans."[17] Mason would have been conflicted not only as a Jeffersonian at heart and a Jacksonian in principle but also as a liberal Democrat with some Whig tendencies. His closest confidant was his sister, Emily, but there is no record of any political discussions with her that might provide clues to Mason's thinking.

With vast amounts of paper money being printed, wild speculation could only follow. To curb such grand-scale speculation and the inflation that accompanied it, Jackson issued his Specie Circular, on July 11, 1836. Speculation did indeed stop for the most part, but with the Specie Circular, Jackson took his quarrel with banks in general and Biddle in particular to another level. Banks failed everywhere, as the Jacksonians found that they could not control the distribution of the government money as they pleased among the various state and local banks.

The currency question, then, "became one of the most troubling political controversies of Jacksonian America, as Andrew Jackson led a successful crusade to destroy the Bank of the United States, to suppress the most commonly used forms of paper money, and to establish a national currency composed of gold and silver coins. Specie was valued for certain purposes but was also scarce and cumbersome to use. Most daily transactions were conducted with paper money which was issued not by the government but by commercial banks."[18] Jackson was a politician, not a financier, and he failed to comprehend that the supply of coin money, or specie, was insufficient for the purchase of public lands. He did not foresee the results of his financial policy: "When people could not get coin money on any terms, land sales stopped. Presently manufacturing stopped and business stopped. Thousands of men were thrown out of work. Farmers could not get acceptable money for their crops."[19] People fell to trading by barter.

The economic depression that fed the Panic of 1837 would change the political landscape as well. In the natural tendency to assign blame for the depression, one can point to "different players, from the White House to the Whigs in Congress to the bankers and the speculators,"[20] even, one concludes, to the natural inclination of humankind toward greed. The Whigs would profit in the short term, both nationally and in Michigan, from the Democrats' failure, and long after he left office, Stevens T. Mason would be excoriated for having brought Michigan to a state of bankruptcy. It cannot be said, however, that Michigan's institutions failed, because the new state simply did not have mature institutions in place or grounded in experience before the bad times hit so spectacularly.

In Michigan at this time, there was a governor who protested his lack of knowledge about financial matters yet was entrusted with the negotiation of a large loan. There was a legislature of some knowledgeable men but also of many backwoodsmen who collectively were unschooled in matters of public financing. There was a state judiciary that wasn't in place until mid-1836. There was a public school system that existed on paper and banks on whose charters the ink was still wet. There was a state with little income and a treasury with only fifty-seven thousand dollars in mid-1836—an amount pitifully inadequate for the needs at hand.

When the money from the federal surplus did start flowing into state coffers, the law of unintended consequences took over. The distribution of the treasury surplus was a factor in the financial disruptions that fed the Panic of 1837. As one writer sees it, "The funds withdrawn from the Bank of the United States in 1833 had been re-deposited in large part in the less populous states. The plan of distributing the surplus . . . was to place it in the states according to congressional representation, which meant that the most populous state received the largest share. In the first half of 1837, millions of dollars of government funds were moved about over the country, causing contraction of loans in some sections and producing inflationary conditions in others."[21] In that way, the distribution of the surplus added fuel to the speculative boom that Jackson was so desirous of stopping.

Once Michigan was in line for payments, the surplus money was to be distributed in installments. But full payment would never be received: "Michigan's first installment, received in January, 1837, was approximately $95,000. The whole amount expected by the State was about $380,000. But the last installment was never paid. The great financial panic broke over the country in the summer of 1837."[22] It is another great irony that Michigan, which took such a strong stand on principle at the First Convention of Assent, at first yielded at the prospect of all those surplus dollars being waved under its nose, only to then see the bulk of these monies evaporate. Michigan, it seemed, couldn't win for losing.

When the legislature assembled on January 2, 1837, some three weeks before the statehood bill was signed, it was with the assumption that the funds and land grants promised by the government were on the table for the taking, and "therefore Governor Mason's message . . . contained recommendations which . . . were carried into legislation and which framed a program suitable to an era of prosperity and an abundance of credit and money."[23] Far be it from Mason to put a damper on the enthusiasm of his legislature or to cast the new state in anything less than sanguine terms. As soon as admission became certain, "the young state launched out, like an heir just emancipated, into the most lavish display of her new freedom and fancied opulence,"[24] said one distinguished jurist.

An act to provide for works of internal improvements, another act calling for a loan of five million dollars to finance them, and yet another act to organize and regulate banking associations followed hard upon each other. But too little thought was given to good planning; transportation routes were projected through areas where settlers had not yet arrived to sink plow into soil. The prospect of building three east-west, transpeninsular railroads and two cross-peninsular canals promised long employment for laborers, but the program was in trouble even as the first spades of dirt were turned.

By now, the effects of the Specie Circular were beginning to be felt: "Since the public land speculation was centered in the West, this meant that a large volume of gold and silver was withdrawn from eastern banks and used to pay for the lands entered in the western land offices, including those in Michigan."[25] With insufficient coin on hand, the banks of the East began to topple, and the panic spread from the banking houses of New York and Philadelphia to all parts of the country. Deprived of eastern money, Michigan was unable to fund its internal improvements. When Governor Mason recommended legislation to suspend the payment of coin for notes, it was already too late to halt the engine of runaway financial depression.

It is always easy to hold up the sins of our predecessors as so manifestly designed to bring about ruin that one wonders why they could not plainly see the same thing. Didn't Michigan's early leaders understand, for example, that the speculation in land values was otherworldly? Didn't they know that tampering with the currency—for example, printing up bales of worthless paper—is the surest means of destroying public confidence in the medium of exchange? Didn't they at least suspect that it was impossible to sustain the kind of economic boom they were hoping for?

For it to have any chance of success, Michigan's far-reaching public works program of roads, canals, and railroads "depended on the continuance of a booming economy; unfortunately it was adopted on the eve of the Panic of 1837."[26] It did not occur to Michigan's leadership that "railways, canals and other great enterprises can only be profitable when they have the sure patronage of a settled country of large population."[27] Michigan had a growing, but not a large, population, and its interior was only marginally settled.

When calling for "the most prudent care" in applications for bank charters, Mason was prophetic. "Excessive issues of notes," he warned, "are calculated to engender overtrading in the community, drive the metallic basis from the country and are apt . . . to be attended with consequences disastrous to the public."[28] But in the very same message to lawmakers, he commented about "something for every constituent" and letting "no local prejudices or attachments misdirect the equal liberality with which you should grant the interests of your constituents."[29] The politics of the pork barrel had made its early intrusion into Michigan political life and, as always, cut across party lines.

Not all were blind to what lay ahead. A serious financial crisis as a result of President Jackson's banking policy appears to have been anticipated in Michigan as early as 1833. "We regret to find," says the editor of the *Detroit Journal and Michigan Advertiser* in its November 27 edition, "that a general feeling of apprehension is felt and expressed by the city papers, of serious embarrassment in the money market."[30] But then along came such distractions as the Toledo War, the drama over statehood, and the writing of a constitution, as well as the riches to come in the distribution of surplus, and caution took a backseat. Then the state government "was overtaken by the financial storm of 1837 while heavily encumbered with its program of internal improvements. Instead of throwing that program overboard, Governor Mason tried matching his financial inexperience with New York and Philadelphia bankers, with disastrous consequences both to himself and his State."[31]

The Panic of 1837 was a severe setback to the young state and its activist governor. Mason had misgivings about his state's liberal banking statute, especially when funds to provide for inspection of banks and enforcement of the act were not provided. That should have sounded the alarm that the state was living in a fantasy land and that expecting backwoods bankers to be on their best behavior at all times was hopelessly unrealistic.

The general banking law gave rise to forty-nine banks in Michigan, forty of which started operations immediately. The law stated that for a bank to begin operations, capital stock of not less than fifty thousand dollars was to be subscribed, and 30 percent was required to be paid in coin. Bank organizers used any number of scams to evade the law and bilk the public. When they didn't have coin in hand, they simply issued notes that pledged the bank to pay to the holder a certain amount of dollars in hard cash. One story told of "a stranger who had lost his way in the woods of Shiawassee County, and toward nightfall, while following what he thought was a trail through the woods, suddenly came to a clearing that contained a large frame structure across the front of which was a conspicuous sign proclaiming it was the Bank of Shiawassee."[32] Another story had a Detroiter making his way to one of these obscure banks to exchange notes for hard money: "The president of the institution received him with cordiality, wined him and dined him, and told him he could not redeem the notes just then, but was expecting a shipment of gold and silver within a few days."[33]

Michigan's attempt to sell five million dollars of internal improvement bonds ran squarely into a European market that was leery of U.S. securities.

The British demand for specie was a further drain on hard currency. Meanwhile, "stories of Michigan's turbulent beginnings and violently partisan politics had appeared in the newspapers along the East coast and such accounts did not convince the bankers that the new state could promise stability and responsible behavior."[34] Bankers and investors love stability, not risk or flamboyant politics, and it was in their hands that Michigan placed its hopes. But the bankers failed Michigan, too.

When the economic bubble burst, it left a trail of failed banks, broken public works projects, and impoverished farmers. When they couldn't get good money, people reluctantly accepted an evil substitute. Knowing that bank notes printed on colorful paper were virtually valueless, they were yet inclined to give such "money" the benefit of the doubt. The joke was that one could wallpaper one's farmhouse with these worthless notes. In panic conditions, the little guy always takes the brunt of the blows, and it was no different in 1837: "The laboring man and the farmer were the chief sufferers. Food prices fell away to such a point that farmers could not afford to bring their produce to town. Employment almost disappeared, as one business after another followed the insolvent banks into failure."[35] Disaffection with Mason showed in that year's gubernatorial election.

In searching for the causes of the Panic of 1837 in Michigan, one report pointed to a decline in immigration to the state during Mason's last years as governor "and to the indebtedness of Michigan businessmen to eastern creditors. Immigrants had represented an important market for Michigan producers, stated a report written by delegates to a bank convention that met in Ann Arbor in the spring of 1838. Because Michigan lacked 'any article of export,' the bankers observed, the nation's economic woes had fallen 'with a peculiar severity on the state.'"[36] The general banking law generated plenty of second-guessing and grist for argument between 1837 and 1839, with Whigs attacking the law on several grounds. They argued "that in loosening state control of banking, lawmakers had compounded the effects of the Panic by filling the state with a greatly depreciated currency. Whigs also asserted that the new law exposed Michigan residents to fraud. They labeled the new banks established under the law 'wildcats' because those who ran them sought to cheat the people out of their hard-earned money."[37]

The Democrats said that they had gone to great lengths to protect Michiganians from such problems: "The banking law protected Michiganians from fraud, they asserted, by placing stringent requirements on the amount of capital and specie each bank possessed, as well as limits on the size of loans and the amount of currency the banks could issue. Bank notes, furthermore, had to be backed by mortgages on real estate or personal bonds. Finally, the law required that the banks formed under the law contribute to a safety fund established in 1836, which would redeem the bills of failed banks."[38] These institutions came to be called safety fund banks.

The financial crisis of 1837 delayed Michigan's development of its internal improvements, and it would be several years before the state successfully tapped into its own wealth. Governor Mason and his legislature were so confident the state's public works would flourish that their unforeseen failure crippled the state's finances. The state went into debt before it had barely begun as a state. The grandiose Clinton-Kalamazoo Canal began with Mason himself turning over the first shovelful of dirt, but after five years and only a few miles of digging, the canal was abandoned. One report had it costing the state more than $350,000 while generating only $90 in tolls. When the state turned its focus on railroads, it wound up losing even more money. Mason's last term found him a scapegoat for all of Michigan's problems, and the Whigs were especially gleeful in helping to dig his political grave.

Historian Bruce Catton has said that Mason "lost everything—his enthusiasm, his popularity and, finally, his job," although Mason took himself out of the running rather than risk sure defeat. "He had caused his state to bite off much more than it could chew," continued Catton, "and when the whole business exploded, he got all the blame." Mason would not be the last Michigan governor to have his political fortunes suffer from economic ill health. One set of statistics shows better than any other how badly the sky turned dark over Michigan: "Sales of government land in Michigan dropped from more than 5,000,000 acres in 1836 to a scant 175,000 acres in 1839."[39]

Mason's successors, William Woodbridge and John Barry, would try to swing the pendulum in the other direction, toward complete removal of the state from all economic development projects, but the legislature would not acquiesce. Not until 1846, when all of the state's railroads, canals, and other internal improvements were either abandoned or sold to private enterprise, would Michigan launch itself into a free market economy. A pattern of economic boom and bust had been established. That pattern would hold well into the twenty-first century. Through the embarrassment of "payless paydays" for state government (1959) and such descriptive slogans as "When the nation catches cold, Michigan catches pneumonia," the state's economy would move like a roller coaster through deep depression and roaring good times. How much these cyclical occurrences are due to national policies can be endlessly debated, but the history of the economy of the Wolverine State is one of robust good times and dismal bad times, with often little in between.

After a new constitution was adopted in 1850, stability returned to Michigan, with agricultural growth and the rise of lumbering and mining. These industries, in turn, paved the way for the state to flex its manufacturing muscles in an industrial economy that paid its workers high wages and turned out quality products, from cars to chemicals. But when the books closed in 1837, all that success was still well in the future. A year that had begun with such bright promise ended with the bitterness that comes from dashed hopes and great expectations.

7 ∼ The Patriot War

Michigan's exposed position on the western frontier left it vulnerable to Indian attack and to mischief from the British. The latter had maintained a strong presence in the Great Lakes because of their forts and the fur trade. In addition, the British found it useful to buy the friendship of the Indian tribes in making trouble against the Americans.

At no time was this more evident than in the War of 1812. Despite a treaty negotiated with the Indians in 1807 involving the southeastern portion of the territory of Michigan, there were constant threats from British-incited Indians. The great Shawnee warrior Tecumseh attempted to unite western tribes, hoping to halt the region's pioneer settlements. He was eventually chased into Upper Canada (now Ontario), and he and his British allies were defeated at the Thames River there (near present-day London, Ontario) by forces led by William Henry Harrison.

The War of 1812 claimed a great tragedy for Michigan along the River Raisin at Frenchtown (now Monroe) on January 22, 1813, when a detachment of Kentucky militiamen under General James Winchester was overwhelmed by a force of British soldiers, Canadian militia, and Indians. The Indians, likely fortified by liquor and angry at their losses from the day before, came back the next day, scalping and murdering the prisoners and wounding those who had been promised safety from the Indians' blood rage. "Remember the Raisin" became a battle cry that motivated the Americans until the end of the war, as the memories of that massacre remained strong from constant retelling.

This is the Michigan lore in which Stevens T. Mason was steeped, a process helped along by the fact that it was the young men from his state of Kentucky who shed their blood on the banks of the River Raisin. He would have known all about the role of Kentucky in the War of 1812, and he would have shared in the general dislike of the British Lion. Now, as if he didn't have enough on his plate in 1837, Governor Mason faced trouble brewing across the international boundary. A rebellion broke out in Canada at the end of 1837, with the rebels, otherwise known as Patriots, often finding support, weapons, and a place of refuge in Michigan for the duration of the rebellion. Governor Mason was soundly criticized by the Canadian government for doing too little to help put down the insurrection.

Mason tried to play it down the middle. He couldn't very well violate neutrality laws by appearing to aid the British in their internal problem, and he was keenly aware of public opinion, held in Michigan and throughout the United States, that the Canadian people had a right to be free and to choose their own government. Mason undoubtedly had those opinions himself, along with a genuine sense of alarm over the vulnerability of Michigan if the British should decide to invade from Upper Canada.

The Patriot War began with revolts against the authorities in both Upper Canada and Lower Canada (Quebec). As one historian explains, "It was an attempt by the French in Lower Canada to overturn the British government and to gain independence, and by the British in Upper Canada to remove from power a selfish ruling group."[1] When the Patriots withheld paying their taxes and took up arms, it looked as though the Mother Country might have yet another revolution on its hands, similar to the one the American colonies had instigated.

At this time, Canada was an oligarchy, into which it had evolved by increments since about 1790. The British Crown had divided Canada into two districts with separate legislatures—one English and the other French. Lower Canada had its own constitution and governor, as did Upper Canada; the people were represented in the lower house of Parliament, but the upper house controlled legislation and wielded power. In Upper Canada, a comparatively small group monopolized government offices, controlled the courts, and dominated business. The "Family Compact," as it was known, had ruled Upper Canada pretty much as it pleased for more than two generations.

The opposition was especially deep-seated in Lower Canada, but it could well be said that grievances of one kind or another went back forty years in both regions. "The poor people," writes one historian, "finding that they had no direct appeal to the crown for redress of their wrongs at the hands of these favorites of fortune, began plotting a rebellion which would compel the home government to take notice of their plight."[2] London did indeed take notice, but in a way that would suppress, not encourage, independence or a weakening of authority.

One of the leaders of revolt in Lower Canada was Louis J. Papineau. His rebellion was quickly put down by force of arms, but such was not the case in Upper Canada, where the leader of the opposition was William Lyon Mackenzie of Toronto, a Scotsman and a member of Parliament. Mackenzie used the newspaper of which he was editor to launch attacks on the Family Compact. Elected five times to Parliament, "he was five times expelled by the supporters of special privilege."[3] To some Americans, that automatically qualified him for hero status.

In December 1837, Mackenzie led an attack on Toronto, in which his troops were defeated. He fled across the border to Buffalo, where he led a propaganda campaign against the government. He was warmly received in Buffalo, and it was from this base of operations that he enlisted a number of American enthusiasts who offered support in liberating Canada. In point of fact, the liberation of Canada was beyond the reach of the Patriots. Support for their cause, while often noisy, was shallow. In no way was the Patriot effort a major military campaign with definable goals.

That said, however, the 1830s were a time of popular uprisings in Europe, and the people of the United States were in sympathy with these movements. To many Americans, a revolt in Canada played to the hearts of those who were all for attaching Canada to the United States. For these Americans, uprisings across the border gave hope that the Union Jack would flutter down the flagpole for the last time and end British meddling that had continued after the War of 1812.

In Michigan, public meetings raised funds and passed measures of support for the Patriot cause. Michigan newspapers argued that the Canadian rebels had "the hands of thousands in the United States to aid them and twelve million hearts beating with sympathy."[4] These expressions gave way to substance: "The formation of armed bodies within the borders of the United States that periodically moved across the border, violating American neutrality laws and jeopardizing peaceful relations between the United States and Great Britain, led British and Canadian leaders to chastise U.S. governmental leaders for sympathizing with and supporting the Patriots."[5]

Even if these incursions across the border had, as their ultimate goal, liberating Canada and uniting its "freedom fighters" with "liberty-loving" Americans, there was no hope for support from official Washington. When the British complained that the Americans were slow to use military force to break up the rebels, the real reason was that America was spread too thin, troopwise, to defend a border from Maine to Michigan. And for all his pro-Patriot leanings, Stevens T. Mason wanted strict adherence to neutrality laws.

After the rebellion broke out, Governor Mason was requested by the U.S. State Department to arrest anyone involved in hostile acts against the British government. Mason promptly issued a proclamation reminding his people of their obligations under international law. But supporters of the rebel cause in Michigan were too numerous to round up that quickly. Meanwhile, Mackenzie's forces had taken possession of Navy Island (in Canadian territory) in the Niagara River, and Mackenzie solemnly announced from there that a provisional government of the republic of Upper Canada had been formed. An American steamboat, the *Caroline*, had been used to carry insurgents from the American side to Navy Island.

On December 28, 1837, a Loyalist force gathered on the Canadian shore to storm Navy Island. The men set the *Caroline* on fire and sent it, engulfed in smoke and fire, down the river toward Niagara Falls. The rebels on Navy Island later regrouped in Detroit, "where they found plenty of ardent sympathizers eager to enlist in the Patriot cause and to aid them with arms, money and other supplies."[6] By the end of the first week of January 1838, groups of Patriots had gathered at various locations on the Detroit River. On the opposite shore were Sandwich, Fort Malden (fortified by the British), and the town of Amherstburg.

The Patriots then raided arsenals in Monroe and Detroit, which yielded about eight hundred stands of arms. On January 6, they seized the schooner *Ann* (moored at a wharf in Detroit), loaded it with the stolen ordnance and more than one hundred men, and headed downriver for Gibraltar, with high hopes of launching an invasion of Canada. Governor Mason was informed by the U.S. government that his job was to recapture the *Ann* and to prevent an attack on a friendly nation.

General Hugh Brady, commander of the military district for the region, had no troops to help Mason, so Mason called out the militia. But because their muskets had been stolen in the raids on the arsenals, the militiamen had to march all the way to the Dearborn arsenal. After hastening back to Detroit, they sailed for Gibraltar, only to find that the *Ann* had already come to grief in Canadian waters. Under the command of Edward Theller, a Detroit water tax collector, the *Ann* had raised anchor and fired some rounds into Amherstburg.

When the Canadian militia opened fire in turn, the *Ann* sustained damage to its rigging and ran aground. Thirteen Americans, including nine Michiganians, were taken prisoner.

On the ninth of January, Mason had written a curious letter to the magistrates of Sandwich. He began, "Persons proceeding from this state and found in arms within the jurisdiction of Upper Canada have lost all claim to the protection of the laws of the United States, and of this State," but he then went on to say, "I cannot permit without resistance any invasion upon the soil of the sovereign and independent State over which I preside as chief magistrate."[7] Mason was saying that he respected neutrality but that his powers were limited and that he would discharge his duties as chief executive only when "a district judge, district attorney and Marshal of the United States call on me 'with the information that the process of the U.S. courts cannot be enforced without executive aid.'"[8] This was doublespeak to the Canadian authorities, but, in truth, the Sandwich magistrates had baited Mason by asking whether he would consider it an invasion "of your country" if the Canadians attacked the Patriots "wherever we can find them." Mason had in fact played an active role in disarming and dispersing groups of Patriots on the Michigan shoreline.

Michigan officials faced at least two major problems in restraining the Patriots. One was the "sense of mission Americans felt in spreading liberty and their corresponding belief that individual rights superseded law; a second was the ambiguous lines of authority between state and federal government."[9] In addition, writes Roger Rosentreter, "During the 1830s, American political thinking was still dominated by ideas popular during the American Revolution. Americans believed England to be ruled by an archaic, oppressive government that was the antithesis of American institutions and America's implacable enemy. Distrust of the British still pervaded U.S. public opinion."[10]

So confident was Governor Mason that the backbone of the Patriot cause had been broken after the *Ann* affair that he informed Major General Winfield Scott, then commanding the Niagara frontier, that "tranquility is entirely restored to this frontier."[11] But just in case, three companies of U.S. regulars were dispatched to Detroit. Public opinion was strongly pro-Patriot, and General Brady was moved to say he would "not be surprised if one-third of the able bodied men of this State would join the Patriots."[12] When it was discovered that arms were stolen from the arsenal at Dearborn and secreted to Detroit, Brady conducted a search, and the weapons were seized.

The Patriots waited until February 24, when between two hundred and three hundred of them crossed the Detroit River on ice to Fighting Island in Canadian waters. The would-be liberators made camp there but were attacked the next day by British troops with artillery. The Patriots broke and scattered back to the Michigan mainland, but not before they had suffered casualties. General Brady's men disarmed the stragglers and arrested the leaders. Then, in early March, another force of four hundred Patriots was routed by the British on Pelee Island, a Canadian island in western Lake Erie.

At that point, the cause seemed hopeless. But the Patriots were only biding their time while continuing to tap into inflamed public opinion. Chastened by his earlier expression of confidence that had proved unfounded, Governor Mason now wrote to President Martin Van Buren and presented an entirely different picture. "You are aware of the exasperated and excited state of feeling in the Province of Upper Canada," he began, claiming, "This unhappy state of feeling is rapidly disseminating itself amongst our own citizens." He talked about the possibility of "an open misfortune between the two shores. This frontier and especially the City of Detroit are vulnerable to our enemy. The most active preparation is going on the other side of the national boundary."[13]

Mason followed up with a letter to Secretary of War Joel Poinsett, setting forth the "defenseless condition of this frontier" and the need for a "competent force to meet an approaching crisis in our foreign relations."[14] Poinsett wrote back to say that Van Buren did not think the contingency warranted measures of the kind Mason envisioned. That reply was to be expected. With U.S. troops tied down in Florida during the long and costly Seminole Wars, the administration didn't want to commit troops it didn't have to the Great Lakes. Hadn't Oliver Hazard Perry cleaned out that area of the British nuisance some years before?

The border stayed quiet during most of 1838, with citizens treated to "the grossest exaggeration . . . on both sides of the line. Thus, in the United States, reports were rife of wonderful 'popular uprisings' all over Canada; while in that province, equally false accounts of sympathy and assured support from this side were employed to bolster the movement, whereas, in fact, there was in neither country any support to justify a moment's continuance of the mad scheme."[15] Canada and Great Britain protested the violation of neutrality laws by armed bodies making occasional forays across the border. In October, George Arthur, lieutenant governor of Upper Canada, came out and said Mason wished the Patriot cause well: "It was even reported that the Michigan governor was a member of the Hunters Lodges, the Masonic-like organization committed to the liberation of Canada."[16] No proof was ever provided that Mason hung around a Hunters Lodge, but it was certain he was walking a tightrope. He was blamed by some "for not having taken stringent enough measures against the Patriots, and by others for interfering with a movement to free Canada from a despotic oligarchy."[17] The outbreaks of the Patriot War that involved Mason's state were distractions from the real problems he was facing as governor. Having to school himself in the nuances of foreign policy and neutrality laws was not what Mason was elected to address.

The Patriots in Michigan made either their boldest move or their greatest blunder in December. On the third of that month, Lucius Bierce, an Ohio lawyer, gathered a band of about 150 men and boarded the steamer *Champlain*, anchored at a Detroit wharf. They crossed the Detroit River and landed, early in the morning, at Walkerville, a couple of miles north of Windsor. The invaders torched a military barracks and guardhouse; several soldiers asleep in the barracks burned to death. When news of all this reached the community of Sandwich, several companies of Canadian militiamen gave battle. The badly outnumbered Patriots fled the scene, only to find that their means of escape back to Michigan, the *Champlain*, was gone. Anything that could float was commandeered, and the remaining Patriots, thirty in number, found safety of sorts. Several were arrested by American vessels guarding the border.

The Battle of Windsor left more than twenty Patriots dead, with several taken prisoner. Four Canadians died as well, and it was a long time before memories of the invasion were erased. For example, a prominent Sandwich surgeon, Dr. John J. Hume, was wantonly murdered on the road by Patriot forces; when news of this atrocity reached the Canadian militia, the commander ordered a firing squad to execute four prisoners his men had captured. Troops from Fort Malden "hastened to the scene of action, and soon all the Patriots were killed, captured, or fleeing for their lives. This Battle of Windsor was the last engagement of the rebellion."[18] Dr. Hume was interred in the old churchyard at Sandwich, where a monument bears an inscription that begins, "SACRED to the memory of John James Hume, staff assistant surgeon, who was infamously murdered and his body afterward brutally mangled by a gang of armed ruffians from the United States styling themselves Patriots, who committed this cowardly and shameful outrage on the morning of the 4th of December, 1838."[19]

Now it was Michigan's turn to fear British reprisals. Three days after the Battle of Windsor, General John R. Williams of the Michigan militia informed Poinsett that he had good information that the British at Fort Malden would attack Michigan once things settled down. Governor Mason regretted that feelings of sympathy for the Patriot cause "should have led any portion of our citizens into an open disregard of the laws of their own country . . . and into a violation of our neutral relations with a foreign power, with whom we are at peace."[20] In March 1839, Mason informed Poinsett "of the military preparations now going on in the neighboring province of Upper Canada. The authorities of that province have now concentrated immediately on the frontier, an effective force of about two thousand men; and in view of a possible collision between the governments of the United States and Great Britain, they seem to be taking active measures of defense."[21] But except for the work of a few agitators here and there, the Patriot War in Michigan had ended.

The postmortems were not over. Governor Mason was rounded on by the British and the Canadians for failing to enforce neutrality laws, and he was not spared on the home front either. The Whigs, through their house organ, the *Detroit Daily Advertiser*, attacked the Democrats for being "spellbound with apathy"[22] or taking actions that were deemed to be absurd. The Democrats fired back; the Whigs, they said, favored the principle that the people were unqualified and incapable of self-government.

When Mason made a point of forbidding Michiganians from volunteering to help the Patriots liberate Canada, the *Pontiac Courier* thought it would have some fun with the chief executive. Reminding readers that "when the governor's political success depended upon the admission of our state into the Union, he contended that the people had an undoubted right to act in all their original capacity, without any regard to the forms of law," the *Courier* concluded that the governor's recent declaration forbidding participation violated the people's will. The paper added that if Michiganians thought it "proper to shoulder their rifles, go over to Canada and join the Patriot cause, they will do it."[23]

Was Mason to be skewered by his own rhetoric? It was a touchy point, because he was remembered for getting fired by Jackson and for poisoning relations with Congress. It was no secret that some prominent Democrats were also ardent Patriots; recall General Brady's remark about "one-third of the able bodied men in this State" joining the Patriot cause if push came to shove. At one point, Mason had to refute a newspaper accusation that he secretly hoped his state's residents would violate neutrality laws.

As a lawyer and chief executive, Mason would have been fully cognizant that the activities of the Patriots were illegal and that any liberation of Canada would have to be an indigenous movement with wide popular support. One writer would say, "The Patriot folly collapsed in a failure which would have been ludicrous, but for the many deluded victims of its vain hopes, and the peril in which it placed the two nations. The inspiration of the movement was twofold—a zeal for liberty without knowledge of the means necessary to obtain it, and the spirit of plunder always so ready as an incentive in such cases."[24] The government had won: "In the aftermath of rebellion, hundreds and possibly thousands of rebels or rebel sympathizers left Upper Canada. Those who stayed could be and frequently were arrested. Two of the rebels of 1837 were hanged."[25] But even though the Patriots failed in their mission, they succeeded in drawing attention to the need for reform. The British government sent Lord Durham to Canada to report on the situation. As a result of his report, reforms were introduced over the protests of the Family Compact: "The way was paved for the establishment of a government which would be responsible to the people of Canada, and in 1849 a fully responsible government was introduced by Lord Elgin."[26]

The political fallout of the Patriot War was still being felt in Michigan in 1841, when there were indications that Patriot backers in the Detroit area would support at the polls only those candidates who favored Canada's liberation. By that time, of course, Mason was gone, and other issues of importance were contending for the state's attention. There isn't much question that Mason was tested by the conflict on his borders, and it matured him in the ways of Washington politicians. The record shows that even though he was conflicted on the issue, his actions in helping to disperse the rebels while paying service to neutrality laws were the proper ones to take.

Stevens Thomson Mason, photograph of a portrait done in oil by Alvin Smith. The original hangs in the House of Representatives in Lansing. (Courtesy State Archives of Michigan.)

Julia Phelps Mason, wife of Stevens T. Mason. She remarried after Mason's death but maintained a great affection for Mason, who she continued to call "my darling." She bore the governor three children. (Courtesy Detroit Public Library.)

Dorothea Mason Wright, the sole surviving child of Stevens T. Mason. She lived to see her father restored to a place of honor. She died in 1916. (Courtesy Bentley Historical Library, University of Michigan.)

Emily Virginia Mason, long-lived sister of Stevens T. Mason. Emily was her brother's official hostess when he was governor. It was through Emily's efforts that her brother's remains were brought back to Michigan and interred on the site of the territorial capitol. (Courtesy Bentley Historical Library, University of Michigan.)

Arthur Holmes, Daniel McCoy, and Lawton T. Hemans (left to right) at Marble Cemetery, New York City. The reinterment committee is standing in front of the slab marking the vault from which they removed the remains of Governor Mason on June 2, 1905, for reburial in Detroit. (Courtesy State Archives of Michigan.)

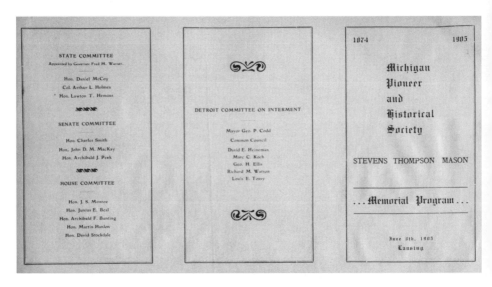

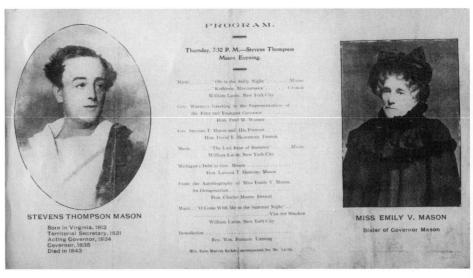

Michigan Pioneer and Historical Society memorial program, June 8, 1905. The inside of the program shows Stevens T. Mason and his sister Emily V. Mason. (Courtesy State Archives of Michigan.)

Hall & Mooney Lith. Buffalo

The capitol building in Detroit. Built in 1828 for $24,500, this building served as the territorial capitol from 1828 to 1837 and as the state capitol from 1837 to 1847. After the state capital was moved to Lansing in 1847, this building served as Union School until it burned in 1893. (Courtesy State Archives of Michigan.)

Statue of Stevens T. Mason in Capitol Park, Detroit, at the base of which are his remains, reinterred in a ceremony on October 27, 2010. (Photo by Jen Luton.)

Inscription on the statue of Mason, from a grateful people of Michigan, in memory of a young man who stamped his name "indelibly on the history of the Commonwealth." (Photo by Jen Luton.)

The tablet a few yards from the Mason gravesite in Capitol Park that marks the spot where the territorial capitol stood. From the building on this site, acting governor Stevens T. Mason led the fight for statehood, prosecuted a war with Ohio over the Toledo Strip, and helped to write the state's first constitution. (Photo by Jen Luton.)

The historical marker in Capitol Park marking Michigan's first capitol, unveiled at a ceremony on October 27, 2011, on the occasion of Stevens T. Mason's two-hundredth birthday celebration. (Photo by Jen Luton.)

8 ∽ The Five-Million-Dollar Loan

If the road to hell is paved with good intentions, Michigan laid down a super-highway in 1837. Along the way, there was enough intrigue, low comedy, high drama, and dirty politics to fill a good-sized novel. There was even a trunkful of cash from which some money came up missing. The story of the five-million-dollar loan and Governor Mason's role in the saga would be talked about for years to come.

In 1837, writes a biographer, "Mason found himself opposed to men who were as clever as himself, and far less scrupulous. They were old hands at technical games which were almost mysteries to him. They were . . . people who were out to skin him at great profit to themselves. They knew Mason was committed to a gigantic public improvement program. They were going to get theirs, and use Mason to get it."[1]

The Michigan constitution had provided the chief executive and his legislature with their marching orders with respect to internal improvements. Michigan moved slowly at first with regard to the constitutional mandate, but along with official statehood came a rush to make up for lost time. Governor Mason outlined a sweeping program of internal improvements and recommended a loan of five million dollars to pay for it. Whether the product of hubris or just plain bad judgment, the ambitious program was far beyond the state's capacity to fund, and five million dollars was an enormous sum for a young state, "which at this time had barely 175,000 in population, was almost wholly agricultural in character, and with a total assessed value of less than 43 million dollars."[2]

Mason, then twenty-five years old, had no expertise or experience in the business he was asked to transact. A bill authorizing a loan not to exceed five million dollars was introduced in the House on January 27, 1837, and passed several days later without a recorded vote. Whigs as well as Democrats supported the measure. The Senate passed the same legislation by a comfortable margin, and the bill was sent to Mason for approval.

The act directed the governor to negotiate loans on the best and most favorable terms that he could obtain; the vagueness of that provision is only exceeded by the wide latitude given to the governor. The act also authorized the issue of state bonds, which were to bear interest not exceeding 5.5 percent and were not to be sold below par. As security, the state pledged its good faith and credit; the expected proceeds of the railroads and canals would go into a sinking fund to pay off the bonds. The proposed loan represented about 12 percent of the state's total equalized valuation.

There are several things wrong with this picture. Entrusting the execution of the loan to one man, without benefit of a board of advisers, was a grave mistake. With affairs of state to attend to, Mason should not have been placed in such a position. In addition, the amount of the loan was out of proportion to the total equalized value of the state. With no funds of its own, the state became a borrower when money was scarce elsewhere, that is, in the banking houses of the East. The thinking seemed to be that if the state just borrowed the money, the future would take care of itself. As a kind of collateral, the state was putting up public works projects whose completion would be far in the future. Admittedly, Michigan's timing was bad, given the speed with which the Panic of 1837 overtook the nation as banks began failing left and right.

Shortly after the legislature adjourned, Governor Mason went to New York to explore the bond market. He went first to John Delafield, president of the Phoenix Bank, a man with good financial connections, who had earlier negotiated a small loan of one hundred thousand dollars for the state. By this time, the financial situation was becoming worrisome, and Mason learned that New York banks were not in a position to handle a loan of five million dollars. Mason agreed to let Delafield contact London financial houses that had satisfactorily managed similar issues in other states (notably, Ohio and Indiana).

Governor Mason returned to Detroit, secure in the belief that Delafield would act in the state's best interest. But the first wave of financial dislocation was being felt in London, and it wasn't long before the economic crisis was affecting the entire United States. In May, New York suspended payments in specie, and from there, depression spread across the country. In June, Governor Mason called a special session of the legislature, which authorized state banks to suspend specie payment. As one historian writes, "The state, however, continued on its course of large expenditures on railroads and canals, believing that the financial troubles were only temporary."[3]

In September, Governor Mason again went to New York to speed up the loan negotiations. This time, he was told that to place the loan under the conditions then existing, the interest rate would have to be raised from 5.5 percent to 6 percent and must be payable in London as well as the United States. Legislation to that effect was introduced and quickly approved. It was clear by now that Michigan was in deep financial straits, and opportunities to assess blame were seized with relish.

The election of 1837 narrowly returned Mason to office. His plurality was tiny indeed, but his party retained control of the legislature. As for the opposition, "although the Whigs had voted for the internal improvements law in the legislature in the spring, now that financial difficulties appeared they opposed the program and blamed the governor and his party for the ills that beset the state."[4] Political opponents came out from every rock and crevice to heap calumnies on Mason, so much so that his inaugural address in 1838 is studded with references to his personal anguish. "However great the censure to which I . . . have been subjected" is followed by "That I may have committed errors I do not pretend to doubt," which, in turn, leads to "Even when my integrity has been assailed, the vilest and worst motives attributed to my conduct, I have only to await the development of time, trust to the good sense and justice of the people, and they will right the wrong done to me."[5] The mea culpas continue with a remark about "an overanxious but erring judgment" and with the lament "if I have failed in my exertions, I sincerely regret it."[6]

Later, in a message to the Senate, Mason urged the appointment of a board of loan commissioners, stating it was wrong in principle to place so much discretionary power in one person: "It gives to the control of one individual millions of the public money without any corresponding check or responsibility." He pointed out what should have been obvious all along: "It is impossible for the executive to bestow that attention to the subject which its importance demands, without the neglect of other duties."[7] The state's troubles provided plenty of opportunity for second-guessing. "It is possible," said one writer, "that Governor Mason was too trustful and put too much assurance in promises."[8] The Whigs would take delight in saying Michigan had sent a boy to do a man's job, another takeoff on the "Boy Governor" moniker.

Finally, though, there was some cause for optimism. Mason had succeeded in disposing five hundred thousand dollars in bonds to Oliver Newberry, a

Detroit shipowner, and another block of bonds had been sent to Great Britain under the care of Delafield, as agent of the state. But if these actions gave reason to hope for a turnaround, they were short lived in nature.

The bad news came in triplicate. The legislature could not be persuaded to approve a bill for an appointed board to assist Mason in conducting bond negotiations. Oliver Newberry reduced his subscription from five hundred thousand to two hundred thousand dollars. European bankers declined to take any of the Michigan issue, on the ground there was no guarantee that payments on the principal would be made in Europe. Only $150,000 had been advanced to the state on the block of bonds Delafield had sent to London.

Again, Mason was left holding the bag. Some of the contracts for internal improvements had been approved, and the legislature had appropriated about one million dollars for this purpose. With the lawmakers getting worried about developments on the bond front, Mason again left Michigan in late April for New York. He received a serious blow upon learning that "only the interest and not the principal could be made payable abroad. The provisions regarding the rate of exchange and the prevalent unsatisfactory financial conditions made the sale in London impossible and the bonds had just been returned to New York and the advance of $150,000 must therefore be repaid by the State."[9]

Mason was crushed. He concluded that foreign sale of bonds was impossible for the time being, so why not try an American outlet? He made the acquaintanceship of Edward R. Biddle, vice president of the Morris Canal and Banking Company, of New Jersey. Biddle was a cousin of Nicholas Biddle, president of the Bank of the United States. Edward Biddle's firm had a high financial standing and was in position to buy large issues of bonds on credit, so it appeared he might be the answer to Mason's problems. Mason, still bereft of instructions other than to get the best deal possible, made an agreement with the Morris Canal and Banking Company. On June 1, 1838, Biddle's firm became the agent of Michigan for the sale of the entire issue. The Morris Canal and Banking Company contracted to dispose of all the unsold bonds at a commission of 2.5 percent on the proceeds of the sale. Under this arrangement, the state would receive less than par value, which was contrary to the law.

However, Mason was assured by the officers of the company that the bonds would sell at a premium or the equivalent of par value. One historian notes, "Considering the stringency of the money market at the time, only the governor's inexperience, his supreme optimism, his knowledge of the urgency of the occasion, or a combination of all three could have made him believe such assurances."[10] It cannot be said that Governor Mason overstepped his authority or that the contract was invalid. He was a lawyer and he had another lawyer, Theodore Romeyn of Detroit, assisting him in the transaction. Except for the feature that the company secured possession of a million dollars in bonds before actual payments were advanced, everything appeared to be on the up-and-up.

With contracts signed and handshakes all around, Mason and Romeyn prepared for the journey back to Detroit on June 8, accompanied by a large amount of cash payment securely locked in a small trunk. Historians do not agree on how much "a large amount" was, although Mason himself places the sum at $10,397. The tale of an old horsehide-covered, brassbound trunk with its purloined goods is worth recounting in brief, if for no other reason than that, as Lawton Hemans puts it, "the trunk and its contents were the occasion of a mystery that supplied gossip for a generation."[11]

Bills of the Morris Canal and Banking Company to the amount of $110,397 were transferred from the company's banking house at Jersey City to the branch in New York; one set of bills included the $10,397 of a balance due on the first payment of the Michigan loan. As Hemans reports, "The money as it was being prepared for shipment was not counted by the Governor, but was several times counted by the bank clerks, who stamped each bill upon the back in red as a protection against robbery on the journey to Detroit. The bills were then done into packages, with the amount of each package marked upon the band of the paper around it; and the various packages were then placed within the trunk, which was then locked and the key delivered to the Governor who conveyed it to the Astor House where it was put in charge of the bookkeeper during the evening meal."[12] After he had eaten, Mason went out that night, quite possibly to court the girl he eventually married, Julia Phelps. Having entrusted charge of the trunk to Romeyn, Mason returned about midnight and found the trunk safe in Romeyn's possession. Each man placed items of a personal nature in the trunk, after which it was taken to Mason's room and locked. From that point on, Mason did not let the trunk out of his sight.

The two travelers headed west, up the Hudson River and through the Erie Canal. From Buffalo, they took a steamer for Detroit. George Catlin reports, "Each man stood watch in turn over that trunk with its precious freight and slept at night with one eye and one ear open."[13] Later, Governor Mason, called on by a subsequent legislative committee of investigation into the affair, would say, "At no time on the journey was the trunk opened by me, nor could I at any time observe that the overcoat on the top had been moved."[14]

When Mason and Romeyn arrived in Detroit, the trunk and its contents were delivered to the Bank of Michigan. But when the trunk was opened in the presence of witnesses at the bank, money was missing; bills had been removed to the amount of $4,630. The deficiency was immediately reported by Mason to Edward Biddle. "Can it be possible," Mason asks, "that an error could have accrued on the part of your clerks in counting? If such is not the case, the money missing must have been abstracted by means of a false key on my journey home. But this I think could scarcely have happened as the trunk was rarely out of my possession."[15]

On the same day that Biddle's firm was apprised by Mason of the loss of the money, it received, through the New York Post Office, a mysterious package containing all of the abstracted bills except for fifty dollars. Mason paid the fifty dollars out of his own pocket to allay any further suspicion. Romeyn and Mason came to a bitter parting of the ways, each suspecting the other of having something to do with the missing money. The fact remains that the only time the trunk was not in Mason's possession was when Romeyn was in charge of it in his hotel room on the evening Mason went out.

The governor's lack of attentiveness over the trunk was election fodder for his political opponents. He was accused of lining his own pockets, prompting him to deny having received so much as a penny's benefit on account of the loan, directly or indirectly. He was made a laughingstock for the mysterious disappearance and reappearance of the money. The theft resulted in no loss to the state, and Mason was eventually exonerated of any possible wrongdoing. Romeyn came under suspicion, but at the time, Mason only said that he would express no suspicion "where no positive testimony exists."[16] The story of the five-million-dollar loan furnished the newspapers and the public with something to talk about for many weeks, leading to still more suspicion and speculation.

It wasn't long before Edward Biddle showed his true colors in the way he maximized returns for the Morris Canal and Banking Company. On November 10, 1838, Biddle informed Mason that the European market was not conducive for Michigan securities. He offered to make an alternative arrangement. The deal was that the Morris Canal and Banking Company, with Governor Mason's consent, would agree to an immediate delivery of the rest of the bond issue ($3,700,000). Biddle's company would be responsible for one-fourth of the issue, and the Bank of the United States of Pennsylvania would take the remaining three-fourths. (This bank, the successor to the Bank of the United

States, whose charter was not renewed, was run by Nicholas Biddle.) The company would pass the entire amount of the loan to the credit of the state at par value, minus the 2.5 percent commission. Mason was over a barrel; the state needed cash, and his agent was urging him to make a quick sale. He wrote back on November 18:

> It is with regret, I perceive that the state of the European market is such as to render the sale of the Michigan bonds a matter of hazard and doubt. My expectation under the contract with your institution was to realize at least par on the stock, and it is with extreme disappointment that I have presented to me the probability of losing the two and one-half percent commission which covers your charges. I still cling to the hope that an immediate sale may not be imperatively necessary, but as the negotiation of this loan has been a most thankless and perplexing undertaking on my part, I feel unwilling to advise you.[17]

Mason agreed to the sale as being in the state's interest, despite the fact that Michigan certificates were being offered at less than their face value, as low as ninety-three and ninety-five cents on the dollar. When, in early 1839, the Bank of the United States of Pennsylvania gave formal guaranty of its obligation to take three-fourths of the bonds, it was a hollow boast. The solvency of both the bank and the Morris Canal and Banking Company was already severely compromised at that time. When both institutions failed in the aftermath of the Panic of 1837, Michigan was left with a debt of more than two million dollars in bonds for which no returns were received. In early 1838, though, both the Bank of the United States of Pennsylvania and the Morris Canal and Banking Company were pillars of the financial world, held in high esteem. The Morris Canal and Banking Company was supposed to be a rock-solid business, but like so many others, it had run itself through the use of government funds, and when these dried up, its lifeblood drained away.

Just before he left office, Mason made one last effort to salvage the situation. He asked Kintzing Pritchette to abrogate the contract with the Morris Canal and Banking Company. "My purpose," said Mason, "is to obtain a return of stock on all installments unpaid. You may accept any reasonable and equitable terms to secure the remaining stock and to protect the state from loss."[18] Despite this praiseworthy attempt to cut the state's losses, the action was pounced on by Mason's political enemies in the legislature. Still, Mason could feel good about one thing: "No criticism from the legislature or from other sources had been directed against Governor Mason for his failure to demand proper security from the bank and the company to fulfill the contract or for the bonds which had been turned over. These institutions were handling millions of dollars of similar securities for other states."[19] Given his options, which were always too few, it is hard to see how Mason could have handled the situation differently.

Pritchette went east as an agent of the state to contract for the abrogation of the loan. Upon proposing a negotiation for the surrender of the bonds not paid for, he was told by the Bank of the United States that all the bonds for which that bank had guaranteed payment had been sent to Europe and were out of the bank's control. Pritchette then went to New York City to take up negotiations with Edward Biddle; several proposals by Biddle were rejected. The upshot of it all was that Pritchette returned to Michigan with proposals that included an offer from the bank to surrender the unsold bonds and a concession from Biddle that the company was indebted to the state for bonds not yet paid in the amount of $737,500.

Much later, with Mason no longer in office, Pritchette's proposals were transmitted to Governor William Woodbridge, who had been elected in November 1839 and who sent them to the legislature. There was a Whig majority in both houses of that body, and neither house was inclined to bail out Mason in any way. Both houses did nothing except appoint committees to consider the proposals, and majority and minority reports were made in both cases. William Jenks put it this way: "The majority report in the Senate was plainly intended as a bitter political attack on Ex.-Gov. Mason, and it denounced his attempt to change or cancel the original contract for the sale of the bonds, disregarding entirely the fact that the interests of the State were being injured by delay, and that the situation demanded prompt action."[20] The story of the five-million-dollar loan ended with bitter partisan politics holding sway, with a Whig legislature more intent on heaping scorn on Mason than on putting the state's interests first.

In opening his message to the legislature on January 7, 1839, Mason tipped his hand on his political future by saying that this was "the last annual communication I shall be called upon to present to the people of the state of Michigan."[21] He tried to explain that a suspension of the internal improvement works "would have proven more prejudicial to the public interests than the sale of stock which has been made."[22] There was no sugarcoating the budget deficit of $7,906. "This deficiency in the revenue is deeply to be regretted," said the governor, who went on to warn about an "embarrassed and bankrupt treasury."[23]

It was not the valedictory Mason deserved for the all the hard work he had done on the loan. He had been let down by men in whom he had put sincere trust, by national policies he was powerless to influence, and by his own legislature, which left him twisting in the wind. The difficulties he had in floating the loan should have alerted wiser heads to a policy of retrenchment where public works were concerned. The ensuing attacks on Mason's character for the mess into which the state had fallen were in such bad taste and so venomous that Mason despaired of ever regaining public esteem.

The collapse of Michigan's banking system will be examined in the next chapter. If it is possible to drown twice over, Michigan did so when its program to finance internal improvements sank along with the banks. As the state lost its financial solvency, its political victims were Mason and the Democrats. Rather than risk ignominious defeat in the next gubernatorial election, Mason took himself out of the running.

But now he at least had the benefit of a life's companion. On one of the governor's eastern trips to negotiate the five-million-dollar loan, he made the acquaintance of Julia Elizabeth Phelps. While visiting at the home of rich New York businessman Thaddeus Phelps, who was assisting on the bond issue, the governor fell for Phelps's dark-eyed daughter. Mason wrote that Julia "had all the charms that ever were bestowed upon the daughters of Eve" and that "in sweetness and real worth, she surpasses every other woman I have ever known."[24] Twenty years old, she was what, in later years, would come to be called a socialite, and she was at ease in the company of the rich and famous.

To all his other worries, Mason now added that of being in love with a girl who was hundreds of miles away. The record is silent on Julia's first impressions of Mason, and Mason himself did not keep a diary, in which he presumably would have recorded tender thoughts for his beloved. He did write to his sister, Emily, about his romance, probably as much to seek approval as anything else. As Kent Sagendorph notes, "Julia Phelps was unquestionably the first girl in his life who had aroused enough interest to become the subject of gushing letters to Emily."[25] The passion Mason felt for Julia does not appear in official communications or in any other documents of like nature, so he somehow kept his mind on the weighty matters at hand while his heart was on her. He was twenty-six at the time, and in all likelihood, Julia was his first intimate experience.

With Julia to think about during his trips to New York, Mason found it even more difficult to concentrate on completing the five-million-dollar loan; he badly needed to focus his energies on compelling state business. When the

Patriot War in Canada erupted, with its potential for armed rebellion on Michigan's borders, Mason had concerns of a different nature. He was regarded by both the Patriots in Canada and their sympathizers in Michigan as a rallying point: "The unfortunate fact that both factions were using the United States as safe ground wherein to raise volunteers and procure arms put Mason squarely in the middle."[26]

Mason stayed in New York for several weeks in late spring of 1838. He was not the man to squeeze concessions from smart New York financiers, and as a result, the bond deal fared badly. Stipulations and conditions were attached, to which Mason, without benefit of expertise, could only parry as best he could. He naively believed that the credit of a state could hold its own with that of the federal government itself, but savvy New York brokers would have none of Mason's line. He was in a hotel not far from the Washington Square district where Julia lived. Evenings found him with Julia in the parlor of the Phelps home.

Sagendorph writes that with Julia, "there was something inscrutable, mysterious, challenging. She was dark, and her brown hair flowed away . . . to cascade down either side of her high forehead, acting as a backdrop for a small, delicate, heart-shaped face and two of the biggest and most soulful eyes in this world. She was small and dainty, as fragile as a doll. Her tightly laced waist seemed so small that Mason thought he could touch his finger tips around it."[27] Unlike the swains who had courted Julia up to that time, Mason came off with the air of a dashing young man of the western frontier who had the charm and grace of an eastern breeding. If there was any resistance on Julia's part, it crumbled quickly.

We don't know when Mason asked Julia to marry him, but it must have been soon after their initial meeting. A fall wedding was agreed on, and Mason couldn't wait to tell friends in Detroit all about it. The speculation began immediately: How would Julia like Detroit? Where would the couple live, and would they start a family soon? The wedding took place at Thaddeus Phelps's home on November 1, 1838, when Mason had just turned twenty-seven. In time, the couple would have three children: Stevens Thomson Mason (1839–43), Dorothea Eliza Mason Wright (1840–1916), and Thaddeus Phelps Mason (1842–47). Only Dorothea—known later as Mrs. Dorothea Mason Wright of Newark, New Jersey—lived to see her father's name exonerated. Stevens T. Mason's own tragic early demise spared him the parent's sorrow of seeing two of his children die young.

9 ❧ Wildcat Banks, Failed Railroads, and Filled-in Canals

Two outstanding events in 1838 do not hint at the extraordinary difficulties that were to follow for the young state. Both involved transportation. Both took place in that exuberance of optimism that marked Michigan's early years under the Boy Governor.

On February 3, the state's first passenger train on the rails of the Central Railroad was scheduled to make its maiden trip from Detroit. The Central, chartered in 1832 as the Detroit and St. Joseph Railroad, was already under construction between Detroit and Ypsilanti when operations were taken over by the state. Railroads were still somewhat distrusted as a reliable conveyance, but it was believed that once the kinks were worked out and decent track was set down, the future had arrived with the steam locomotive.

A large gathering of people came to see the train make its departure for Ypsilanti. Speeches were made, bells were rung, and Governor Mason and his party stepped into their carriages, equipped with various creature comforts. The first passenger car was dubbed the *Governor Mason,* and all went well until the return trip, when the locomotive developed boiler problems. The train broke down in Dearborn, and a team of horses had to be dispatched from Detroit to fetch the governor, who arrived home around midnight. History does not record whether he retained his sense of humor about his namesake car having to be dragged home.

A celebration of like nature took place at Mt. Clemens in July when Governor Mason turned over the first shovelful of dirt on the Clinton-Kalamazoo Canal. This great ditch was proposed to cross the peninsula, linking Lake

St. Clair on the east with Lake Michigan on the west and utilizing inland streams, including the Clinton and Kalamazoo Rivers. Visitors came from miles around to partake of an outdoor banquet at a dollar per plate, prepared by a local hotel, as well as to drink champagne and listen to the oratory.

After a thirteen-gun salute and band music, onlookers were ready to observe the governor roll up his fancy dress shirt for the duty of shoveling. There were reports that most of the celebrants were "tight as a brick." District marshal Conrad Ten Eyck said, "Someone must stay sober and I am that man."[1] The Clinton-Kalamazoo Canal turned out to be the most notable failure of Michigan's internal improvements program. Only twelve miles of canal were dug between Mt. Clemens and Rochester, and canal boats ran only briefly. Records show "tolls of the first year totaled $46.90 and the second year the tolls fell to $43.44 when the project was abandoned."[2] When the money ran out, payrolls couldn't be met, and disgruntled laborers took to vandalizing the canal. Time and weather did the rest, so only remnants can be seen today.

Governor Mason had used his message to the legislature in the first days of 1838 to attack "overbanking" as the cause of the country's economic problems and to call for "curtailment of excessive credits and the gradual suppression of unlimited issues of bank paper."[3] He argued that the attempt to substitute paper for real capital "disturbs the natural laws of trade. Competition is the best regulator of every branch of industry."[4] But Mason seemed to want it both ways; he endorsed measures to insure the continued circulation of local bank issues, and he went out of his way to assure lawmakers that he had confidence in the solvency of the banks of the state.

The economic times must be seen in their political context. Politically, the state was Jacksonian in character, believing, along with Jackson, that bankers and their ilk were hostile to free institutions. "From 1835 to 1839, the wing of the Democratic Party led by Governor Stevens T. Mason, Senator John Norvell and young Kinsley S. Bingham controlled the state. This 'radical faction' "was composed of the thorough-going reformers in the state; representatives of frontier conditions professing the purest type of frontier philosophy. . . . Their constituents were small farmers, laborers and debtors, a class which was hostile to chartered banks, monopolies and slavery. In response to the popular outcry against the chartered banks, the 'radicals' supported the free banking law."[5] Put another way, the people wanted their legislators to make banking more democratic and open to anyone who wanted to get into the business.

When the legislature passed the free banking law in March 1837, with hardly a dissenting vote or murmur from the press, permission was given to form banking associations by fulfilling certain conditions. In 1837, there were fifteen chartered banks in Michigan. Detroit had a population of about ten thousand at that time. Fifteen banks should have been sufficient to the financial needs of a frontier state, but the radicals carried the day. Under the liberal banking statute, forty-nine banks were organized, most of which actually started operations: "Money had been in great demand during the real estate boom of the past few years, and the establishing of banks which could issue notes that would pass as currency seemed an easy way to provide additional funds."[6] The wildcat banks that sprouted like mushrooms in the most unlikely places are a remarkable story in the history of American banking.

The banking law might have worked in normal times, but 1837 was destined to be a signal year in the nation's economic fortunes. President Jackson's vendetta against Nicholas Biddle and the Bank of the United States had resulted in relaxing controls on state banks. When Jackson deposited U.S. funds in some of these banks, he increased their capacity to issue paper notes. But then his Specie Circular issued in 1836, which ordered banks to accept only gold or silver in payment for public land, helped to cause a shortage of hard cash. Banks all over the country suspended specie payment.

"I did not join in putting down the Bank of the United States to put up a wilderness of local banks," fumed Senator Thomas Hart Benton. Yet it was the passing of that "hydra of corruption" (Jackson's term for the Bank of the United States) that "appeared to clear the way for a plague of secondary monsters that seemed less controllable but every bit as vicious as their parent."[7] The dispute between Biddle and Jackson, always noteworthy for its bitterness, became epic in scale; when the time for reason and compromise became irretrievably lost, Biddle resorted to bare-knuckle tactics. "This worthy president," he sneered of Jackson, "thinks that because he has scalped Indians and imprisoned judges he is to have his way with the Bank. He is mistaken."[8] But as the government steadily drained its funds at the Bank of the United States into the new depositories—or "pet banks," as they were called—Biddle had no choice but to call in loans to compensate for the loss: "Businessmen who normally depended on Bank credit to finance their affairs faced a money shortage. From a period of relative prosperity, the nation's commercial centers quickly felt the sting of panic."[9]

It was at that point, shortly before Jackson issued the Specie Circular, that Biddle lost all distinction between the public good and the well-being of his bank. He hoped to parlay national distress to create political pressure for a rechartering of the Bank of the United States: "Biddle consciously pushed the contraction further than necessary. A short and sharp recession became his deliberate tool for political influence. When the Bank of the United States unexpectedly refused to renew the notes of its customers and demanded repayment instead, the money market suddenly dried up."[10] Businesses failed, unemployment rose, and although the poor suffered most when jobs disappeared, everyone felt the hard times. When Biddle reversed himself and expanded the bank's loans, the economy improved. When his charter was allowed to lapse in 1836, Biddle obtained a state charter and continued operations through the Bank of the United States of Pennsylvania.

To put matters in the broadest possible perspective, Biddle's bank

symbolized the dramatic changes that were rebuilding the American economy and altering the meaning of independence in the lives of ordinary citizens. For Americans who supported these changes, the Bank was a legal and necessary bulwark of an orderly, credit-based economy. For Americans who opposed these changes, the Bank was far more sinister. Because the Bank was a creation of the federal government, it depended on political support for its existence. When disagreement about the future of the American economy led to political disagreement during Jackson's presidency, the friends of banking . . . faced serious public challenge. In fact, the related questions of banking and the economy became central to the political conflicts of the era.[11]

The conflicts of the era were eye-openers in many respects: "Jacksonian Americans learned that money could hardly be taken for granted, that its influence over society was far from neutral, and that power over money could be used to remake the social and economic landscape in previously unimagined ways. In particular, the value and supply of money could be manipulated to stimulate economic growth or to slow it down to encourage a broad distribution of the benefits of economic change, or to concentrate economic power more tightly."[12]

In Michigan, the legislature sanctioned the suspension of specie payments for one year, presenting a gift-wrapped opportunity for the unscrupulous to make a lot of money. New banks were formed whose purpose was to print a ton of beautifully colored paper notes that were not redeemable in gold or silver. People accepted these notes anyway: "People in general did not know how to get along without money and when they could not get good money, they reluctantly accepted bad money, knowing it to be of doubtful value, but hoping to find some other person who would accept it."[13] Money in the form of bank notes became, it was said, as plentiful as strawberries in June.

The term "wildcat banks" seems to have many fathers. Some say banks were so named because of their vicious practices or because many sprang up in the Michigan woods where only wildcats roamed. George Catlin says the description "wildcat" arose from the fact that "several fraudulent banks made large issues of currency. The engraving and printing were done by a few firms which . . . economized their engraving expenses as much as possible, and many of the bills bore an engraving of a wildcat or panther."[14]

Some of the banking associations organized under the free banking law were legitimate, "but many were pure note manufactories, located at points difficult of access and used to promote speculation, frauds and swindles. Bonds and mortgages on 'city lots' in the wilderness constituted collateral; wildcat banks held the notes of other wildcat banks as capital."[15] The gullible were gulled, and the shysters took full advantage of nonexistent regulation. Perhaps the most notorious of the wildcat bank stories was that of Brest, near Monroe, "whose chief asset as a city was a colored map and prospectus of itself, which showed broad avenues lined with palatial homes, busy docks and warehouses, and noble vessels bearing the commerce of all lands."[16] The only trouble with this rosy-hued picture was that Brest was a figment of somebody's imagination. There were, in fact, many Brests.

With credit available for the asking and colorful notes "backed" by the local bank as the medium of exchange, the result was that towns with churches and broad avenues were platted where there was only wilderness. Maps were distributed purporting to show prospective buyers where their riches were to be made. In the aura of general prosperity, nothing seemed too remote or out of the question. People were caught up in the mania of buying one day and hoping to sell later at a large profit. Dunbar relates that "a canal was surveyed from Paw Paw to Lake Michigan and this was to be lined its full length by mills and factories. A great university was planned. All over the State, towns grew up like mushrooms—on paper."[17] A visitor to one of these paper cities described entering a river that "hardly admitted our canoe. Harbor there was none. Churches, houses, mills, people all were a myth. A thick wilderness covered the whole site. Even those marks of advancing civilization, the surveyor's marks, were wanting."[18] In the interior, new cities and villages appeared faster than surveyors could plat them.

The inspections of the banks were a haphazard operation. There were too few inspectors to begin with, and many of the banks were hidden in the woods, so inspectors had little knowledge of their whereabouts. When bank organizers learned of an approaching inspection, they sent specie on ahead, so that "the same bags of coin were passed from bank to bank, just ahead of the inspector, and sworn to be the property of each bank." On one occasion, "the unexpected return of the inspector . . . led to the discovery that the bank had in cash exactly $34.20 to support a note circulation of $20,000."[19] Despite their lack of hard cash, the banks issued notes that pledged the bank to pay to the bearer so many dollars in hard coin on demand. The law required that all banks had to keep on hand a stipulated amount of gold and silver in proportion to their issue of paper notes. But because there wasn't sufficient silver or gold in Michigan to comply with the law, the banks got by with specie certificates, "certifying that the specie had been received to be held on deposit."[20] The idea was to stay one step ahead of the inspector and out of the law's reach.

Wildcat bank promoters used every dodge in the books to promote their nefarious schemes. When there wasn't resort to swindle, incompetent and inexperienced managers added to the general aura of "anything goes." Banks difficult to reach or find were beyond the law, and their promoters provided little or no security. Inevitably, the crash came. Shortly after Michigan approved its program of public works, banking houses in the east announced that they could no longer redeem their notes in gold and silver. The Panic of 1837 was on; bank notes depreciated in value, and business stopped. In Michigan, the wildcat banks collapsed; of the forty-nine that were organized, only seven remained in 1839, and in the meantime, the state was flooded with the worthless paper notes of dead banks. The state Supreme Court in 1844 declared the general banking law of 1837 unconstitutional, and a year later, "there were only three banks in Michigan, all of them operating under special charters."[21] It is ironic, as Lawton Hemans points out, that Charles W. Whipple, who was speaker of the House of Representatives when the law was enacted, "should later have been the judge to deliver the opinion declaring the law unconstitutional and that the Honorable Alpheus Felch, late Banking Commissioner, should have been one of the judges to concur in the decision, and that the attorney to present the question before the court should have been Theodore Romeyn, a Detroit lawyer . . . whose name had been connected in no enviable relation as stockholder, director and general promoter of some of the wildest of the wildcat banks of Michigan."[22] This is, of course, the same Romeyn who accompanied Governor Mason on the trip west with the trunkful of money.

The bank issue became an important factor in state politics. Whigs and Democrats united on deploring overexpansion of state banking as bringing on the crisis, but then each tried to fix blame on the other: "The Whigs pointed to the many banks chartered by the Democratically-controlled legislature; the Democrats responded that the Whigs were the bankers and speculators. In support of this, they capitalized on the fact that the Whig gubernatorial candidate in 1837 was a Detroit banker, Charles C. Trowbridge, and attempted to show that the majority of Michigan bankers were Whigs."[23] The Whigs attacked the opposition as "the Rag Party" because of its support of the free banking law and called for investigations.

On April 16, 1839, the general banking law was permanently suspended by the legislature, and free banking was a dead issue in Michigan. Elsewhere, the national Democratic Party, which had a lot of explaining to do for the economic crisis precipitated by Jackson, increasingly turned against banks and pushed for hard currency. In Michigan, the Democrats split into factions, and a great shift in attitudes toward banks occurred: "Nowhere was this shift as sudden or as dramatic as in Michigan following the defeat of the Jacksonians in the election of 1839 led by William Woodbridge."[24] The Mason wing of the party was held in disfavor by other Democrats, with the result that Stevens T. Mason's departure from office was eagerly anticipated by some within his own party. The Boy Governor had fallen a long way from the heady days of the Toledo War and statehood celebrations.

A letter from Marshall dated November 2, 1833, and signed by A. Wilding arrived in the office of Governor George B. Porter. Wilding said that he had sent the Detroit papers a communication for publication "on the importance of constructing a railroad through the interior of Michigan" and that he had "suggested a method by which the necessary funds could be raised." He concluded that the railroad "is an object of great importance and if it comes into effect, would without doubt confer great honor on the Executive of the Territory as well as increase the prosperity of the country in a very great degree."[25]

Flattery of Porter aside, the governor's correspondent was on to something. But his vision was too limited. Porter's successor, Stevens T. Mason, would call for not one but *three* railroads to run across the peninsula. They were to be the centerpiece of a bold program that would catch Michigan up to its competitors and open up the interior for development and prosperity. It was as clear as the hand before your face that Michigan's water resources and favorable terrain were transportation-friendly. All that was needed was a plan, a cooperative legislature, and a funding mechanism. The profits from these large-scale public works would pay them off in short order.

Michigan's confidence in railroads as a mode of transportation was evident by the fact that up to 1837, "the territorial and state legislatures had granted charters to no less than twenty railroad corporations."[26] The first of these, the Pontiac and Detroit Railway Company, was established by an act bearing the date July 31, 1830. This was the first chartered railroad in the Old Northwest. It was reorganized as the Detroit and Pontiac Railroad in 1834 and was the forerunner of the Grand Trunk Western Railroad. The Detroit and St. Joseph Railroad Company was chartered on January 29, 1832, and was designed to connect Detroit with the St. Joseph River, deep inland.

But the state's most famous pioneer railroad was the Erie and Kalamazoo, chartered on April 22, 1833. The plan was to connect Port Lawrence (later Toledo) with Adrian and then extend westward to a point on the Kalamazoo River. This was one of the railroads that had banking powers, and its notes circulated freely as money. Construction of the road was completed to Adrian by the fall of 1836, using solid oak rails topped by an iron strap, which had an annoying tendency to pop loose. In 1837, the Erie and Kalamazoo took possession of a locomotive to replace horses; this was the first steam locomotive to operate west of the Alleghenies.

Although it was easy to get a charter, building a railroad was a different matter altogether: "Railroad construction was still very decidedly in an experimental stage. Although thousands of dollars had been subscribed to the Detroit and St. Joseph railroad project by Detroit people, it did not have a mile of line in operation in 1837. It was because the legislature wanted action that it launched the State into the business of building and operating railroads."[27] Lawmakers did so over Governor Mason's objections. And so, in his message to the legislature of January 2, 1837, Mason said he had submitted "to each railroad company within the state, the proposition of transferring to the state their respective charters."[28]

Earlier, the House Committee on Internal Improvements had issued a remarkable report on Michigan's prospects for development. The report gave a routine rundown of facts relating to the system of improvements in other states. But then the committee outdid itself in lifting up Manifest Destiny: "Whilst every state in the Union . . . is contending for the meed of glory, should Michigan withhold her young and vigorous arm, in coping with her renowned rivals, for her share of the honors to be meted out to those who shall accomplish the greatest work of improvement, and perform the greatest services to mankind? Your committee would do injustice to themselves and the state, did they hesitate to recommend the most active and liberal legislation in favor of the great and all absorbing subject of internal improvements."[29] This glowing prose was followed by the committee's call to action: "Your committee are of the opinion that the legislature will be fully justified, not only in incorporating all companies for railroads and canals of a feasible character, that may be applied for, but in using the credit of the state for the purpose of raising means to take a direct interest in most of them."[30] In other words, the state would leave no stone unturned in the mad rush to accelerate development of the interior by a vast network of roads, canals, and railroads.

How was all this to be accomplished? The committee recommended legislation authorizing the governor to borrow on the credit of the state the sum of three million dollars; that a board of internal improvements be constituted, "with power to appoint a competent chief engineer, the board to have full power and authority to control and direct the execution of all laws relating to internal improvements"; and that a tax of one mill on the dollar be levied to pay the interest "on such sums as may from time to time be borrowed."[31] With that, the committee awaited the action of its legislative colleagues. It wasn't long in coming. Three million dollars were considered too paltry a sum. The board of internal improvements was formed, and its members were named; the difficulty was finding a competent chief engineer: "The shortage of experienced civil engineers was a particularly serious problem."[32] There was also a shortage of trained railroad engineers, many of whom "were merely men who had picked up some know-how while working in a subordinate capacity on some eastern railroad."[33] But Michigan was a state in a hurry, maybe with something to prove to its neighbors, and so it went into the railroad business with all appropriate haste.

The master plan called for railway systems that would cross the state roughly parallel to each other. The Michigan Northern would run from Palmer on Lake St. Clair to Grand Haven. The Michigan Central would extend from Detroit to St. Joseph on Lake Michigan, and the Michigan Southern would have as its terminals Monroe on the east and New Buffalo on the west. It was believed that rapid settlement would provide plenty of traffic and, therefore, profits to the state. Visions of wealth and prosperity swayed the head of Governor Mason and like-minded Michiganians, for whom the future was a covey of chuffers bearing settlers, the products of agriculture, and other freight to busy towns along the rights-of-way.

Problems appeared quickly. In his State of the State message of January 4, 1838, Governor Mason could proudly report expenditures for "complete surveys of the northern, southern and central railroads," but he accurately predicted, "Routes of the different railroads will give rise to disputes generated from conflicting local interests."[34] There was yet another caveat: "For some time to come," said Mason, "our public works will prove but a limited source of revenue to the state; and we are already borrowing money without providing available funds to meet the interest or principal on our loan."[35] A year later, Mason was able to report, "The central railroad is under contract as far as Jackson, being a distance of seventy-eight miles from Detroit, and locations are now in progress as far as Kalamazoo, one hundred forty miles from Detroit. By the agreement with the contractor, that portion of this road between Ypsilanti and Ann Arbor should have been ready for the iron rails . . . but from some cause is not as yet completed. On the southern road, thirty miles as far as Adrian will be ready for laying the iron early in the ensuing spring; it is under contract as far as Hillsdale."[36]

In 1840, the report was decidedly mixed. The central route was completed to Jackson, and cars were regularly running the thirty-eight miles from Detroit to Ann Arbor. Expenditures from May 1837 to December 1839 were $757,076. Receipts for the calendar year 1839 for that portion of the central railroad from Detroit to Ann Arbor were $61,154.84, down $24,000 from the previous year. "The expenditures during the same period for running cars, repairs to road, machinery, etc.," reported Mason to the legislature, "have been $44,451, leaving a profit to the sinking fund of only about $16,703."[37] The southern road was nearly completed to Adrian, and the sum of $60,120 was expended for clearing and grubbing about 110 miles of the northern road between Port Huron and Lyons.

As Mason had predicted, there was bickering over the selection of the exact routes. Everyone believed the railroads should pass through their settlement. It wasn't long before speculators were creating paper cities in the wilderness, serviced by a railroad whose whistle you could hear if you put your ear on the track, except that there mostly was no track. Where there was track, the lines were often badly constructed.

To make matters worse, the state's limited funds "were dissipated through a combination of dishonesty, naivete and mismanagement."[38] The national crisis swept through Michigan, and cash dried up. When cash was short, the state issued scrip, described as "a kind of state treasury note which circulated hazardously at a woeful discount."[39] Scrip, of course, inspired confidence in nobody, but what could the state do? Borrowing was out of the question, hard money was in short supply, and businesses everywhere were failing, along with the banks.

It proved detrimental that the state, not private interests, was building the railroads: "No one had a financial interest in building them efficiently. The Michigan Central and the Michigan Southern both had tracks that were too fragile to support heavy loads, and each had major flaws that proved to be dangerous and costly. Levi Humphrey, a Mason appointee to the Board of Internal Improvements, had manipulated the results of the bids to construct the Southern, so that his friends would win the contracts. They then charged three–four times the market price for supplies. The Board's records were falsified to cover that their budget was overspent."[40] Michigan learned the hard way how little the cost of building railroads was then understood. The ineptness of the authorities in managing railroad construction, the drama that accompanied the negotiation and renegotiation of the five-million-dollar loan, and the sheer scope of the plan, both in terms of railroad trackage and the sums committed to the projects, combined to bring Michigan to its knees in debt. As one historian laments, "Over-optimism, sectional jealousy, political bickering, plain mismanagement and some dishonesty marked the affairs of Michigan's improvement plans."[41]

Of course, some things would never change. The pork barrel is a fixture in national, state, and local politics. When Michigan passed its "something for everybody" internal improvements law, lawmakers were only doing what came naturally. A legislature is the sum total of many individual parts, and each of those parts has a constituency. "To get any portion of the program accepted," reports Dunbar, "it was necessary to have something attractive for every section of the State with any considerable population. It was a case of all or nothing."[42] One legislator wrote his constituents to assure them, "Since a railroad from Monroe to New Buffalo was now a certainty, your property is now doubled in value—you must have a hearty rejoicing."[43] When it comes to pleasing the folks back home and burnishing their own reelection chances, lawmakers are inclined to vote for the all rather than for the nothing.

With the benefit of hindsight, it would have been far wiser for the state to have concentrated its energies on one railroad, the Central, which was easily the most advanced in construction of them all. The northern route would run through a portion of country as yet largely undeveloped and would, in fact, have the least to show for it when the bottom fell out. (The state did not build a mile of the northern road.) The southern route fell well short of its intended goal on the Kalamazoo River. By the time the state got out of the railroad business, "the Michigan Central and the Michigan Southern would prove to be viable projects, but only to a limited degree. The Central did in fact show profits right up to its sale to private ownership in 1846. In the course of building westward, most of the railroads' operating profits were spent on construction, a minimum amount on maintenance, and none to pay interest on the state's internal improvement bonds. They were subject to the ill effects of the post-1837 depression. State indebtedness reached $4.1 million in 1846."[44] That was the year Michigan sold its railroads to private chartered corporations.

Mason's successor, William Woodbridge, would say of internal improvements, "This scheme, so bold in its conception, so splendid in its design, so captivating to a fervid imagination, but yet so disproportioned to our present local wants and so utterly beyond our present means, must be given up. Every consideration of prudence forbids the further prosecution of this work."[45] The acts authorizing the sale of the Michigan Southern and the Michigan Central to two private business interests passed easily. The Southern was sold for five hundred thousand dollars, the Central for two million. As Frank Elliot notes, "Approximately three million dollars had been spent by the state to construct those roads. The money that had been spent on the Michigan Northern was not recoverable. The speedy completion of the Central by 1849 and the Southern by 1852 seemed to confirm the state's wisdom in getting out of the railroad business."[46]

Still, with the ultimate success of the Central, it can rightly be said that Stevens T. Mason opened the railroad era in Michigan. The first railroad passenger car made in Michigan was named after Mason, as was the first steamboat built in western Michigan, at its launching into the Grand River. A federal land grant in 1852 enabled construction of the canal and locks at Sault Ste. Marie, which would have pleased Mason mightily.

Unfortunately, what began with such high hopes of success ended with the state insolvent. Most of his people had nodded their heads in agreement when Governor Mason had said earlier, "The period has arrived when Michigan can no longer, without detriment to her standing and importance as a state, delay the action necessary for the development of her vast resources of wealth. Nature has bestowed upon us the highest advantages of climate, a fertile soil and peculiar facilities for commerce; and with a prudent and wise forecast to be exercised by the legislature and the people; we cannot fail soon to reach that high destiny which awaits us."[47] But that was the high-spirited language of January 1837. Only three years later, the governor would look back on his administration and say, "No party action was brought to bear upon the subject; and the error, if error there is, was the emanation of that false spirit of the age, which forces states as well as individuals, to over-action and extended projects. If Michigan has overtaxed her energies and resources, she stands not alone, but has fallen into that fatal policy which has involved in almost unparalleled embarrassment so many of her sister states."[48] Mason correctly assessed the times. He bravely shouldered his share of the responsibility for the loan agreement that fell apart, for the twin bankruptcies of the canal company and the bank with whom he had contracted, for the indebtedness into which the state was plunged, and for the failure of "a cherished policy" (as Lawton Hemans puts it) that Mason had hoped would raise Michigan into the first rank of states.

Michigan's confidence in railroads as the transportation hope of the future was only exceeded by its confidence in the canals portion of the state's internal improvements. The canal projects were the most imaginative in terms of reach. Inspired by the Erie Canal and the quick profits that followed its completion, the leaders of the new state saw no reason why Michigan could not match New York's success. The need to transport farm products to market without having to make the long trip to Chicago and then through the Straits of Mackinac argued for a cross-state canal. The state's rivers were its natural highways.

Unlike the railroads, canals were a familiar means of transporting goods and passengers. Their success was proven, whereas the railroads' was only speculative. Michigan's southern neighbors, Ohio and Indiana, had supported construction of canals with considerable outlays of money: "Ohio's legislature had authorized the construction of two canals across the state in 1825. Though not completed, considerable sections were in operation by 1837, and it was believed that they had contributed much to the prosperity of the state. Indiana had several canal schemes before 1837; the work had started on one canal in 1832."[49] It was thought that Michigan's system of rivers and navigable streams would link the big lakes Michigan and Huron and pay big dividends. The canal fervor traced its origins to President George Washington, who called canals "fundamental to nationhood" and who envisioned a system of canals that would bind the nation together and transform the country into a world power. Completion of the Erie Canal proved that from an engineering standpoint, few obstacles would stand in the way of a canal.

The main canal in Michigan was the Clinton-Kalamazoo Canal, which came at a cost of about sixteen to eighteen thousand dollars per mile of construction. Its total length would be 216 miles, with surveys showing a ditch thirty-two feet in width at bottom and holding water to a depth of five feet. The highest elevation would be near Pontiac, and most of the route would provide no great problems from an engineering standpoint. Plans called for a canal wide enough for boats to pass, with a fifty-foot-wide channel. Towpaths, turning basins, and rights-of-way would all have to be secured. At a point a short distance from Mt. Clemens, where the proposed canal would meet the Clinton River, a town of Frederick was platted, with great expectations that it would become a port. As it turned out, Frederick was a casualty of the canal, its name joining that of others hoping to cash in on the prosperity of internal improvements.

A second canal would link the waters of the Saginaw and Grand Rivers, utilizing the Maple River and the Bad River as connectors. This canal would measure forty-five feet in width and carry water at a depth of four feet. Numerous locks would need to be constructed on this canal, which never came remotely close to fruition. A third canal, authorized in a separate act of the legislature, would be surveyed with an eye toward bypassing the rapids of the St. Marys River at Sault Ste. Marie. The amount of twenty-five thousand dollars was appropriated for this canal if the survey and engineering reports proved favorable. In addition, money was set aside to clear certain rivers of impediments to navigation and to make other necessary improvements

With monies earmarked for each of these projects, a board of commissioners on internal improvements provided oversight for survey, construction, and operations. Again, Governor Mason provided the vision: "The practicality of uniting the waters of Lake Michigan with those of the eastern part of the state has long been conceded. The headwaters of the Grand River flowing into Lake Michigan might be connected with the waters flowing into Lake Huron or the Black River of St. Clair. I am credibly informed that a canal fourteen miles in length would unite the headwaters of the Looking Glass River with the headwaters or tributaries of the Shiawassee; the Huron may be connected with the Red Cedar, and the Raisin with the headwaters of the St. Joseph or Kalamazoo."[50] The board of commissioners echoed the governor's rosy-hued outlook: "There is no doubt in the public mind as to the superior advantages of canals over railroads . . . when heavy and bulky articles are to be transported. This canal (the Clinton-Kalamazoo) will do all the heavy transportation to and from the navigable waters of the Grand and Kalamazoo Rivers. This improvement will place Michigan before any of her sister states in the works of internal improvement early and wisely conceived and vigorously prosecuted for the benefit of her citizens."[51]

After the governor journeyed to Mt. Clemens to open the Clinton-Kalamazoo Canal, it wasn't long before work began, and the woods filled with men laboring with picks, shovels, and wheelbarrows. It was all very labor-intensive: "Lack of steam shovels and modern excavating equipment necessitated the placing of the burden on human brawn."[52] At first, things went well, albeit slowly. Towns sprang up to accommodate the work gangs. The great work crawled toward Utica and then Rochester. Mason would later report purchase of materials for fourteen locks and expenditures of $109,650. As for the Saginaw Canal, he reported, "Five miles are under contract, one mile of which is completed. Expenditures are $22,256. Improvements on the Grand and Kalamazoo Rivers are progressing with as much rapidity as the means at the command of the Board of Internal Improvements would permit."[53] Work at the St. Marys River was, unfortunately, "interrupted by the unauthorized interference of the authorities of the United States. The reservation of lands by the United States, for military or any other purposes, vests in the federal government no authority to interfere with an important and needful exercise of jurisdiction by our own Legislature."[54] So Mason staunchly maintained. But this reference to the dispute at Fort Brady was tilting at windmills.

In his last official communication to the people of Michigan, Mason reported total appropriations for all works of public improvements at $2,118,000 and expenditures of $1,510,315. "Your system, however, is as yet in its infancy,"[55] he confidently said, but it was in fact in its death throes. With the Morris Canal and Banking Company going bankrupt, there were no funds to pay the laborers, and when the money ran out, the men on the Clinton-Kalamazoo Canal left their jobs. In 1846, a committee of the legislature officially declared the canal to be a failure. And so a canal that began with high hopes and hoopla never went into use beyond the first twelve miles or so. Careless work by contractors, sloppy oversight, unanticipated adverse conditions, and then the shortage of hard money combined to saddle the state with abandonment.

It is certain that the state prosecuted its program of internal improvements with more energy than wisdom. Leaving aside the conditions of uncertainty and panic from the national depression, Michigan's plan was flawed from birth. When Governor Mason recommended that the state be a stockholder in private railroad and canal companies, he couldn't make his recommendation stick. He went along with the idea of something for everybody, but he was beholden in that to his governing partner, the legislature. That was exactly the problem: the state was subject to sectional pressures, and the legislature bends and flows with local needs. The result in 1837 was "prosecuting projects for which there was no present economic need in order to allay objection and secure support for other projects for which there might be said to be present economic necessity. As there had been contests between sections that each and all might partake of the benefits from improvements that were to be constructed at the expense of all, so now there began to be contests between localities of the same section for the location of the particular improvement that was no longer divisible."[56]

Governor Mason hadn't yet left office when, in April 1839, the legislature reduced the board of commissioners to three members. In the election of that year, the Whigs criticized both the system and its management, to good effect with the electorate: "The people realized they had undertaken too sizeable a task; running the works after they were built would be a bigger job still."[57] Consider the colorful language of a Senate committee's report a few years later: "The control of such a complicated mass of business as would arise from directing the transportation of freight and passengers . . . and superintending all the financial concerns of this vast system, would indeed form a nucleus around which would gather a horde of greedy, half-starved political hacks, whose sole aim would be self-aggrandizement—in whose midst corruption, intrigue, and deception would riot in unlimited freedom."[58]

A House committee in 1840–41 issued a long report on Michigan's improvement program, in which it made no accusation of major dishonesty. But the incompetency and gross excesses, especially pertaining to the wildcat banks, were too evident to admit of any whitewash. And there is no denying that the state's financial problems "were further enhanced by her own peculiar banking and currency situation."[59] Later administrations would take steps to reform banking practice and to restore and preserve public credit. When Michigan received a delayed donation of five hundred thousand acres of land from the federal government to be used for promoting internal improvements, these lands were sold to meet past obligations rather than for new developments.

What Michigan should have learned from the canal building fiasco was not to plan and build so extravagantly during a depressed national economy; financial problems slowed the canal projects in their tracks. Michigan's leaders also needed to read the signals sent out by President Jackson. Early in his administration, Jackson had vetoed a bill to provide federal funds for a road in Kentucky, saying, in his veto message, that he opposed lavish expenditures for internal improvements. He recommended instead that the national debt be paid, which resulted in a treasury surplus. Finally, the Whigs made hay with Governor Mason's failure to get a good deal on the sale of the state's internal improvement bonds. Mason's inexperience in high finance and later allegations that he used the sale of the bonds to enrich himself and some of his cronies were damaging.

The immediate postmortems were to be especially harsh on Mason and the Democrats. The Whigs' successful gubernatorial candidate William Woodbridge chose to focus on the fiscal mess he had inherited from Mason. Not content to leave the discredited former governor alone, Woodbridge found means to associate him with bribe-taking in the case of the five-million-dollar loan. It is a pity that so remarkable a public servant should be remembered in history as the implacable foe of the state's first governor and that his hatred should take the form it did, as we shall see in the next chapter.

William Woodbridge served his state for thirty-six years, in all three branches of government, and no name is more prominent in the early annals of Michigan. Michigan governor Robert McClelland (1852–53) would say of Woodbridge, "With the exception of General Cass, there was no man who did more to mold the character of the state than Governor Woodbridge."[60] In 1828, President Adams appointed Woodbridge chief justice of the territory, a position he held for four years. But when it came time for his reappointment, President Jackson let it lapse; Woodbridge took this as a "contemptuous ejection." Since Stevens T. Mason was a protégé of Jackson, Woodbridge allowed his generous endowment of anger to fall on the youth.

In the early 1830s, the fortunes of Woodbridge and Mason became commingled during the fight for statehood, with Woodbridge taking the anti-statehood position. Later in Mason's tenure as governor, the resentment by Woodbridge at times crossed the line of acceptable political behavior. When the Whigs took office, Woodbridge was sixty years old, and Mason was only twenty-eight. In his last years, Woodbridge preferred the life of a recluse, dying of emphysema at age eighty-one in 1861; he was buried in Detroit's Elmwood Cemetery, not far from Lewis Cass. He outlived his party, the Whigs, by many years, and he outlived his sworn enemy, Stevens T. Mason, by almost two decades.

10 ～ Final Disheartenment

The Boy Governor's downward trajectory and fall into disgrace could be dated to his reelection in 1837, when he squeaked out a victory of a few hundred voters over Charles C. Trowbridge. His considerable appeal and independent feistiness seemed to have lost their charm with his people. If the achievement of statehood and his spirited prosecution of the Toledo War were the apex of Mason's public life in Michigan, the events of 1837 and after would provide a sad denouement to his political career. The fact that he was hounded out of Michigan speaks volumes about ingratitude, fickle opinion, and short memories. Only his marriage to Julia and subsequent fatherhood helped to ease the sting of his public setbacks.

In his correspondence with family and friends during this period, we see a wiser, more mature man. There is less of the impetuous Hotspur and more of the deliberative, canny politician. He would recall the words of his father, written in 1835: "Politics are fascinating, but altogether delusive, and I think a poor broken-down politician the most miserable of society. Even one honorably retiring is soon forgotten, and he sickens from neglect. I have seen so much of this unprofitable life that I look upon your course as full of hazards and disappointments, as that of every politician must be. But take care not to progress too rapidly and be not ambitious of promotion. When it comes regularly and unsought for, it has some stability and secures a foundation to build on."[1]

In 1838, Mason was still only twenty-six years old. He didn't have a sensible older brother or his father on the scene to help him in his decision making. A good portion of his young life had been lived in public scrutiny. In the process, "he had learned something of the insincerity of the praise that sometimes follows success, and the injustice of the blame that sometimes follows failure."[2]

We know that he became disheartened at times—that would only be normal—but he bore his trials with grace and dignity. He may have been conscious that as the first governor of his state, he was not unlike George Washington, who set the tone for all succeeding presidencies in how he viewed the powers and responsibilities of his office.

When Stevens T. Mason began his second term in January 1838 with the assembling of the third legislature, he would have seen some men who would provide the leadership for Michigan in the coming decades. Among them were Kinsley Bingham, John S. Barry, Robert McClelland, and, of course, William Woodbridge. These men and others would attempt to restore the state to solvency, to complete the program of internal improvements, and to point the state in the direction of a free market economy that would give rise to strong private industries.

Mason would spend a lot of time away from Michigan in 1838, mostly in New York. That afforded him more time to see Julia and to make wedding plans, but that happy circumstance was accompanied by the knowledge that the financial deal worked out the previous fall wasn't going smoothly. He must have known, with a sinking heart, that he was the wrong man to match skills with eastern financiers and canny businessmen such as Edward R. Biddle. Here, Julia would have been a source of solace, after Mason came to her place from a long day's negotiation with the financiers.

Back home, surveys on the Southern Railroad were stopped for lack of funds. A return of cholera hit construction crews on the Michigan Central, necessitating a work stoppage. The legislature had authorized an increase of the interest rate on the bonds to 6 percent, up from the original 5.5 percent. When Mason, still trying to get the best deal possible, negotiated an agreement that was less than satisfactory, his critics let him have it with both barrels.

Worse was to come. The state election of 1839 was held in an atmosphere of bitter recrimination. In addition, "Michigan's wildcat banks had folded, and the paper notes they had issued, which were held by thousands of Michigan citizens, had become worthless. Little public land was being sold and immigration into the state had sharply slowed. Prices for farm products had dropped disastrously."[3] The party in power was blamed, and even within the party, factions were forming.

With Mason declining to run for reelection, the Democrats held a state convention in Ann Arbor on September 19, 1839, for the purpose of selecting a successor. The delegates settled on Elon Farnsworth, a competent judge, as their nominee, paired with Thomas Fitzgerald for lieutenant governor. The unkindest cut of all was the silence the convention kept on Stevens T. Mason. It was a great omission that the convention passed no resolution commending him or his administration for his service to the state. This would normally be an opportunity for delegates to whoop it up in a show of appreciation for their retiring standard-bearer. There could have been no more humiliating insult than the fact that Mason was ignored.

In his final address to the legislature, Mason had taken an optimistic view of the financial and economic condition of Michigan and its people, expressing hope for the future: "Though sensible my exertions have not met the success I could have desired, I trust they will be considered as having been directed by an earnest desire for the public good. And if my official relations to the people of Michigan have been attended with any injurious consequences to their interests, I am consoled by the persuasion that those evils will find their correction in the patriotism of the legislative branch of the government, and in the wisdom of those who may succeed me."[4] The charity he extended to his successor was not returned. Woodbridge would respond to kindness with savagery; he early threw out hints that Mason had lined his pockets from a fee-splitting deal he had cooked up with Biddle. When the money from the trunk came up missing, that was further "proof" to Woodbridge that Mason was running a scam on the people of Michigan. Woodbridge's Whigs would portray Mason as "a worthy successor to Benedict Arnold"[5] and guilty of youthful indiscretions.

Before the election campaign began, Mason had some news of a personal nature to report—the birth of his first son, Stevens Thomson Mason, Jr., in New York, on August 1, 1839. In a letter to his mother, the proud father says, "I have only time before the closing of the mail that at 1 o'clock this day, Master Mason made his entrance into the City of New York, amidst the firing of cannon and the shouts of thousands. The steam ships Great Western and British Isles are now passing out to sea, bearing the news to the old world. The young gentleman is of prodigious size, black eyes, black hair and withal, the greatest praising of the age. Julia is, as the ladies say, 'doing kindly well.' She sends her love and a kiss to you all from the boy. I must not omit to say that the youngster has a dimple in his chin, and is said to be the image of his father."[6] We don't know whether Julia concurred in that judgment, but the new father is quick to write again the next day, "By Julia's instructions, I send you a lock of the baby's hair. Instead of being black, it turns out to be a dark brown, but will in time assume a still darker shade. I wish you could see the little fellow taking his morning nap. Julia only needs you and the girls to make his happiness complete."[7] Mason then assured his mother of his intention to put the Mason family coat of arms on the baby's cup.

Even though Mason was not a candidate and, in fact, took little part in campaign activities that year, he was still a prominent target for the Whigs. Sensing blood in the water, the Whigs dredged up the border war with Ohio and castigated Mason for weakness in yielding the Toledo Strip. The failure of the wildcat banks, the conduct of the five-million-dollar loan, and the general administration of state affairs were fair game for Whig politicians and the Whig press. When the Whigs paired James Wright Gordon of Marshall with Woodbridge at the top of the ticket, a slogan was born: "Woodbridge, Gordon and Reform!" This slogan, writes Lawton Hemans, became the campaign shibboleth of the party: "It was a time when for reasons that were logical and for reasons that were fallacious there was potency in the word 'reform.'"[8] It worked for William Henry Harrison, too, who rode reform, lubricated by hard cider and the slogan "Tippecanoe and Tyler Too," into the White House.

The Whigs in Michigan were aided by the Democrats' dispirited campaign. But even though the Democrats were split, they could still agree on how to dish it out. They reminded voters of the Whigs' Federalist origins and labeled Woodbridge "a filcher from the U.S. Treasury, a disfranchiser of foreigners and the poor, and an office seeker in his dotage."[9] Yet the attacks on personalities from both sides—portraying Mason as a Benedict Arnold and Woodbridge as a tyrant judge—didn't change the fact that bankruptcy and ruin were threatening to engulf Michigan. Woodbridge and Gordon won easily, and the Whigs won majorities in both houses of the legislature.

The political career of Stevens T. Mason ended after eight years as governor, acting governor, and territorial secretary. He turned twenty-eight on October 27, shortly before the vote that carried Woodbridge to victory. He had a means of livelihood at hand and a bright future in Michigan, if one allowed for the possibility of a political comeback and convenient short memories. He was a family man who stood to gain a nice inheritance some day, and when the bad times passed, people would remember his pluck in the Ohio affair and his persistence in preparing Michigan for statehood. He had vote-pulling power—everybody knew that. He was handsome, articulate, and possessed of an easy affability. But what might have been would never be, and Mason's cup of sorrows was far from drained.

Upon the expiration of his term in January 1840, Mason hoped to establish a thriving law practice with his longtime friend Kintzing Pritchette. But first, there were the duties of office to attend to, specifically one last opportunity to address the people of Michigan. It was the custom, in those days, for the departing governor to send a farewell message to the legislature. At first, Mason wasn't going to present a final State of the State message, out of courtesy to Woodbridge. But then he thought better of it, thinking it to be his rightful due.

Two years earlier, in his second inaugural address, Mason had taken the high road of gentle self-criticism: "However great the censure to which I may at times have been subjected, . . . I have not willingly jeopardized the interests of my constituents. That I may have committed errors, I do not pretend to doubt, but I can truly say they have not been errors of intention."[10] Now, his official departure was the time to clear the air and to present to the people a final accounting. But his leave-taking would be the occasion for another humiliation.

Mason had just learned of his mother's death in New York, and thus it was with a heavy heart that Mason sent his message to Woodbridge for the expected routine approval. The message, conciliatory in tone and inoffensive, set off a firestorm. It had been given to the newspapers for publication, "in anticipation of its delivery at the opening of the session," but "upon presentation to the Legislature it was denied acceptance, treated with resolutions of ridicule and sarcasm and denied a place in the records of the State."[11]

The governor's treatment at the hands of the Senate was reported in the Senate journal of January 6, 1840. A resolution was offered informing Mason that the Senate "is not prepared to receive any communication from him." The resolution was amended to read that the communication from Mason "is regarded as disrespectful to the Senate, justly entitling him to its censure." The next day, Benjamin Witherell moved to have the message read; the motion lost by a vote of 6–10. He then moved that the message be printed; that motion lost by the same vote. Witherell then moved that Governor Mason's message be the order of the day for the next Thursday; that motion was amended by Mr. Hawkins to read "for the next 4th of July."[12] One can imagine the guffaws that greeted this taunt by Hawkins.

The discourtesy shown to Mason by the Whigs was not disavowed by their leader, Woodbridge. The new governor had, in fact, suggested that Mason prepare a farewell message; somewhere along the line, Woodbridge changed his mind. Perhaps having read the message prior to its transmission to the legislature and taking note of its polite tone, he decided its statesmanlike approach was worthy of contempt. He told the editor of the *Detroit Advertiser,* the Whig newspaper, that "Mason had used the utmost effrontery in trying to get such a message on the record."[13] When this was published, the Democratic papers published the complete text of Mason's message. When the vulpine Woodbridge encouraged Mason, the former may have been hoping for an opportunity to show up the latter publicly; if so, Mason fell for the bait. The legislature's refusal to accept the message as a public document had Woodbridge's full endorsement.

When the Whig house organ then published a story saying Mason never had Woodbridge's permission to write a farewell address in the first place, Mason demanded an explanation from Woodbridge as to the truth or falsity of the newspaper story. "I regret to see it stated in the morning's paper," Mason began, "that I had not received your concurrence in my determination to prepare an annual message . . . My right to transmit this message, I have never for a moment yielded; but I am unwilling to rest under the imputation of treating you with discourtesy, or with having asserted that which will not be borne out by your own testimony. You will oblige me therefore by saying how far this statement of the paper is true."[14] Woodbridge, in reply, would smoothly say, "I am incapable of doing you injustice or even to evince toward you other than the courtesy I have always received from you."[15]

Mason's letter to the governor had the effect of making the former appear to be on the defensive, writing letters questioning the motives of the chief executive and coming off as a sore loser and a publicity hound. From his estate at Springwells, Woodbridge would assure Mason of no unkind feelings on his part and, as for an official explanation, would say, "I at least had duties to perform of too grave a character to warrant me in suffering my mind to be diverted from them."[16] Mason let the matter drop, but the attacks on his character were only warming up.

Woodbridge vented his personal hatred for Mason by tearing down the previous administration's accomplishments, beginning with the internal improvements program. He said it had to be given up, in its entirety. His vindictiveness then showed in allegations of irregularity and gross incompetence in the negotiation of the five-million-dollar loan, with Mason made out to be "a bungler of colossal stupidity."[17] No facts were cited to show that Mason's conduct was other than exemplary, but throughout Woodbridge's governorship, he lost no opportunity to challenge Mason's reputation for honesty.

So what *did* Governor Mason say in his farewell address? He didn't sugar-coat economic conditions, and he acknowledged that some internal improvements would have to be abandoned. He listed the problems of the state and warned against compromising the school system. He wanted the state university to be protected at all costs, and he requested appropriations for a geological survey and a state penitentiary. Then he concluded on a personal note.

> My official relations with you, fellow citizens, now terminate, and it only remains for me to take my respectful leave. On reviewing the period of my connection with the executive branch of the government of Michigan, I find much both of pleasure and pain. Pleasure derived from the generous confidence reposed in me by my fellow citizens, and pain for the many unkind emotions to which my position has given rise . . . I part from official station without one sigh of regret.
>
> I cannot be insensible to the many errors I may have committed. But I derive consolation from the reflection that they will be amply repaired by the services of one whose experience is acknowledged, whose ability is known and whose patriotism is unquestioned. Michigan shall have my earnest and continued desire for her prosperity and welfare, and my earnest and fervent prayer that He who holds in His hands the fate of nations . . . will bestow upon her every blessing a free and enlightened people can desire.[18]

Lawton Hemans writes, "It was hardly to be expected that a communication so void of all that might be occasion for offense would be received with contumely or disrespect, but the virus of bitter partisanship was still active and the Whig majority was still exultant if not arrogant in their victory."[19] The disheartened Mason now sought the security of private life and the challenges of a law practice. In May, he and his wife moved into the larger quarters of the Norton House in Detroit. Emily Mason wrote to a friend to say, "I am so delighted that my brother Tom and Julia are to have Mr. Norton's house, it will be charming."[20]

A legislative committee that had been formed to investigate the handling of the bond sales now took up its work. Mason, who was weary of all the second-guessing of his and Pritchette's negotiations, was more than willing to have an investigation of his actions, saying, "As there are many circumstances connected with this negotiation which admit of explanation, . . . I would court the most rigid inquiry."[21] He should have known better; the political climate was still hostile, and with Woodbridge as instigator, the committee was a "fishing expedition" right from the start.

Chaired by DeGarmo Jones of Detroit, the committee was out to make political capital of the loan deal. There was no pretense of fairness about the committee's work. Testimony from Mason was refused, and there wasn't much for the committee to do except to poke around in the correspondence between Mason and the Morris Canal and Banking Company. The goal was "to find something upon which to base a charge that Mason and Pritchette had received a slice of the fee paid to the Eastern bank at the time the contract was signed."[22] And if committee members couldn't find something of interest, maybe they'd contrive something.

The report was a mockery. On March 10, 1840, Woodbridge received his copy of the report and quickly ordered twice the usual number of copies printed. After the Whig version was read into the record, Woodbridge adjourned the legislature before the minority Democratic version could be placed into the record. The Whig version made it appear as though all the correspondence that passed among Mason, Pritchette, the Morris Canal and Banking Company, and the Bank of the United States "had been unearthed through the diligence and astuteness of the committee."[23] Lamenting the "daring fraud" upon the interests of the state, as well as negotiations that must have been "entirely illegal," the report noted that the credit of the state was "irretrievably gone."[24] The committee ignored the fact that Pritchette had attempted to regain Michigan's bonds under instructions from Mason, who had written to Michigan's auditor general of his "deep apprehension that loss might occur to the State from its sale of five million dollars of bonds to the Bank of the United States and the Morris Canal and Banking Company in consequence of the unprecedented depression in the money market."[25] Mason went on to say that he had instructed Pritchette to obtain the return to the state of 2.5 million dollars in bonds.

A minority report, signed by Samuel Etheridge of Coldwater, "set forth the well-established fact that the very matter the Whigs were yelping about had been foreseen and thwarted by Governor Mason long before the Whigs were in office."[26] That document went on to show that Mason had worked to prevent further losses to the state and that any allegations of improprieties on his part were baseless. Portions of the minority report are worth reproducing here.

Should the purchasers of the State bonds fail to meet their engagements with the State, it is difficult to imagine an occurrence fraught with the consequences more fatal to the future prosperity of Michigan. Burdened with the interest on five million of dollars for twenty years and the principal at the expiration of that period, without having received but little more than two million of that amount, is a picture calculated to startle the boldest. Had such a catastrophe occurred, as there was every prospect, without any effort to prevent it, when would the sound of the clamor have ceased against the Executive for his culpable remissness in neglecting the most vigorous measures to save the State.[27]

The language is that of Mason himself, who had maintained a long silence to the attacks on his character. It may be that he used the Democratic minority report to try to set the record straight. The catastrophe that Mason feared did in fact occur, but it was less damaging in its results than feared. Who but Mason himself would have been most sensitive to "the clamor against the Executive," and who but Mason would have wanted to make clear to future generations that he took steps to avert a greater catastrophe? The report concluded,

No effort has been spared to place the monetary affairs of our State before the world in their worst possible form. These constant and clamorous assertions of the absolutely desperate condition of Michigan are everywhere producing the most disastrous effects, and in the end, these predictions of ruin will bring about their own fulfillment. No motive appears strong enough to prevent every good thing from being dragged into the political arena. Every good custom and well established principle vanishes before the demand for political capital. No art is too low, no tongue too base to be used in trumpeting to the world everything which seems calculated to ruin the credit of the State abroad and depress her interests at home, provided that a political object can be obtained.[28]

Such was the state of affairs now that Mason was out of office, with the Whigs in control, the Democrats reduced to quarreling factions, and Mason the object of vicious personal abuse. Julia, appalled by the attacks against her husband and, by now, pregnant with Dorothea, longed for New York and family. The law partnership with Pritchette could hardly succeed when Mason was under a cloud. All he had fought to accomplish for Michigan was in danger of being torn down by the Whigs.

Yet Mason was still a popular figure. There are reports of him attending political gatherings and being acclaimed as a hero. Hemans describes such an event: "On the evening of the 'Democratic Jubilee' a vociferous crowd filled the City Hall to overflowing. The meeting was no sooner organized than there was a shout of 'Mason! Mason! Mason!' The ovation which greeted his arrival and subsequent address showed that he still had a place in the hearts of the people."[29] The fact Mason was popular despite the debacles of the five-million-dollar loan and the wildcat banks is testimony to the open and unaffected nature of his persona.

Mason's evident claim on the loyalty of his friends and followers would have gnawed at Woodbridge. In the back of the old man's mind was the scenario of a Democratic return to power, with Mason triumphant. Even if Mason personally did not lead a comeback, there he was, practicing law in Detroit, right under Woodbridge's nose. For Woodbridge, success would not be achieved until Mason had been driven from Detroit and so tainted with scandal and shame that generations to come would revile the name of Mason.

In 1840, a presidential campaign was in full swing, and Mason found himself drawn to political rallies, where he was asked to speak. Elected on the basis of his war record and a popular slogan, William Henry Harrison served for only a month before becoming the first president to die in office. Woodbridge resigned the governorship but continued to exercise the duties of that job until he accepted election to the U.S. Senate on March 4, 1841. But before he left Michigan, Woodbridge made one more effort to smear Mason. The five-million-dollar loan was to be investigated yet one more time.

Woodbridge thought that if he could dig up more charges against Mason and make them stick, he could put the Boy Governor behind bars. Woodbridge drew up a plan linking Mason to conspiracy and embezzlement. Mason's innocence of any such crimes "made it necessary for Woodbridge and his cohorts to forge documents, present perjured testimony, hide witnesses, change records, and in general concoct a wholly synthetic case."[30] Because Woodbridge had access to the records and Mason did not, he could keep the files off-limits to Mason's supporters. In addition, neither Mason nor his allies would be given a chance to speak in defense.

The opening move was Woodbridge's. He presented to the legislature a document purporting to be a bill in chancery on the part of the state of Michigan against the Morris Canal and Banking Company and addressed to the chancellor of the state of New Jersey. Woodbridge didn't miss a trick; Mason was in the East on business at the time and wouldn't return until the opening of the navigation season in the spring. Woodbridge had plenty of time to do his dirty work and no moral scruples to impede him.

The document demanded the return of money alleged to have been steered Mason's way during contract negotiations. Apparently, no such chancery bill ever was sent to the New Jersey official, but the document was submitted as "evidence" to the finance committee of the state senate, chaired by DeGarmo Jones. The chair then said that a most secret investigation was going on and that Governor Mason was at the center. What he didn't say (and probably didn't need to) was that the whole thing was a frame-up and that his committee was the judge, jury, and executioner.

With the handwriting so clearly on the wall, Mason's friends rallied. Benjamin Witherell in the Senate volunteered to serve as his defense counsel. Jones cut him off by denying him the right of producing or cross-examining witnesses before the committee. Witherell then took the matter to the floor of the Senate, where he demanded a clear statement of the charges, if any, against Mason. Witherell was silenced by a party-line vote. With no right of attorney, no access to the records, and a hostile "jury" sitting in judgment, Mason, in absentia, was a helpless victim.

Communications were dispatched in haste to Mason in New York. He was needed, the letters said, to use his popularity to offset the pending miscarriage of justice in the legislature. Even if he were denied any opportunity to present his case before the committee, maybe his presence in Detroit would give Woodbridge pause. Or maybe the Whig lawmakers would come to their senses and see that what they were doing was character assassination. Maybe enough of them would have the gumption to stand up to their former leader. That was not likely, though.

Mason and Julia came west as fast as winter conditions would allow but did not arrive in time. The investigating committee made its report on March 27, 1841, amid great secrecy. Publication of its sordid details would soon follow, but until then, Mason's friends could only surmise the report's contents through guesswork. The committee was not going to take any chances on rogue copies making their way to the newspapers; the report was kept from view, and its contents were not divulged by anyone.

When the contents did go public, the result was a sensation. Governor Mason was charged with embezzlement and corruption. The committee's star witness was none other than Theodore Romeyn. Before the committee in 1839, at its first investigation, Romeyn had testified that he had never, directly or indirectly, drawn any money from the state for personal advantage; "neither have I received from Governor Mason," he had said, "any accommodations or advances."[31] But now Romeyn was willing to say under oath that he had been present with Governor Mason at the time the contract was signed and that Mason had received financial profit from the state's loan. That this statement contradicted his earlier testimony seemed not to bother the committee. The report went on to say that the state treasurer had begun direct negotiations with the Morris Canal and Banking Company, under authority of the legislature, with the object of securing the unpaid installments on the loan.

The acceptance of Romeyn as a credible witness was all the more surprising because he had just been convicted of fraud and was awaiting sentence. Now he was saying that both he and Mason had been paid by the directors of the Morris Canal and Banking Company for enabling them to collect a fee. Romeyn, by most accounts a slippery character, "seems to have been willing to admit his own lack of honor so that he might assist in besmirching the reputation of Governor Mason."[32] Governor Mason never came out and said so, but he suspected Romeyn of knowing something about the disappearance of money from the trunk.

Not much seems to have been made of Romeyn's professed guilt. One account has him throwing himself at the mercy of the legislature, but as that body was doing Woodbridge's bidding in this saga of slanders, Romeyn was safe from punishment. As for the committee, "Its purpose was served by the release of statements of allegations of wrongdoing which it did not attempt to prove, but which it did not allow to be disproved."[33] Alarmed at how cynically he had been framed, Mason now attempted to prove his innocence to the slander that the committee had passed against him.

Mason appealed to the legislature to hear him out, but he was refused. One by one, the doors closed against him. Not a word in Mason's defense was allowed into the records, and even the newspapers seemed to lose interest in his troubles. Then, on top of everything else, he received a personal letter from Romeyn saying, among other things, "I think if I could see you in person that we could arrange answers that would be more satisfactory than if published without consultation."[34] Mason had no intention of doing business with the devil and fired off a withering reply of rejection.

Mason wrote to his brother-in-law, Colonel Isaac S. Rowland, saying, "I have received and read in the last day or two the report on the five million dollar loan. A greater combination of falsehood and misrepresentations was never collected together. I have a plain story to tell in answer, and every unprejudiced mind won't fail to understand and believe."[35] With that, Mason issued, on May 11, a lengthy defense in pamphlet form, which was addressed "TO THE PEOPLE OF MICHIGAN." He would go over the heads of the people's representatives to the people themselves; surely they would understand.

In his pamphlet, Mason traced the conduct of the negotiation of the five-million-dollar loan from its beginnings. He responded to each allegation with page after page of documentary proof of his innocence. The state treasurer's story about his alleged discoveries was declared to be false. DeGarmo Jones of the finance committee and his associate James M. Edwards were termed "my violent personal and political enemies, pliant instruments to aid their work of infamy."[36] Correspondence that Mason had kept from the Morris Canal and Banking Company indicated that the loan deal was advantageous to Michigan. The men who had so maliciously pursued him had, in all cowardice, carried on their business when Mason wasn't around to answer charges. The pamphlet was, all in all, a telling document, which concludes with Mason sick at heart and hoping to be remembered as he once was.

> I have thus, fellow citizens, endeavored to place before you a full answer to all the accusations preferred against me. While I am free to acknowledge that there is no external reward as dear to me as the good opinion of my fellow citizens, even to secure that reward I would not mistake the grounds of my defense.
>
> I act as a private citizen unjustly and ruthlessly assailed. Circumstances render it probable that I shall never again be a candidate for your suffrages. I have therefore no political purpose to effect. I strike in defense of my name and all that is dear to me. I have left your service poorer than I entered it, and if I have any earthly boast, it is that I have never intentionally wronged the public. That I have felt the imputations cast against me I do not pretend to deny, but the consciousness of my own integrity of purpose has afforded me an inward pride and satisfaction that the world cannot rob me of. To the people of Michigan I owe many obligations and with the last pulsation of life I shall acknowledge and remember their kindness.[37]

At the age of twenty-nine, Mason had finished public life in Michigan, frustrated and hurt, his character blackened and dragged through the gutter. He was depicted as a crook, "the man who had caused the wave of bankruptcies and disasters which history says made up most of the period wherein he held office."[38] Satisfied that Mason was crushed, Woodbridge left the state for the imperial splendor of the U.S. Senate—a place more deserving of his gifts than that provincial backwater whose people bestowed high honors on a stripling.

It must have been a living purgatory for Mason to be seen on the streets of Detroit in the summer of 1841. His own black mood may be glimpsed in a letter he wrote to a friend in New York: "Detroit at present is as dull and quiet as the tomb. Everybody seems to be awaiting the promised arrival of better times."[39] But writing to the same friend a month later, Mason exhibited a lively interest in current politics, before announcing a momentous decision.

John Barry was nominated for governor on the simple ground that the western part of the state was entitled to the candidate this year. Thus far, my name has been left out of the question, and I think the policy of the Whigs will be to let me alone. If we can elect Barry, I shall leave the state contented. I am here long enough to see the Whigs cutting each others' throats, and to feel that every personal enemy I have is politically as dead as a doornail. DeGarmo Jones, and all of the legislative clique who assailed me last winter, have been dropped by their own friends, and in their stead men have been nominated of as decent a character as the Whig ranks could afford.

I have made an accurate estimate, and I am satisfied we can live for $1,600 a year, $800 each, which be about one half it would cost abroad. In this estimate, I allow $400 for a house and three servant women.[40]

Thoroughly disheartened, Stevens T. Mason made plans to leave Detroit. His wife knew all along that her husband needed a change of scenery. "Thomson has fully made up his mind to leave Detroit next fall and settle in Baltimore," she wrote to a friend, adding, "He has had every encouragement by the good people there to locate among them."[41] Mason's furniture was sold at auction; his bedrooms, kitchen, parlor, and hall were emptied, "so that nothing but bare walls remained to tell the tale."[42] The money from the auction was used as moving expenses.

But before Mason left for good, there were some loose ends to tie up. He persuaded one Detroit newspaper to let him get some things off his chest, whereupon he called Romeyn a liar and offered further proofs of his own innocence. And then there was the touching story of one of his last public appearances: "They gave him a supper last night and when he rose to speak he was so choked he could not utter a word and finally giving way to his feelings, he cried like a child which . . . proved so infectious that there were handkerchiefs drawn out and heads held down without number."[43]

Without question, the slanderous campaign against Mason was a low point in the history of the state of Michigan. Try though we may to understand the character of the times (when free speech was in its rawest forms), nothing excuses the suspension of due process for Mason in facing his accusers. Securing a false confession from Romeyn and then stating that the ex-governor had taken a bribe were equally reprehensible. Excessive partisanship may be seen in our own age, but Woodbridge turned it into a vendetta of unprecedented venom.

When Woodbridge left for the Senate, his legislature dissolved into intraparty squabbling. To their credit, the Whigs in power worked to meet the economic crisis: "Tax deadlines were extended, government spending was slashed, . . . and the state's commissioners of internal improvements were forbidden to enter into any further construction contracts. In addition, recognizing the need to create a stable currency with which to pay taxes and move crops, Whig legislators passed a currency act in 1840 which authorized the state to issue drafts that would serve as the basis for loans from solvent banks so that the government could meet its payments to contractors."[44] But then Woodbridge left the state for Washington, and "nothing the Whigs ever did for Michigan approximated the loss they caused when they drove Mason out of Detroit, embittered, humiliated and crushed in spirit."[45]

In some eyes, Mason was like a biblical prophet without honor in his own country. There was vindication, of sorts, in the report of the joint committee of the House and the Senate on the subject of the five-million-dollar loan bonds, but Mason didn't live to see it. This committee, chaired by Digby V. Bell, issued a report on February 13, 1843, saying that it was in receipt of a communication from Charles Butler, Esquire, of New York, "in behalf of the larger portion of the bona fide holders of the five million loan bonds of this state, negotiated with the Morris Canal and Banking Company, and the United States Bank." As reported by the committee, this communication explained that "had all the installments of the five million loan been received, as they became due, and been applied in the construction of public works, as they undoubtedly would have been, it was reasonable to suppose that those works would have been in a condition to yield a revenue adequate or nearly so, for the payment of interest on all the bonds issued, but the failure of the parties from whom the remaining installments were due was consequently productive of great embarrassment and injury to the state, and necessarily left her in a very unprepared situation to pay interest on her debt from the proceeds of her public works."[46]

After presenting a financial statement for 1841–42, the committee said, "It will therefore be seen that even upon those bonds for which the State has received consideration she has already paid more than double the amount of interest, that has been received as net proceeds from all the public works to the close of the last fiscal year; and of bank stocks, it is well known that the State has never been possessed of any."[47] The committee opposed any direct tax on the people for purposes of paying off the bondholders, suggesting, "that the best means in the present power of the State to offer . . . would be to fund the interest from July 1, 1841, to January or July 1, 1844, and issue new bonds for the interest then due, by which time the state works would be completed to Marshall and Hillsdale, our treasury notes absorbed and cancelled, and the State in a situation to commence the punctual payment of interest on all her bona fide bonds."[48] The public works to which the committee made reference are the Michigan Central and Michigan Southern railroads. Both railroads would be completed and would make money for their owners, thus justifying Governor Mason's determination to link the state's internal improvements with the railroad.

The year 1841 wasn't all wormwood for Stevens T. Mason. The University of Michigan opened in Ann Arbor, with Mason an ex officio member of the Board of Regents. The architects had designed a pair of classroom buildings, the northernmost of which was given the name Mason Hall. It is still there today, graced with an appropriate plaque, but hard to find on a campus at which Mason would blink his eyes in astonishment. He and John Pierce designed well; a higher education establishment that began with the state university in Ann Arbor grew to include the nation's pioneer land-grant university, Michigan State University in East Lansing, and a model teaching training college in Ypsilanti that is today Eastern Michigan University.

In bricks and mortar, the University of Michigan has grown far beyond the first building Mason watched being constructed. Its growth in outreach and influence would no doubt please Tom Mason, who had such a parental interest in "his" university that he even cared about the living quarters of the first students. Kent Sagendorph writes, "No one believed that such an institution could be created, much less maintained, out there in the depths of a Michigan forest nearly a thousand miles from New York and Boston. The University authorities declare in their own history of the institution that Mason's mind saw it originally, not as just another school, but as the most influential state university in the Union."[49]

Mason never fully recovered from the damage done to him by political forces in Michigan. His psyche was shattered, his self-esteem torn to ribbons. Being unable to prove his innocence and to restore his good name meant that his usefulness to Michigan was over. Where once there were plaudits, now there was only pity. He seemed to have the life and spirit extinguished in him. When he tried to put the pieces together, it didn't happen. Unfairness, rejection, ingratitude—Mason faced them all. Perhaps it was his youth that made the disillusionment so complete; his belief in the basic goodness of the people shone through his several messages to the legislature. When he was thrown to the lions and nobody spoke out for him, the rejection was unbearable. As a politician who occupied a unique place in his state's early life, Mason would have been very conscious of his place in history. "It has never been contended that the verdict of the people sustained the charges made, but unfortunately their judgment could not be entered as was the slander in the annals of the State,"[50] Hemans writes. Mason had to content himself that the people, for all their fickleness, still held him in high esteem.

The law firm of Mason and Pritchette was a natural development, given the two men's long ties. Pritchette had come to Michigan in 1831 with Governor Porter and soon formed an attachment to the young Secretary Mason. When Mason became governor, his first appointment was of Pritchette as secretary of state. Now the two were reunited, and it is not hard to imagine the likeable Mason making the personal connections while Pritchette did the main work in the law office.

But the records show that there wasn't much business, and as a result, Mason was importuned by Julia and her family in New York to seize the opportunities the big city offered. Mason was no doubt conflicted; he wanted to show he could make it on his own in Detroit, but he also wanted to please his wife. There was his family to think of, and with the wolf knocking at the door, the decision to go east was made. Mason, it seems, wanted to keep some distance from his wealthy father-in-law, not out of a personal dislike, but from a feeling of independence that a long solitary existence had fostered. In the fall of 1841, Tom Mason left Detroit for the last time. He would not return for sixty-four years, after which time a grateful state was ready to make amends.

What must have been his thoughts as he and his family boarded the steamer for the trip east? What went through his mind as he stood on deck while Detroit receded from view? No brass bands played at his departure, and there were no speeches of appreciation. If he had had a key to the city, they probably would have demanded it back from him. Since he and his father had arrived in 1830 he had witnessed a decade of momentous events, and Stevens

T. Mason had had his hand in all of them, guiding and shaping the destinies of the territory turned state.

Mason could have recalled the wars he had been in. The Black Hawk War never amounted to much as far as the territory was concerned, but it was a time when the people felt threatened and looked to Mason for leadership. He gave them plenty of that quality during the dispute with Ohio as well and was raised to hero status for that. He hewed to a position of neutrality in the Patriot War, while sympathizing with the Canadians fighting for greater freedoms. He had stood up to the federal government in the Fort Brady affair; to his mentor, Andrew Jackson, and the peace commissioners in the Toledo War; and to Congress in the terms it dictated for statehood. There was a lot in his political career to be satisfied with and to offer no apologies for. With a break here or a twist of fickle fortune there, it might have all turned out differently.

But now, on the cold deck of a steamer on Lake Erie, it was time for Mason to put reflections and any self-pity aside and rejoin Julia and the children. She would have been thrilled to leave Detroit and the hateful politicians who had ruined her husband. His own health needed looking after, and New York was just the place to put him on the mend. She expected that they would, of course, stay with her father until such time as Tom would put enough money aside to afford a home. Mason, however, put his foot down and announced that the family would find a proper place of its own. One can infer the marital discord that accompanied this decision. When Mason was unable to secure such a place, he arranged for Julia and the children to move into a boardinghouse on Leonard Street, near Broadway. He then learned that he couldn't even practice law in New York, there being no reciprocity between that state and Michigan. So with the family in humble dwellings and poverty raising its ugly head, Mason had to become a law student all over again.

Tom's father wrote from Washington to say that Baltimore offered some advantages, but his son turned him down. "I have made up my mind, both as a matter of economy and as a source of health for the children, to find quarters in some cheap boardinghouse on Staten Island or the Jersey shore," he wrote, "the very moment I see a certain indication of the arrival of spring."[51] Spring hadn't yet arrived when Tom wrote to his father about heavy household expenses, "the hourly expectation of an addition to our household," uncertainty about living arrangements and his professional prospects, and doubt about the wisdom of having left Detroit, "where living was cheaper and income more certain."[52]

Mason had earlier shared concerns about his economic livelihood with his good friend Charles Anderson. "The lawyers in New York are moaning most loudly the want of business," he wrote, adding, "This is a sad prospect, but still I do not despair. I shall have at my command available means for two years at best, and if I cannot get into business by that time, why I can only starve, or do what is nearly as bad, come back to Michigan and live on politics. For the winter, we shall board and next spring possibly go to housekeeping in a small way. For myself, I should prefer boarding for a year or two, but in this I must yield to Julia and the extent of our family."[53]

His third child, Thaddeus Phelps Mason, arrived on March 11, 1842. "Julia has instructed to convey to you at once," Mason wrote to his father, "the important intelligence that she has presented you with another grandson. The young gentleman made his appearance this morning about 4 o'clock. He is a fine healthy baby, and thus far has established great proficiency in the arts of sleeping, eating and bawling."[54] The new father informed his sister Kate, back in Detroit, that her nephew is "remarkably large, has blue eyes and dark hair. The other two children are lost in wonder at seeing a baby in their mother's room this morning."[55]

With three young mouths to feed and a wife to support, Mason moved his family to Staten Island, from which he took the ferry to his office. He gained admission to the bar and thought he was discerning progress in his personal fortunes. He informed his father that in New York, "The best way to get ahead is to keep up appearances and seek the society of those who can benefit me. However much it may be at war with my nature, I am gradually becoming an apt pupil of the modern school."[56]

His work, he said, put him in the constant company of the most prominent businessmen of New York: "I have made acquaintances of great value." He shared news of national politics with his father and talked enthusiastically about the impending "utter annihilation" of Henry Clay.[57] The talented young man of such unusual experience on the western frontier seemed ready to make a name for himself in New York, to raise a family that would be accepted in the highest levels of society, and to erase from his mind so much of recent history in Michigan. Of course, that didn't happen.

11 ~~ Death and Remembrance

There is a life-size portrait of Stevens T. Mason hanging in the House of Representatives at the state capitol in Lansing. Attributed to Alvin Smith in 1837, when Mason was campaigning for reelection, the painting is a remarkable likeness of Michigan's first governor as contemporary accounts describe him. The portrait was first on view in the old state capitol in Detroit and was presented as a gift to the House of Representatives in March 1837, only a few weeks after statehood. It is "one of the few surviving items which tie together Michigan's early statehood era and the present."[1] It is eye-arresting and rarely fails to elicit questions from visitors as to the identity of the man.

In the painting, Mason stands before a bust of George Washington, his hand lightly resting on a desk bearing the great seal of the state of Michigan. He holds a folded document in his right hand; his left is placed on his hip, fingers splayed. He looks off into the distance, a slight smile playing on his lips. Dark, wavy hair, somewhat receding at the temples, sets off a face that is intelligent-looking and brimming with optimism. The jaw is determined, the eyes steady; his tailoring features a white linen shirt with lace cuffs, under a knee-length velvet waistcoat. Well-cut trousers round out the figure of a young man of more than average height.

The whole demeanor of the man in the portrait is that of someone who wears the mantle of leadership with supreme confidence. That depiction of Stevens T. Mason is not consistent, however, with what we know of him in the final months of his life. The contacts he made with New York businessmen do not seem to have steered meaningful work his way, and his time was spent doing the work of a public defender. He wrote to his father to say that his only capital consisted of hope, energy, and perseverance. He missed the familiar

streets of Detroit and his friends in Michigan, particularly Kintzing Pritchette. If only he had stayed over Julia's objections, he would have witnessed the
demise of the Whigs and perhaps led a resurgence of the Democrats. Or if he
had returned to Virginia, where the Mason name was honored and respected,
a thriving law practice and active public life would have been assured. Why
hadn't he thought of that earlier, when the hounds of hell were assailing him
in Michigan?

Mason needed what all politicians crave, which is the roar of an approving
crowd and recognition. A politician deprived of this nourishment is one for
whom any substitute is never quite the same. He missed speaking opportunities and the stir caused by his appearance at a public function. He may have
been on the outs with Julia over money, his job, and his prospects. Was the
dream of that beautiful home he had promised her always to be replaced by
the cheap reality of the boardinghouse where they resided? What were his
enemies doing back in Michigan, where he couldn't defend his name against
further calumnies?

In late 1842, Mason seemed to be stumbling through life. Emily visited
her brother on Staten Island and filled her diary with the sad changes that she
noted had come over Tom. He seemed to be increasingly morose, moody, and
absentminded. It wasn't long before even "keeping up appearances" became
onerous. His heart wasn't in his work, his family, or himself. Little was known
of depression in those days, and Mason was left to deal with his personal
demons on his own. What comfort Julia and the children provided can only
be surmised.

December brought two much-anticipated events. There was an invitation
from the writer Washington Irving to attend a New Year's Eve ball, and from his
friends on Staten Island came an invitation to address a meeting of the Lyceum
Society on the history of the Northwest. Now here was a topic Mason could
sink his teeth into. He not only brought a passion for history into the discussion but also was a major player. He could bring a decade's worth of personal
experience with men and events into this lecture. It was due to his leadership
that Michigan had prevailed in its long struggle for statehood. He was men-
tored by the great Cass, crossed swords with the veteran Woodbridge, and
collaborated with Pierce in devising a model educational system.

"Our land," his speech to the society began, "has been from its earliest history a land of wonders. Every step which has marked its discovery, its settlement, its early history, its glorious revolution, and its astonishing subsequent

progress, has exhibited events which were in their individual and separate importance of thrilling interest to the human family, and which have formed unitedly a chain of incidents before unparalleled."[2] And on it went in that vein, his listeners entranced from having the subject explained with such insightfulness by a man who had helped to shape the history of an important part of the Northwest. It is not hard to imagine an animated Stevens T. Mason, eyes flashing, describing his efforts at the head of the Michigan militia during the Toledo War or explaining the necessity of the Second Convention of Assent. The lecture was a huge hit, and Mason returned home with his spirits rejuvenated. This was the last public event of his life. Fittingly, it was one that made frequent mention of the state to which he gave so much.

The New Year's Eve ball was a place for an aspiring barrister such as Mason to be seen, "a great social affair in the best old Knickerbocker tradition, with a guest list that read like the index to the Social Register."[3] Maybe, thought Mason, 1843 would bring a turnaround, and his clients would be well heeled, not the penniless down-and-outers he had so far been forced to represent. Maybe, instead of the deadly routine of defending vagrants, Mason would work on cases that provided a stiff challenge to his legal training.

Mason took sick upon his return from the ball and was running a fever. The day being a holiday, no doctor was available on short notice, and Julia was in despair until the evening, when a neighborhood physician was found. His prognosis was one that could have been given by any layperson: the patient was running a fever, and it would have to run its course. In the meantime, plenty of rest and liquids were prescribed. But Mason wasn't resting and he wasn't keeping anything down. His father had arrived from Louisiana after receiving letters from Emily describing his son's changes; now John Thomson Mason hurried to the boardinghouse and into the bedroom where his son lay, burning with fever and barely conscious. On the fourth of January, another doctor was called in; after an examination, he concluded the patient had pneumonia. By this time, the disease was too far along to admit of cure, and Stevens T. Mason was drifting into and out of consciousness. He died in the early morning hours of January 5, with Julia and his father at his bedside. He was just thirty-one years old.

The shock of the death vigil took Julia in its full grip. Her husband's last breath sent her into a spasm of weeping. The grief for Julia over the death of her husband would still be fresh when Stevens Thomson Mason, Jr., just three years old, died on January 27, 1843. Thaddeus Phelps Mason died at age five in 1847, and only Dorothea, born in 1840, lived into a ripe old age; she died in 1916. For Julia, losing a beloved husband and her firstborn son all in less than a month was almost too much to bear.

Upon his son's death, John T. helped to settle Julia down before the heart-broken father composed himself long enough to write the tragic news to his daughter Kate Mason Rowland at Detroit. His letter to her is dated January 5, 1843, from New York.

> I attempted to write you last night but found myself unequal to the task, and am now little better prepared to announce to you a most heartrending event. Our light afflictions for the past year we bore not without repining, but they were temporary and susceptible of alleviation. Now we have to summon to our aid the strength we possess, and call to our relief the only power that is capable of it—the power of religion—the trust in God that all His ways are best.
>
> Your beloved brother is no more—I cannot yet realize the awful truth. But it is nevertheless so. He now lies a corpse in this house. His sickness was not considered dangerous until two hours before his death, and it was so sudden, so calm and so free from pain that to look upon him at this moment the serenity of his countenance cheats you into the belief that he still lives.

There follows a description of his son's early signs of sickness and of the doc-tor's recommended treatment. John T. recounts being told by Dr. Mott that his son was dangerously ill, that he had only a brief time to live, and that there was nothing that could be done.

> His predictions were, alas!, too true, and at three o'clock he expired without a groan, and in such entire absence of pain, that he seemed to fall into a com-posing sleep. Little did we apprehend that it was the sleep of death. Julia is in a state of distraction and I can hardly tell the character of my own mind. I shall write to you again in a day or two, but it is impossible for me to afford consolation other than your own minds will present; a submission to the will of God—to whom I commend you and pray that He may give you strength to sustain you under the heartrending calamity which it has been His pleasure to award us. Your affectionate father, JOHN T. MASON.[4]

A great stillness settled over the boardinghouse, punctuated by sounds of weeping. Mason's father-in-law was informed of Tom's death, as were other family friends. It was agreed that he would be interred in the Phelps family vault in Marble Cemetery in New York. When it came time for burial, the body was placed in a mahogany casket, in which was placed a silver plate bearing his name and the date of his death. But the casket didn't fit into the narrow space allotted to it, and so the handles had to be removed. Finally, the casket and its contents slid into its niche in the side of a high stone wall. A marble slab covered the hole and was cemented in. To passersby, the simple inscription read, "Stevens T. Mason, died January 5, 1843."

The news of Mason's death reached Detroit on January 12. Political animosities were put aside in a great upwelling of feeling for the late governor. With one voice, says his biographer, "his old friends and his former political enemies joined in tributes to his memory."[5] The city came together as Americans often do in times of great grief. The *Detroit Free Press* provided this account:

It becomes our painful duty to announce to the citizens of Michigan the death of one of their most esteemed and valued friends, Stevens Thomson Mason, the first Governor of the Peninsular State . . . He died suddenly in New York City, aged 31 years, . . . the much honored and universally beloved friend of Michigan—the gifted orator, the talented statesman, the high-souled patriot, the warm-hearted, frank, generous, noble and magnanimous friend . . .

Were we to speak of the distinguished ability with which he administered the government of the late Territory of Michigan, as Secretary and Acting Governor, while he was yet scarcely twenty-one years of age, to which office he had been appointed by the sagacious and patriotic Jackson, or still later, of the state, for the first four years of its existence, we should repeat what is familiar to every citizen of Michigan.

The death of Governor Mason will be felt deeply by the people of Michigan. Few men were more deservedly respected; no one could be more generally beloved. As a politician, he was zealous, patriotic and consistent. He was a statesman of enlarged views. The political principles of Thomas Jefferson were his guide. The largest liberty of the largest number was the polar star in his political creed. He was a man of great integrity and pure patriotic feeling. He was remarkably distinguished for a degree of good humor and vivacity, and in generosity of character, was an ornament to human nature. Of Stevens T. Mason, it may truly be said, in the language of the darling poet of nature: "His life was gentle! And the elements so mixed in him that nature might stand up and say to all the world—this was a man."[6]

Other newspapers were also warm in their praise. Even the *Detroit Advertiser,* house organ of Woodbridge's Whigs, was moved to say, "We cannot forbear to mingle our tears in the general sorrow. His career here was indeed an uninterrupted political struggle, and yet few men have left behind them more personal friends among all parties, and now when the hand of death has laid him low we cannot but count ourselves fortunate to have been permitted to have been of that number. *Vale, amice, vale!*"[7] It was an unusual gesture for the *Advertiser* to make, but the spirit behind it was genuine.

The legislature was not to be outdone. It fell to Senator William L. Greenly, Democrat from Adrian and later governor of Michigan, to formally announce to the Senate the death of Michigan's first governor. On January 15, he rose from his seat to address that body.

> Mr. President—since our adjournment on yesterday, the mournful intelligence has been received of the death of the Honorable Stevens T. Mason, the former and first Governor of our state. The first political relations of his life were with us, and as soon as he had attained his majority he was by the almost unanimous suffrages of our people elected to the chief magistracy of our State . . . THERE-FORE BE IT RESOLVED, that we deeply sympathize with the relations of the late STEVENS T. MASON, in their sudden and afflictive bereavement, and in this public manner would tender our heartfelt tribute to the memory of . . . an individual who was deeply imbued with all the sterling virtues of public, social and private life.[8]

The House passed a similar resolution, and a joint committee from both houses was appointed to prepare public funeral services.

A day of mourning was held on Sunday, January 15, at the Episcopal Church of St. Paul, where Mason had attended services. A large gathering of Detroiters watched a solemn funeral procession headed by the Brady Guards, with notables from the military, state, and city government trailing behind. There was no casket to view, no body to bury, and the wonder of it all was that the same men who had driven Mason out of the state, disgraced, and crushed in spirit, were there to march in the procession and to nod in agreement at the lauds and tributes. The sorrowing family in New York and Detroit would have derived some satisfaction from the testimonies of respect for the late governor. And Mason himself would have delighted in the crowds lining the sidewalks. With his death and memorial service, Stevens T. Mason faded from public view. When Lansing became the new state capital in 1847, the portrait of Mason moved to that city and took its place in the statehouse.

Little is known of Julia's whereabouts following her husband's death. In 1846, Emily Mason corresponded with a friend regarding the engagement of Julia Phelps Mason to Harry McVickers. For her part, Julia wrote of her husband-to-be,

> Mr. McVickers belongs to one of our best and oldest families. You know my penchant in this respect, he is exceedingly agreeable, clever and intelligent, indeed often witty and humorous in conversation, extremely enthusiastic and warm in his feelings, good tempered and has always been an excellent son, his mother thinks him perfection.
>
> His person, it is true, is much against him and kept me wavering some time. He is sans doubt excessively ugly, and this such a contrast to my darling [Stevens Thomson Mason] . . . [H]is figure is handsome and his hands and feet remarkably delicate and beautiful, and withal his ugliness has a good expression.[9]

This less than flattering depiction of her intended is the last we hear from Julia Phelps Mason, who died in 1870 at age fifty-two. She buried a husband and two small children. That she would still refer to Mason as her "darling" while planning a second marriage is a good indication of the strong affection she retained for him. Her father-in-law, John T. Mason, died in 1850, and Tom and Julia's surviving child, Dorothea, would live to see her father restored to a place of honor.

Emily Mason, who was her brother's official hostess when he was governor, lived a long and productive life. It was she who famously reminded people that her brother was deposed from office for one month and then elected governor in the next month—for her, vindication of the first order. She was a prolific writer who provided many descriptions of Detroit in the 1830s. Two brief examples will suffice here. She wrote of the cholera epidemic in Detroit,

> With this terrible cholera we lost many of our friends, and among others, our dead old "Granny Peg," my mother's faithful nurse, a Guinea negro who could never be converted to Christianity. She died in my arms, and I went out into the night to find the "death cart" which passed the streets day and night, calling "Bring out the dead!" One evening a charming young man from Boston sat

with us on the doorstep, sipping a mint julep (thought to be a prevention of the disease). He was, well, gay at parting; by the morning he was dead.[10]

Of the time when a famous travel writer came to town, she reported, "All the distinguished persons who came to Detroit were entertained by the governor, and among others, I remember Harriet Martineau, with her formidable ear trumpet, and of whom we young people stood very much in awe."[11]

Following the death of her brother, Emily Mason moved to Fairfax County, Virginia. At the onset of the Civil War, she left her home and offered her services in the Confederate hospitals. She served as matron at Greenbrier, White Sulphur Springs, Charlottesville, Lynchburg, and Richmond, Virginia. To obtain money to educate the orphan daughters of Confederate soldiers, Emily collected and arranged *The Southern Poems of the War*, published in 1867. She also wrote *Life of Gen. Robert E. Lee*, published in Baltimore in 1871. After the war, she spent fifteen years in Paris, most of the time as an assistant principal of an American school for young ladies.

It was through Emily and Dorothea Mason Wright that Lawton T. Hemans, a lawyer who lived in the city of Mason, arranged to have the body of Stevens T. Mason returned to Michigan. Emily, it seems, "had always desired to have the mortal remains of her brother brought back for their final resting place to Detroit, the scene of his youthful prominence."[12] There had been talk in the legislature about bringing Governor Mason back, but nothing was done until 1905. By then, a transformation had taken place. A legend was beginning to grow, as more people began to wonder about this pivotal historical figure. Who was the "Boy Governor," and why had he been so reviled? What was there about him that seemed so compelling? What was the real story behind the famous painting in the Detroit Institute of Arts about the first election in Detroit, with Governor Mason in the foreground? Was all that stuff about scandal and profligate spending true? Debaucheries, bribe taking, public drunkenness—did the history of the times verify any of this?

With the passage of years, the people of Mason's state could place him in perspective. He came to be appreciated as a leader who had taken Michigan from a frontier territory to a dynamic state in only a decade. His acts of defiance driven by youthful ardor came to be admired for the forthrightness and deliberateness with which they were taken. He bestowed on early Michigan a high idealism and devotion to public service worthy of emulation by his successors. Americans are great believers in fair play, and a fair assessment of Mason's role was long overdue. Always a romantic, dashing figure, Mason, decades removed from his early death, came to achieve a stature that fully accords with the young man's management of momentous events. As with any person's mark of greatness, the good has to be taken with the bad, the sound and mature instincts with the suspension of good judgment, the profound with the profane. But when we view him in his historical perspective, the shadowy figure forgotten by history takes on real-life form.

With Hemans providing the impetus, public interest began to grow over plans to bring back the Boy Governor. News of Hemans' efforts got around, and Emily's nonagenarian status gave the story an "I was there" cachet. The legislature appointed a committee, with Hemans as one of its members, to supervise the removal of Mason's body to Detroit. Governor Fred M. Warner took a personal interest, as did Detroit mayor George P. Codd, who arranged for the City of Detroit to landscape Capitol Park and prepare it for a burial site.

The committee of Hemans, Daniel McCoy of Grand Rapids, and Arthur Holmes of Detroit, went to New York and secured permission to examine the Phelps vault, where they found the remains in their mahogany casket. The identity was established by the silver plate on the casket bearing Mason's name and the date of his death. Emily, Dorothea, a grandson, and a grand nephew, along with the committee, then acted as escort to the remains as they were borne by train to Detroit.

The Michigan Central train arrived in Detroit at 8:15 a.m. on June 4, 1905. It was met by Company A of the Detroit Light Guard, representing the military group of which Governor Mason was once a member. The casket, still without its handles, was draped with an American flag and carried down Jefferson Avenue to the armory. Long lines of spectators viewed the "homecoming" of the first governor. At the armory, the casket rested on a catafalque of purple, with a huge national flag as a backdrop. The ceremony had been set for 2 p.m., and an audience of two thousand persons was on hand. The venerable Emily Mason was escorted to the speakers' platform, and it was noted that she walked with a firm step.

The first speakers were mercifully brief. The Reverend D. M. Cooper, pastor emeritus of the Memorial Presbyterian Church, related a story of how he had taunted Governor Mason as a child, only to be taken aside by the governor and given "the sweetest, most fatherly talk imaginable." Mayor Codd spoke next, followed by Governor Warner, the presiding officer of the occasion. The principal address was given by Clarence M. Burton, at the time president of the Michigan Pioneer and Historical Society. He told of what Mason had accomplished, beginning,

> We are assembled here this afternoon to pay tribute to the memory of one of the men who made our State; whose hand and brain guided our territory through its last years, and who helped to lay the solid foundation of the commonwealth over which he was the first to preside.
>
> If the citizens of Michigan take pride in our just and liberal laws; in the results of the great internal improvements of canals and railroads; in the numberless schools that . . . crown the hills of our country; in the splendid university that gives a name to Michigan throughout the civilized world, let them remember that the man above all others, who worked to accomplish these ends, was Michigan's boy governor.
>
> Separated for more than half a century from the land he loved so well, he has been returned to us today, and his ashes will repose on the spot where the greatest achievement of his life took place—the site of the first Capitol of a mighty State. Here let him rest in peace and let there be erected above him a monument with suitable inscription, so that the present and future generations may truthfully say that Republics are not always ungrateful, and that our beloved state has done proper honor to one of its most faithful servants."[13]

With the tributes over, a crash of military music signaled departure from the armory. The casket was carried to a waiting hearse, with Emily Mason leading the procession into the street. The funeral cortege was formed, the line of march being from Jefferson Avenue to Woodward Avenue, up Woodward to Michigan Avenue, on Michigan Avenue to Rowland Street, and on Rowland to Capitol Square. The bell at City Hall tolled at intervals of one minute.

A spectacle the likes of which the two-hundred-year-old city had never seen presented an inspiring sight, according to one newspaper account. The mounted policemen so impressed the onlookers that they would have broken out into applause were it not for the solemnity of the event. "Hardly the sound of a voice was heard," reported the *Detroit Tribune*, "as the procession marched slowly to the place of interment, taking twenty minutes to go that short distance."[14] When the grave was excavated, it was found to rest on the very foundation stones of the territorial and first state capitol. Upon arrival at the small square, the police on guard presented arms, and officers of the First

Infantry formed ranks on either side of the path. The band played "Michigan, My Michigan," and Emily Mason, tears welling, took her place under the pavilion. The other Mason family relatives followed, and then came the notables of public life. As the casket was slowly lowered into the earth, a benediction was pronounced, the bugler played "taps," and the ceremony was over. For the witnesses to this historic occasion, Governor Mason finally was resting in his native soil.

The next day's newspapers treated the occasion as a landmark event in the state's history. Under the headline "Mason Buried in Foundation Ruins of First Capitol," the *Detroit Tribune* began its lengthy coverage as follows: "With the solemnity and impressiveness peculiar only to the obsequies of a departed statesman, all that remained mortal of Stevens Thomson Mason, the first governor of the state of Michigan and familiarly known as 'the boy governor,' was laid in the ruins of the foundation of the first capitol of the state. As the thousands watched and listened in profound silence with unflagging attention, they were carried back in mind three-quarters of a century, when this remarkable man, forceful, determined, masterful, directed the affairs of the commonwealth of Michigan."[15]

Two days earlier, the *Detroit Journal* had opened several columns of type with the headline "Our Boy Governor Comes Back to Us." Stevens Thomson Mason, the writer opined, "is our one romantic figure. One can almost see the triumphal entrance into Detroit of this bright-faced youth, as proud and elated over the great honors that had come to him as any lad of scarce 20 years could possibly be, for he bore a commission with the great Andrew Jackson's name at the bottom of it, designating him in his father's stead as secretary of the territory of Michigan."[16] The columnist recounted how the stripling had turned the town on its head after the indignation meetings that greeted his appointment: "All the histories of the times speak of the manliness and generosity and boyish grace with which Stevens T. Mason met this critical and embarrassing situation. It was only a few hours before some of those who had been most outspoken against him were his most earnest partisans. Everything turned out all right in the end, and he is to be adjudged a wise and successful as well as highly popular ruler."[17] The columnist went on to say that when the internal improvements plan went awry and the state failed to get a decent return on the bonds it sold, Mason "was not held at fault in any way except as lacking experience."[18] To that, one can almost hear Mason saying, "You could have fooled me!"

Three years later, at the unveiling of a statue of Mason at Capitol Square

Park, the same newspaper picked up on the idea of Mason as a romantic figure in language that might have made the Boy Governor blush. One staff correspondent wrote, "Stevens Thomson Mason is the most romantic figure in Michigan history. The years have caught great folds of glamour and romance about him—he is like the heroes of Indian history in Michigan, Hiawatha and Pontiac and Tecumseh, covered with a legendary brilliance. With the erection of a monument of suitable impressiveness, the increase of the study of Michigan history in schools will increase the romantic luster that surrounds him in the minds of our people."[19]

In March of 1907, as though to atone for the shabby treatment given to the Boy Governor, the legislature had approved funds for a statue of Mason in bronze at the place of his interment. U.S. senator Russell Alger procured a sufficient quantity of bronze, melted down from ordnance at Fort Michilimackinac. A sculptor, Albert Weinert of New York, was accorded the honor of fashioning a suitable likeness of Mason.

At the unveiling of the statue on May 30, 1908, Emily Mason was again in attendance. Flanking the monument were two curved marble end pieces that served as spacers at the base of the monument. The inscription read,

> The Tribute of MICHIGAN to the Memory of Her FIRST GOVERNOR, Whose Ashes Lie Beneath, Called to the Duties of Manhood While Yet a Boy, He So Acquitted Himself As To Stamp His Name Indelibly on the History of the Commonwealth.

With the Honorable Thomas W. Palmer serving as chairman of the unveiling ceremonies, the invocation was given by the same Reverend D. M. Cooper who had spoken at Mason's homecoming three years before. Palmer described Mason as "of tall and elegant figure with such a face as Longfellow's Excelsior might have embodied if that ideal had been portrayed on canvas."[20] He recalled a Mason who was "debonair in manner, robust and hearty in his association with men, attractive to women and children, deferential to age and genial with all."[21]

Emily Mason, assisted by Dorothea Wright, unveiled the statue, to "great applause as the national colors fell from the monument."[22] The crowd then settled back to hear the principal address, given by the Reverend Walter Elliott of Washington, D.C., who was acquainted with the governor's sister. The clergyman gave his audience their money's worth of rhetoric, before yielding to

Lawton T. Hemans, who was given the pleasurable task of formally turning the monument over to the city of Detroit. It was a bit of an awkward moment, as Hemans was sharing the speakers' platform with Governor Fred Warner, to whom he would narrowly lose in the gubernatorial election that year. Hemans said, "It is befitting that the ashes of Stevens T. Mason should commingle with the soil already hallowed as marking the birthplace of a state and that above the silent form in sculptured bronze should teach with precept and example the lessons of patriotism and of courage, of loyalty and the joy of service."[23]

The erection of the Mason monument at Capitol Square Park seemed satisfying all around. The *Detroit Journal* called it "a sadly belated honor" and recalled how Mason "came into office in a strange land under the most hostile auspices and was hounded out of the state by party feeling of unimaginable bitterness and vindictiveness." The paper regarded the monument as tangible evidence of his people's affection: "The hatreds of the old days are buried with the enemies who affronted him. It is love and admiration that now remain."[24] The last word of the ceremony belonged to Dr. James B. Angell, president of the University of Michigan, who praised Mason for his valuable services in protecting the interests of the university. Then the captains and the kings departed, the band instruments that had played "America" were put away, and the bronze statue of Stevens T. Mason kept a lonely vigil in a small triangular park in the city. One would think the controversy surrounding the Boy Governor would be over for all time, but one would be very wrong.

The years rolled by, and Tom Mason's Michigan became an urban industrial state, noted for manufacturing, especially automobiles. The 1835 constitution of which he was so proud would be replaced several times. The transportation system he envisioned would evolve in ways beyond his thinking. The railroads he wanted built served the state well before going into decline. Highways would crisscross the state and serve every burg and hamlet. On the sparkling surface of the Great Lakes would ride, low in the water, those noble, workaday vessels bearing the raw materials of extracted wealth. The wisdom of accepting the mineral riches of the Upper Peninsula for those bullfrog ponds of the Maumee River would serve as evidence that Mason had put one over on Ohio.

Controversy followed the Boy Governor in death when, in the 1950s, it became necessary to move Mason's remains once more. Traffic planners in Detroit called for a widening of city streets around Capitol Park and for location of a bus station on Griswold. The Weinert statue (by now gathering a patina of pigeon droppings) and the burial vault under it were in the way. The old necessarily gives way to the new, and at the time, Detroit needed that small green park for other uses. Now it was time for another generation of Michiganians to focus on who this man Mason was.

The state senate opened discussion about the state's "right" to the body of its first governor and called for interment in the capitol grounds at Lansing. The city of Mason thought it had a claim, too, and before long, the Boy Governor was making headlines again, fueled by squabbling politicians. Detroit, however, was not of a mind to part with the remains of Mason, and so plans were made to move the vault and the statue to the south end of the park. But first, he had to be disinterred, and the remains in the casket had to be reidentified as truly those of Mason.

In what appeared to be a circus atmosphere, there are accounts of a historian providing a running commentary to onlookers as the casket was unearthed. Curt Haseltine, a reporter for the *Detroit Free Press*, covered the event under the headline "Past Is Bared at Capitol Park," dated June 2, 1955.

It was an historic event Wednesday when a crane hoisted the huge stone slab cover from the crypt. Detroiters crowding the fence felt the past peering over their shoulders. They looked down at the shards of past construction crumbling in the dirt and realized that here Michigan was born, here Michiganders have lived, worked and died, that here in what was now a little island between steady streams of traffic men of vision had wrought a sturdy foundation for a glorious future.

As workmen dug into the earth, they saw hand-made bricks from the original Michigan State Capitol, bits of charred wood from the fire that destroyed Capitol High School, and even got a glimpse of all that's mortal of Michigan's first governor, Stevens T. Mason. The mahogany and rosewood of the 113-year-old casket was badly deteriorated although the zinc lining held firm. The lid fell apart as the casket was hoisted from its resting place.

A small metal plate lay near the head of the casket. It was so corroded it was hardly legible. It read, "Stevens T. Mason, First Governor of Michigan. Removed from New York City to Detroit, Michigan, June 4, 1905." When Mason is reburied in Capitol Park later, it will be with the rites of the Episcopal Church of which he was a member. Robert E. Palmer, assistant curator of the Detroit Historical Museum, was on hand to gather up every fragment to assure both reverent handling of Mason's remains and complete historical coverage.[25]

The Harris Funeral Home, established in 1910, was chosen to store the casket and its remains until such time as the park was finished and the body reinterred.

Six months after the governor was disinterred, he was ready for a reinterment service, set for December 5, 1955, at Capitol Park. The honorary pallbearers for this second reinterment included Brigadier General Lester Maitland, representing Governor G. Mennen Williams, and Norman Hill, representing Detroit mayor Albert B. Cobo. (Apparently the state's chief executive and the Motor City's mayor had more pressing commitments.) Other pallbearers were City Council members Mary V. Beck, Edward Connor, Del A. Smith, Eugene I. VanAntwerp, Blanche Parent Wise, and Charles N. Youngblood. Also at the scene were representatives of city departments, a handful of elected officials of the City of Detroit, representatives of veterans' organizations, and historical organization officials, including Dr. Lewis G. Vander Velde of the Michigan Historical Commission.

A detail from the 425th Infantry Regiment was drawn up on the sidewalk facing the statue. The casket was borne from the hearse by members of the City Veterans Post serving as pallbearers. As the casket passed between the double lines of the infantry detail, it was preceded by clergy, followed by descendants of the Mason family and children of Mason Elementary School, who had the honor of placing a wreath. The ceremony was brief, including a prayer, a volley by the infantry detail, taps, and a benediction. The grave was sealed, and Stevens T. Mason seemingly would not be disturbed again.

More years passed. In the 1980s, one historian wrote of Mason's memorial, "Crowded against the sidewalk at one end of the small triangle which is all that remains of Capitol Park, the statue stands on its high base above indifferent passersby . . . The streets are wider, the green park less, the history largely forgotten."[26] On November 25, 2009, came a stunning announcement in the *Detroit Free Press* that the city's Downtown Development Authority was making plans to relandscape Capitol Park and that, in the process of reconstructing the park, Governor Mason would have to be moved from his present location to the middle of the park.

Historians cringed; hadn't the governor been moved often enough? The *Detroit News* told of how workers digging in a downtown park for the remains of Stevens T. Mason "marked the third time his eternal slumber has been disrupted by hammers, drills and shovels. When the governor's remains were last exhumed 55 years ago to make way for a bus terminal, a badly damaged casket, zinc lined, contained the intact skeleton of Mason and a few scraps of cloth."[27] Apparently the authorities in 1955 hadn't left exact plans as to where the casket was buried (it was off-center from the statue), and so workmen had to probe around a bit before discovering the box.

On July 1, 2010, the governor was disinterred, and his casket was taken—yet again—to the Harris Funeral Home for storage. On October 19, the Michigan State Capitol Tour and Information Service announced plans to have Stevens T. Mason lie in state in the rotunda of the capitol building. This was an honor only bestowed on three other Michigan governors—Frank Fitzgerald in 1939, Chase Osborn in 1949, and George Romney in 1995. The flag-draped casket made the journey from Detroit to Lansing, and citizens were invited to pay their respects on the appointed date.

On Monday, October 25, 2010, the body of Governor Mason arrived at 5 p.m. at the state capitol. His casket was escorted into the building by the National Guard. The doors opened on Tuesday at 8 a.m., and viewers had until 5 p.m. to file past the casket. The rotunda is always an impressive place, with its display of flags, and it was especially so when sheltering the first governor's casket. All that was missing were the Brady Guards.

In 1837, a Michigan military company known as the Brady Guards received its colors from Governor Mason. This was Mason's contribution to the first Michigan flag, as the company flag was blue, with the new state seal on the obverse. The elegant standard presented by Mason was accepted by his brother-in-law Isaac S. Rowland, who was then serving as the company's captain. The Brady Guards were organized on April 13, 1836, General Hugh Brady being a native of Detroit. Brady died on April 10, 1851, and a week later, the company disbanded. So there were no colorful Brady Guards on the occasion of the viewing of Governor Mason's casket in 2010. When the day was over, his remains were taken back to Detroit for interment.

The next day, October 27, was the 199th anniversary of Mason's birth, and plans had been made to honor him with a special ceremony. It was a bright, sunshiny day, albeit windy, when a crowd began to gather at Capitol Park. The newly restored Mason statue had been moved to the center of the park. The park, small to begin with and now devoid of trees, was dwarfed by the tall buildings of downtown Detroit. Atop his pedestal, the governor faced west amid swirling automobile traffic. Onlookers came to satisfy their curiosity as to what the assembly of people and television coverage were all about. Mason's flag-covered coffin arrived in a long black hearse, along with a six-member honor guard provided by the Michigan National Guard.

At 1 p.m., the ceremony began. A historical perspective was given, followed by several tributes. Robert S. M. Mason, a great-great-great-grandnephew, represented the late governor's family. The honorary pallbearers included former governors William Milliken and James Blanchard and former attorney general Frank J. Kelley. As before, neither the state's chief executive nor the mayor of Detroit attended the event.

Silence prevailed over the park as the Reverend S. Scott Hunter, dean of the Cathedral Church of St. Paul, read the Episcopal rites with which Mason was so familiar. "And now," intoned Hunter, "let us lay our brother to rest." With that, the honor guard slid the metal coffin into the vault below the statue, and at 1:47 p.m., the ceremony was over. A little more than a century earlier, Emily Mason had stood in this park as a living link to events at the dawn of statehood.

The next day's *Detroit News* predictably headlined its story "State's First Governor again Laid to Rest in Capitol Park," the park's renovation having led "to the third—and presumably—final move"[28] for the state's most restless statesman. The *Detroit Free Press* headlined its story "Laid to Rest—Again" and quoted Kerry Chartkoff, a historian of the state capitol building, as saying that the governor's reburial in an aboveground vault was "to give him more prominence at the renovated grounds. He's a symbol of the renewal of the city itself."[29]

With the fourth burial of Stevens T. Mason, it may have seemed to some that his peregrinations were symbolic of a state on the move. Controversy had been Mason's companion in death, as witnessed by the competition over where his remains should finally rest. Even that magnificent painting by Smith hanging in the House chamber didn't escape insult, when House pages in 1970 damaged the portrait with an errant softball. The portrait was warehoused until 1977, when the seventy-ninth legislature authorized repairs that included its restoration and preservation. Jean Frazier reports, "Years of inadequate storage had rapidly deteriorated the canvas and its image. Five months of meticulous work, which involved at least four hundred working hours, lots of patience, and the expertise of Richard Galleriani and Theresa Hensick, were required to restore and renovate the Mason portrait."[30] It was an "all's well that ends well" story, assuring citizens of Michigan that the combination of modern technology and time-tested techniques would keep the Mason portrait for posterity.

It seems to be Mason's fate to be put away, forgotten, and subsequently rediscovered. In comparison with the pomp and circumstance of his burial in 1905, the 1955 ceremonies seemed almost indecently brief. Then he was forgotten again, his statue and gravesite lost in the canyons of the great city until the present time, when this transformational figure again rose from the past to command another generation's attention. The process of reinstating his good name actually began early, with one of his immediate successors in office, Alpheus Felch. He knew Mason, of course, and made these remarks at the Michigan Semi-Centennial:

> Governor Mason entered upon the duties of the chief executive office of the state while a very young man, called by the people with enthusiasm and unanimity. He held office during the period in which the foundation stones of the new Republic under the national constitution were laid. The present institutions of the state received their origin and largely their form during those years. Governor Mason showed more than ordinary ability in treating the gravest subjects of public concern, both in his extensive correspondence and in his many messages to the legislature.
>
> In the performance of all executive duties Governor Mason was untiring in his zeal. As a man he was genial, kind and companionable, and his personal popularity never ceased. I never recall the stirring incidents and great events of those early times in the history of our state but that the youthful governor stands before me a true emblem of the new commonwealth in its youthful aspirations and high purposes.[31]

Michigan would have gotten off to a very different start if its fortunes had been left to the cautious old men of the territory rather than to the bold, youthful Mason. His elders were apprehensive of demanding statehood as a right and were doubly apprehensive of crossing Old Hickory and the national government. Think of it—a mere territory making a clamor about being a state without the benefit of enabling legislation, asserting its right to a boundary bestowed on it by a defunct document, the Northwest Ordinance. None of it made sense, and the wise men of the territory would have held back, let the "normal" processes take their course, and consulted among themselves as to which path prudence dictated. It took a leader like Mason to take the status quo and turn it on his head, and it took a visionary to shape and mold the way he did, using the ways and means at his disposal. One of the speakers at the ceremonies unveiling the Mason monument in May 1908 said it best:

The ideal leader of free men should be like Stevens Thomson Mason, a man driven right onward by youthful ardor and steadied by a judgment worthy of more mature years. Providence . . . gave us a youth for our first governor, a man in that part of his life which is at once the truest and most visionary. He was a young hero for a young state.[32]

Mason had his faults, of course. He failed to understand the viciously partisan nature of the Whigs and their brand of politics. He was inclined to put too much faith in the people, when they tend to be motivated by baser instincts. He could be presumptuous, as when he pushed statehood without the consent of Congress, while citing the "Tennessee precedent." The dubious legality of the Frostbitten Convention did not seem to bother Mason much, but his zeal and impetuousness had cast him as a suspect leader to the men in Washington—a Hotspur who didn't understand the meaning of discretion and who needed to be taught a lesson about politics. He had sent out mixed signals during the Toledo War—at once conciliatory and bellicose. He could be respectful of Governor Robert Lucas and brashly dismissive. His internal improvements plan was too grandiose for a fledgling state, and he may have gotten ahead of himself in selling the legislature on its sustainability. But in that, Mason knew his people, and his people wanted easy money, jobs for all, busy towns on every railroad line, and a thriving state.

On some of those "gravest subjects of public concern" that Governor Felch mentioned, Mason was ahead of his time. He was an outstanding humanitarian, as when he repeatedly called for reform of imprisonment for debt. He said it was "a time-honored relic of barbarism which has failed of its object."[33] He called for humane treatment of penitentiary inmates and proposed that prisoners be trained in a useful, self-supporting trade. He thought the question of slavery was one best left to the states to decide, but as to its morality, he was very clear. He not only deplored the practice but said it was an alarming subject, "perhaps involving our permanent existence as a united nation."[34] He used one occasion to ask, "Why do we permit the value of the Union to be questioned? Why do we listen to selfish calculations of the balance of power between the North and the South? Do we American citizens begin to distrust and fear each other? Cling to Michigan, but live and act for your country, your whole country."[35] (He had "your whole country" underlined in his text.) As for the First Amendment, he said, "The freedom of the press is a home-bred right, an ancient and sacred prerogative of the people."[36]

When Stevens T. Mason died, he was not old and full of years, with gray hair and grandchildren. He did not die covered with honors or in the comfort of a fine home. But he is remembered for being faithful to his moment in history, for fully embracing the walk that was worthy of his calling, and for investing public service to his adopted state with grace, dignity, and integrity.

On July 12, 2010, I stood beside Governor Mason's open casket and viewed the remains of the Boy Governor. A plaque on the outside of the slightly rusted metal container read, "Stevens T. Mason, Died January 4th, 1843, Aged 31 Years." Inside the casket, another plaque read, "Stevens Thomson Mason, First Governor of Michigan, Removed from New York City to Detroit, Michigan, June 4th, 1905." I was in the basement of the Harris Funeral Home on the east side of Detroit. The Harris firm had been asked to store the casket and its remains, disinterred from Capitol Park downtown, until such time as the reconstruction of the park was finished and the governor could be reinterred. When the employee who had escorted me into the basement walked away to attend to other business, I was left alone with Governor Mason.

All that remained in the satin-lined casket was a skeleton, held together by string. The skull rested on a white pillow; the facial bones had deteriorated, but the jawbone was intact, as were two attached molars. Descriptions of a man above six feet tall fit well with what I was viewing. I let myself drift back in time to when the remains of the man in front of me was carrying on a lively correspondence with his family.

He once wrote to his sister Kate to express his "disapproval of women in politics,"[37] and again three years later, he cautioned her against "reading newspapers and interest in politics."[38] As for the day's fashions, he exclaimed, "Had I an empire of my own, I would as strictly quarantine the approach of fashions as I would that of a contagious fever."[39] On one occasion when he wrote Emily to say he was unwell, he thought he had better quickly assure his mother that "I am myself again and that you need entertain no apprehension for me."[40] The affection Mason showed to his mother was more than returned. She once wrote to her son to say that a gentleman in her boardinghouse had read one of Mason's messages to the legislature and that it showed "considerable judgment for one of your age." She then got to the point: "I shall expect to hear from you at least once a week. Your father says I could not be happy anywhere without you—I only wish, my dear boy, when you get a wife that she may be as much devoted to you as your old Mother is."[41] For Mason's mother, her son was always "My dear Thomson"; she, in turn, was "Mama."

In my mind's eye, I saw Governor Mason tipping his hat and smiling to all as he attended St. Paul's Episcopal Church on Sunday. He wasn't one to wear his religion on his sleeve, but he made frequent references to the Deity and the Supreme Ruler in his messages, as, for example, when he promised to "exhibit a just interest for the public morals, and a due regard for the great truths of our holy religion, . . . and seek to prevent religious intolerance that would seem to worship God the avenger, rather than God the Father."[42] I saw the youthful chief executive jumping on a sled and careening down a hill toward the Detroit River as one of the old stories related. I envisioned him helping the victims of cholera as they were brought into the capitol building. I imagined him meeting Woodbridge on the street with a polite gesture of deference.

The funeral home attendant reappeared, and my reverie was broken. The Michigan of the 1830s became the Michigan of the modern era, all haste and bustle, with too little reverence for history. After one long last look, I took my farewell of the Boy Governor and contented myself with the historian's satisfaction of having a privilege few others have shared—peering through a window into the past that afforded a glimpse of the Boy Governor himself.

✑ Epilogue

Acclaimed in some segments of the eastern press for challenging President Jackson and standing up to the venerable Robert Lucas of Ohio, Stevens T. Mason was just as quickly disowned as a popular hero when Michigan's economy plunged. He suffered the fate of all politicians who, having achieved some measure of success, are rejected when times and political fortunes turn against them. Mason, however, fared better than some. His popularity in Michigan remained high, and he was lauded in death as a man of integrity and virtue. As the decades passed, a legend built up around him, and succeeding generations of Michiganians were moved to learn more about this Boy Governor. In modern terms, he was rehabilitated, although that seems much too clinical a term to apply to him.

With Mason, so much is speculative. If he had lived, would he have attempted a comeback in Michigan? Had he been successful, would he again have come to national attention? Would he have played a strong role in anti-slavery efforts? In his short life, he was a powerful influence on his times, but due to his placement on the western frontier, he yielded the lion's share of attention to his contemporaries in the East. Mason made headlines during the struggle for statehood and during the Toledo War, but men such as Clay, Webster, and Calhoun enjoyed larger pulpits and wider audiences.

The state's case in the Toledo War was never adjudicated before the U.S. Supreme Court as Mason had fervently hoped it would be, which is ironic, because he was confident of victory before that tribunal. He did not live to see the mighty locks at Sault Ste. Marie constructed, which is one of his greatest legacies. At the time of his own death, he was struggling to make ends meet. The Mason story has its share of sorrow, disappointment, and broken dreams.

In *Michigan History* magazine, Jean Frazier called Mason an "activist, liberal Democrat, progressive thinker, astute politician, precocious youth and social charmer."[1] He was all those things, as well as a scapegoat for all of Michigan's problems at the end of his second term. It has also been said that he had heroic responsibilities thrust upon him when still a youth, and that is true; fortunately for Michigan, his gifts included a great insight not only into issues of the gravest public concern but into the needs of the future as well.

Andrew Jackson saw so much promise in Mason that he bestowed a presidential appointment on him at the age of nineteen. Some scholars, in trying to read the Jackson mind, have called this appointment Old Hickory's idea of a practical joke on the Whigs; but that is not likely. When Jackson was famously provoked into calling Mason "that young Hotspur," his comment may have been tinged with admiration at the young man's spunk. In Michigan's pantheon of heroes, Mason is overshadowed by the redoubtable Cass, who served longer and in more government positions. Yet it is Mason who captures our attention today, as the young man who courageously believed he had "right on his side." That is a good way to be remembered.

Notes

Chapter One

1. Peter L. Bernstein, *Wedding of the Waters* (New York: W. W. Norton, 2005), 27.

2. Kent Sagendorph, *Stevens Thomson Mason: Misunderstood Patriot* (New York: E. P. Dutton, 1947), 47.

3. Patricia J. Baker, "Stevens Thomson Mason," *Great Lakes Informant*, ser. 1, no. 5 (2001): 1, Michigan Historical Center.

4. Major W. C. Ransom, speech before the Historical Society of Michigan, January 26, 1871, in Michigan Pioneer and Historical Collections, vol. 6, 1883, 110. Michigan Pioneer and Historical Collections is a series of volumes created from materials that were presented at meetings of the Michigan Pioneer and Historical Society. These volumes are available at a number of libraries throughout the state, including the Ann Arbor District Library. The series is particularly useful to studies of early Michigan.

5. Lawton T. Hemans, *Life and Times of Stevens Thomson Mason* (Lansing: Michigan Historical Commission, 1920), 34.

6. Kent Sagendorph, *Michigan: The Story of the University* (New York: E. P. Dutton, 1948), 52.

7. Jon Meacham, *American Lion: Andrew Jackson in the White House* (New York: Random House, 2008), prologue.

8. Ibid., 82.

9. Sagendorph, *Stevens Thomson Mason: Misunderstood Patriot*, 84.

10. Hemans, *Life and Times of Stevens Thomson Mason*, 36.

11. Baker, "Stevens Thomson Mason," 1.

12. Quoted in Meacham, *American Lion*, 289.

13. Letter of August 22, 1830, John Thomson Mason Papers, 1787–1850, Burton Historical Collection, Detroit Public Library, Detroit.

14. Quoted in Hemans, *Life and Times of Stevens Thomson Mason*, 89.

15. Sagendorph, *Stevens Thomson Mason: Misunderstood Patriot*, 131.

16. Silas Farmer, *History of Detroit and Wayne County and Early Michigan* (Detroit: Silas Farmer, 1890), 962.

17. Letter of July 26, 1831, MS/Mason, Stevens Thomson, 1831–1842, Mason Papers, Burton Historical Collection, Detroit Public Library.

18. Ibid.

19. Letter of August 1, 1831, box 1, Stevens T. Mason Papers, Bentley Historical Library, University of Michigan, Ann Arbor.

20. Letter of December 20, 1831, box 1, Stevens T. Mason Papers, Bentley Historical Library.

21. "Accounts and Claims between S. T. Mason and U.S.A.," box 3, Department of State, Michigan State Archives, Lansing.

22. Letter of January 4, 1832, William Woodbridge Papers, 1780–1861, Burton Historical Collection, Detroit Public Library.

Chapter Two

1. James Z. Schwartz, *Conflict on the Michigan Frontier: Yankee and Borderland Cultures, 1815–1840* (DeKalb: Northern Illinois University Press, 2009), 92.

2. Brian C Wilson, *Yankees in Michigan* (East Lansing: Michigan State University Press, 2008), 36.

3. Howard Peckham, *The Making of the University of Michigan, 1817–1992* (Ann Arbor: Bentley Historical Library, University of Michigan, 1967), 3.

4. Ibid., 8.

5. *Michigan Manual, 2001–2002* (Lansing: Legislative Service Bureau, 2002), 6.

6. Willis Dunbar, *Michigan: A History of the Wolverine State* (Grand Rapids: William B. Eerdmans, 1965), 135.

7. C. Warren Vander Hill, *Settling the Great Lakes Frontier: Immigration to Michigan, 1837–1924* (Lansing: Michigan Historical Commission, 1970), 2.

8. Don Faber, *The Toledo War* (Ann Arbor: University of Michigan Press, 2008), 31.

9. Vander Hill, *Settling the Great Lakes Frontier*, 3.

10. Cass, in a June 7, 1824, message to Territorial Council, quoted in George Weeks, *Stewards of the State* (Detroit: *Detroit News*; Ann Arbor: Historical Society of Michigan, 1987), 10.

11. Quoted in Kent Sagendorph, *Michigan: The Story of the University* (New York: E. P. Dutton, 1948), 45.

12. Sagendorph, *Michigan: The Story of the University*, 46.

13. Harry L. Watson, *Liberty and Power: The Politics of Jacksonian America* (New York: Hill and Wang, 1990), 25.

14. Charles Sellers, *The Market Revolution* (New York: Oxford University Press, 1991), 392.

15. Ibid., 393.

16. Ibid.

17. Wilson, *Yankees in Michigan*, 2.

18. Quoted in George N. Fuller, *Economic and Social Beginnings of Michigan* (Lansing: Wynkoop Hallenbeck Crawford, 1916), 486.

19. Quoted in N. B. Sloan, "Citizenship in the Public Schools," in Michigan Pioneer and Historical Collections, vol. 38, 1909–11, 612.

20. Dunbar, *Michigan: A History*, 201.

21. Bruce Catton, *Michigan: A Bicentennial History* (New York: W. W. Norton, 1976), 73.

22. Ibid., 68.

23. Schwartz, *Conflict on the Michigan Frontier*, 79.

24. Ibid.

25. Ibid., 4, 5.

26. Ibid.

27. Catton, *Michigan: A Bicentennial History*, 69.

28. John T. Fierst, "Rationalizing Removal: Anti-Indianism in Lewis Cass's North American Review Essays," *Michigan Historical Review* 36, no. 2 (Fall 2010): 11.

29. Ibid., 15.

30. Ibid., 32.

31. Watson, *Liberty and Power*, 107.

32. Dunbar, *Michigan: A History*, 218.

33. Kent Sagendorph, *Stevens Thomson Mason: Misunderstood Patriot* (New York: E. P. Dutton, 1947), 120.

34. Lawton T. Hemans, *Life and Times of Stevens Thomson Mason* (Lansing: Michigan Historical Commission, 1920), 155.

35. Ibid., 56.

36. Ibid.

37. Dunbar, *Michigan: A History*, 219.

38. Catton, *Michigan: A Bicentennial History*, 82.

39. Fuller, *Economic and Social Beginnings of Michigan*, 503–4.

40. Quoted in Justin L. Kestenbaum, *The Making of Michigan, 1820–1860: A Pioneer Anthology* (Detroit: Wayne State University Press, 1990), 17.

41. Emily Virginia Mason, "Autobiography of an Octogenarian, 1830–1850," in Michigan Pioneer and Historical Collections, vol. 35, 1907, 248–52.

42. Harlan L. Hagman, *Bright Michigan Morning* (Brighton, MI: Green Oak Press, 1981), 10.

Chapter Three

1. Letter of March 1, 1933, Stevens T. Mason Papers, Burton Historical Collection, Detroit Public Library, Detroit.

2. Letter of June 30, 1833, Stevens T. Mason Papers, Burton Historical Collection, Detroit Public Library.

3. Kent Sagendorph, *Stevens Thomson Mason: Misunderstood Patriot* (New York: E. P. Dutton, 1947), 151.

4. Ibid.

5. Alec R. Gilpin, review of *Black Hawk: An Autobiography*, edited by Donald Jackson, *Michigan History* 40, no. 3 (September 1956): 378.

6. Bruce Catton, *Michigan: A Bicentennial History* (New York: W. W. Norton, 1976), 85.

7. F. Clever Bald, *Michigan in Four Centuries* (New York: Harper and Row, 1954), 191.

8. Box 42, Executive Office Series, Mason Papers, Michigan State Archives, Lansing.

9. Letter of May 22, 1832, Stevens T. Mason Papers, Burton Historical Collection, Detroit Public Library.

10. Letter of May 23, 1832, Stevens T. Mason Papers, Burton Historical Collection, Detroit Public Library.

11. Quoted in Lawton T. Hemans, *Life and Times of Stevens Thomson Mason* (Lansing: Michigan Historical Commission, 1920), 77.

12. Harlan L. Hagman, *Bright Michigan Morning* (Brighton, MI: Green Oak Press, 1981), 36.

13. R. Carlyle Buley, *The Old Northwest Pioneer Period, 1815–1840*, vol. 2 (Bloomington: Indiana University Press, 1950), 59–60.

14. Ibid., 80.

15. Bald, *Michigan in Four Centuries*, 192.

16. Letter of October 26, 1832, box 1, Stevens T. Mason Papers, Bentley Historical Library, University of Michigan, Ann Arbor.

17. Quoted in Hemans, *Life and Times of Stevens Thomson Mason*, 91.

18. Quoted in ibid., 317.

19. Patricia J. Baker, "Stevens Thomson Mason," *Great Lakes Informant*, ser. 1, no. 5 (2001): 2, Michigan Historical Center.

20. Willis Dunbar, *Michigan: A History of the Wolverine State* (Grand Rapids: William B. Eerdmans, 1965), 210.

21. Stevens T. Mason Papers, Box 154, Executive Office RG 44, Michigan State Archives, Lansing.

22. Hagman, *Bright Michigan Morning*, 42.

23. Box 2, folder 17, Stevens T. Mason Papers, Bentley Historical Library.

24. Emily, from her diary, quoted in Sagendorph, *Stevens Thomson Mason: Misunderstood Patriot*, 172.

25. Letter of December 12, 1833, John Thomson Mason Papers, 1787–1850, Burton Historical Collection, Detroit Public Library.

26. Letter of March 7, 1838, box 1, folder 11, Stevens T. Mason Papers, Bentley Historical Library.

27. Letter of April 16, 1833, Stevens T. Mason Papers, Burton Historical Collection, Detroit Public Library.

28. Letter of October 13, 1833, Stevens T. Mason Papers, Burton Historical Collection, Detroit Public Library.

29. Letter of December 15, 1833, Stevens T. Mason Papers, Burton Historical Collection, Detroit Public Library.

Chapter Four

1. Charles Sellers, *The Market Revolution* (New York: Oxford University Press, 1991), 111.

2. Harry L. Watson, *Liberty and Power: The Politics of Jacksonian America* (New York: Hill and Wang, 1990), 94.

3. Lawrence Frederick Kohl, *The Politics of Individualism: Parties and the American Character in the Jacksonian Era* (New York: Oxford University Press, 1989), 5.

4. Ibid.

5. Watson, *Liberty and Power*, 29.

6. Ibid., 47.

7. Ibid., 48.

8. Sellers, *Market Revolution*, 111.

9. Kohl, *Politics of Individualism*, 122.

10. Ibid., 132.

11. Quoted in Brian C Wilson, *Yankees in Michigan* (East Lansing: Michigan State University Press, 2008), 72, taken from Martin J. Hershock, *The Paradox of Progress: Economic Change, Individual Enterprise, and Political Culture in Michigan, 1838–1878* (Athens: Ohio University Press, 2003).

12. Kohl, *Politics of Individualism*, 65.

13. Ibid., 119.

14. Ibid.

15. Ibid., 101.

16. Ibid., 35.

17. Clinton Rossiter, *Seedtime of the Republic* (New York: Harcourt, Brace and Company, 1953), 449.

18. Kohl, *Politics of Individualism*, 14.

19. Kent Sagendorph, *Stevens Thomson Mason: Misunderstood Patriot* (New York: E. P. Dutton, 1947), 175.

20. Ibid., 178.

21. Letter of September 10, 1834, Stevens T. Mason Papers, Burton Historical Collection, Detroit Public Library, Detroit.

22. Letter of November 10, 1834, Stevens T. Mason Papers, Burton Historical Collection, Detroit Public Library.

23. Letter of September 20, 1834, Stevens T. Mason Papers, William L. Clements Library, Ann Arbor, MI.

24. Message of November 19, 1834, Stevens T. Mason Papers, Bentley Historical Library, University of Michigan, Ann Arbor.

25. Ibid.

26. Quoted in Lawton T. Hemans, *Life and Times of Stevens Thomson Mason* (Lansing: Michigan Historical Commission, 1920), 44.

27. Willis Dunbar, *Michigan: A History of the Wolverine State* (Grand Rapids: William B. Eerdmans, 1965), 245.

28. *Journal of the Proceedings of the Convention to form a Constitution for the State of Michigan, begun and held at the Capitol in Detroit on May 11, 1835,* p. 222, Michigan State Archives, Lansing.

29. Quoted in Hemans, *Life and Times of Stevens Thomson Mason,* 72.

30. Quoted in ibid., 207.

31. Ibid.

32. Roger Rosentreter, "The Quest for Statehood," *Michigan History* 71, no. 1 (January–February 1987): 41.

33. Quoted by Anna May Soule in "The Southern and Western Boundaries of Michigan," in Michigan Pioneer and Historical Collections, vol. 27, 1896, 350.

34. Hemans, *Life and Times of Stevens Thomson Mason,* 133.

35. Frank E. Robison, "The Michigan and Ohio Boundary Line," in Michigan Pioneer and Historical Collections, vol. 11, 1887, 222.

36. Hemans, *Life and Times of Stevens Thomson Mason,* 139.

37. Letter of February 20, 1835, Stevens T. Mason Papers, Bentley Historical Library.

38. Address to the legislature, February 6, 1835, Robert Lucas Papers, Toledo–Lucas County Public Library, Toledo, Ohio.

39. Sagendorph, *Stevens Thomason Mason: Misunderstood Patriot,* 202.

40. Letter of April 18, 1835, Stevens T. Mason Papers, Burton Historical Collection, Detroit Public Library.

41. Letter of May 9, 1835, Stevens T. Mason Papers, Bentley Historical Library.

42. *Cleveland Whig,* edition of April 22, 1835, and *Detroit Journal,* edition of June 19, 1835, from the *Annals of Cleveland, 1818–1935,* vols. 18–19, part 1 (Cleveland, Ohio: Works Progress Administration, 1938), State Archives of Ohio, Columbus.

43. Letter of May 9, 1835, Mason Papers, Bentley Historical Library.

44. Letter of August 21, 1835, Mason Papers, Bentley Historical Library.

45. Hon. Edward W. Peck, "Disputed Questions in the Early History of Michigan," in Michigan Pioneer and Historical Collections, vol. 11, 1887, 156.

46. Letter of August 28, 1835, Stevens T. Mason Papers, Burton Historical Collection, Detroit Public Library.

47. Michigan Pioneer and Historical Collections, vol. 35, 1905–6.

48. Message to the legislature, February 1, 1836, box 2, folder 20, Stevens T. Mason Papers, Bentley Historical Library.

49. L. G. Stuart, "Verdict for Michigan: How the Upper Peninsula Became a Part of Michigan," in Michigan Pioneer and Historical Collections, vol. 27, 1896, 403.

50. Address on laying the cornerstone of the new courthouse for Lenawee County in Adrian, June 28, 1884, Lewis Cass Papers, William L. Clements Library.

51. Address at the Detroit ceremony reinterring Governor Mason, June 4, 1905, Lewis Cass Papers, William L. Clements Library.

52. Stevens T. Mason Papers, Bentley Historical Library.

53. Don Faber, *The Toledo War* (Ann Arbor: University of Michigan Press, 2008), 136.

54. Letter of February 21, 1836, box 5, Lucius Lyon Papers, William L. Clements Library.

55. Quoted in Dunbar, *Michigan: A History*, 257.

56. Quoted in Roger Rosentreter, "Michigan's Quest for Statehood," in *Michigan Visions of Our Past*, ed. Richard J. Hathaway (East Lansing: Michigan State University Press, 1989), 88.

57. W. V. Way, *The Facts and Historical Events of the Toledo War of 1835* (Toledo, Ohio: Daily Commercial Steam Book, 1896), 48.

58. Alec R. Gilpin, *The Territory of Michigan, 1805–1837* (East Lansing: Michigan State University Press, 1970), 172, 173.

59. Stevens T. Mason Papers, RG 56-26, box 200, Department of State, Michigan State Archives, Lansing.

60. Ibid.

61. Letter of November 13, 1836, reprinted in the *Michigan Argus*, Stevens T. Mason Papers, Bentley Historical Library.

62. Ibid.

63. Letter of November 14, 1836, reprinted in the *Michigan Argus*, Stevens T. Mason Papers, Bentley Historical Library.

64. Reprint from *The Globe*, Jan. 11, 1837, Stevens T. Mason Papers, Bentley Historical Library, University of Michigan, Ann Arbor.

65. Quoted in Rosentreter, "Quest for Statehood," *Michigan History*, 21.

66. Reprint from *The Globe*, Jan. 11, 1837, Stevens T. Mason Papers, Bentley Historical Library, University of Michigan, Ann Arbor.

67. Quoted in Gilpin, *Territory of Michigan*, 176.

Chapter Five

1. John Kern, *A Short History of Michigan* (Lansing: Michigan History Division, Michigan Department of State, 1977), 25.

2. Willis Dunbar, *Michigan: A History of the Wolverine State* (Grand Rapids: William B. Eerdmans, 1965), 306.

3. Clark F. Norton, "Early Movement for the St. Mary's Falls Ship Canal," *Michigan History* 39, no. 3 (September 1955): 257.

4. Ibid., 259–60.

5. Anna Reid Knox, "Michigan State Rights," in Michigan Pioneer and Historical Collections, vol. 30, 1905, 165.

6. Norton, "St. Mary's Falls Ship Canal," 262.

7. Letter to Mason, June 20, 1839, from MS/Woodbridge, Wm., Jan.–Sept. 1839, box 38, Burton Historical Collection, Detroit Public Library.

8. Knox, "Michigan State Rights," 167.

9. Message to the legislature January 2, 1837, the Stevens T. Mason Papers, Bentley Historical Library, Ann Arbor, quoted in George Weeks, *Stewards of the State* (Detroit: *Detroit News*; Ann Arbor: Historical Society of Michigan, 1987), 17.

10. Ronald E. Seavoy, "Borrowed Laws to Speed Development: Michigan, 1835–1863," *Michigan History* 59, nos. 1–2 (Spring–Summer 1975): 39.

11. Dunbar, *Michigan: A History of the Wolverine State*, 270.

12. Seavoy, "Borrowed Laws," 42.

13. Ibid.

14. Ibid., 43.

15. Kern, *Short History of Michigan*, 27.

16. Message to the legislature, January 2, 1837, Stevens T. Mason Papers, Bentley Historical Library, University of Michigan, Ann Arbor.

17. Willis Dunbar, *Michigan through the Centuries*, vol. 1 (New York: Lewis Historical Publishing, 1955), 201.

18. Box 2, folder 20, Stevens T. Mason Papers, Bentley Historical Library.

19. Ibid.

20. Message to the legislature, January 2, 1837, Stevens T. Mason Papers, Bentley Historical Library.

21. Message of March 8, 1838, Stevens T. Mason Papers, Bentley Historical Library.

22. John Davis Pierce, "Origin and Progress of the Michigan School System," address to the Pioneer Society of Michigan, February 3, 1875, in Michigan Pioneer and Historical Collections, vol. 1, 1874–76, 45.

23. Alan S. Brown, "The Northwest Ordinance and Michigan's Quest for Excellence in Education," *Michigan History* 71, no. 6 (November–December 1987): 26.

24. Ibid.

25. Howard Peckham, *The Making of the University of Michigan, 1817–1992* (Ann Arbor: Bentley Historical Library, University of Michigan, 1967), 18.

26. Brown, "Northwest Ordinance," 27.

27. Letter of November 30, 1836, box 186, Superintendent of Public Instruction, Michigan State Archives, Lansing.

28. Dunbar, *Michigan: A History of the Wolverine State*, 331.

29. George B. Catlin, *The Story of Detroit* (Detroit: *Detroit News*, 1926), 382–83.

30. Elizabeth M. Farrand, *History of the University of Michigan* (Ann Arbor: Register Publishing House, 1885), 34.

31. Ibid.

32. Burk A. Hinsdale, *History of the University of Michigan* (Ann Arbor: University of Michigan, 1906), 22.

33. Peckham, *Making of the University of Michigan*, 21.

34. Hinsdale, *History of the University of Michigan*, 23.

35. Ibid.

36. Erich Walter, ed., *Our Michigan* (Ann Arbor: University of Michigan Press, 1966), 11.

37. "Proceedings of the Annual Meeting," Michigan Pioneer and Historical Society, Michigan Pioneer and Historical Collections, vol. 35, 1905–6, 16.

38. Quoted in Larry R. Massie, *Voyages into Michigan's Past* (Au Train, MI: Avery Color Studios, 1988), 61.

39. Dunbar, *Michigan: A History of the Wolverine State*, 335.

40. Peckham, *Making of the University of Michigan*, 20.

41. Quoted from *Ann Arbor Argus*, cited in Kent Sagendorph, *Stevens Thomson Mason: Misunderstood Patriot* (New York: E. P. Dutton, 1947), 280.

Chapter Six

1. F. Clever Bald, *Michigan in Four Centuries* (New York: Harper and Row, 1954), 212.

2. Harry L. Watson, *Liberty and Power: The Politics of Jacksonian America* (New York: Hill and Wang, 1990), 25.

3. Rev. Walter Elliott, quoted in *Unveiling Ceremonies of the Mason Monument, May 30, 1908*, p. 12, Mich. F 566 M43P76, 1908, Michigan State Library, Lansing.

4. Art. XIV, sections 8, 9.

5. Douglas H. Gordon and George S. May, "The Michigan Land Rush in 1836," *Michigan History* 43, no. 1 (March 1959): 6.

6. Ibid.

7. Gordon and May, "Michigan Land Rush," 6–7.

8. Willis Dunbar, *Michigan: A History of the Wolverine State* (Grand Rapids: William B. Eerdmans, 1965), 261.

9. George B. Catlin, *The Story of Detroit* (Detroit: *Detroit News*, 1926), 343.

10. Watson, *Liberty and Power*, 138.

11. Charles Sellers, *The Market Revolution* (New York: Oxford University Press, 1991), 180.

12. Watson, *Liberty and Power*, 97.

13. Lawrence Frederick Kohl, *The Politics of Individualism: Parties and the American Character in the Jacksonian Era* (New York: Oxford University Press, 1989), 29.

14. Ibid., 46.

15. Ibid., 60–61.

16. Ibid., 96.

17. Ibid., 115.

18. Watson, *Liberty and Power*, 35.

19. Catlin, *Story of Detroit*, 344.

20. Jon Meacham, *American Lion: Andrew Jackson in the White House* (New York: Random House, 2008), 342.

21. George N. Fuller, ed., *Centennial History of Michigan*, vol. 1B (Chicago: Lewis, 1939), 255.

22. Ibid.

23. Ibid., 256.

24. Quoted in ibid.

25. Ibid.

26. Dunbar, *Michigan: A History*, 271.

27. Catlin, *Story of Detroit*, 345.

28. Message to the legislature, February 1, 1836, Stevens T. Mason Papers, Bentley Historical Library, University of Michigan, Ann Arbor.

29. Ibid.

30. George N. Fuller, *Economic and Social Beginnings of Michigan* (Lansing: Wynkoop Hallenbeck Crawford, 1916), 67.

31. Fuller, *Centennial History of Michigan*, 303.

32. Dunbar, *Michigan: A History*, 264.

33. Ibid.

34. Harlan L. Hagman, *Bright Michigan Morning* (Brighton, MI: Green Oak Press, 1981), 89.

35. Kent Sagendorph, *Stevens Thomson Mason: Misunderstood Patriot* (New York: E. P. Dutton, 1947), 266.

36. James Z. Schwartz, *Conflict on the Michigan Frontier: Yankee and Borderland Cultures, 1815–1840* (DeKalb: Northern Illinois University Press, 2009), 58.

37. Ibid., 63.

38. Ibid.

39. Bruce Catton, *Michigan: A Bicentennial History* (New York: W. W. Norton, 1976), 109, 108.

Chapter Seven

1. F. Clever Bald, *Michigan in Four Centuries* (New York: Harper and Row, 1954), 216.

2. George B. Catlin, *The Story of Detroit* (Detroit: Detroit News, 1926), 338.

3. Bald, *Michigan in Four Centuries*, 216.

4. Roger Rosentreter, "Brigands or Paragons: Michigan Officials during the Patriot War," *Michigan History* 73, no. 5 (September–October 1989): 25.

5. Ibid.

6. Catlin, *Story of Detroit*, 338–39.

7. Letter of January 9, 1838, RG 44, Canada Correspondence, box 2, Executive Department, Detroit, Michigan State Archives, Lansing.

8. Ibid.

9. Rosentreter, "Brigands or Paragons," 27–28.

10. Ibid.

11. Letter of February 2, 1838, Stevens T. Mason Papers, Burton Historical Collection, Detroit Public Library, Detroit.

12. Quoted in Rosentreter, "Brigands or Paragons," 26.

13. Letter of March 6, 1838, box 151, Patriot War folder, Stevens T. Mason Papers, Michigan State Archives, Lansing.

14. Letter of March 10, 1838, box 151, Patriot War folder, Stevens T. Mason Papers, Michigan State Archives, Lansing.

15. Clark Waggoner, *History of the City of Toledo and Lucas County, Ohio* (New York: Munsell, 1888), 74, Michigan State Library, Lansing, Mich.

16. Rosentreter, "Brigands or Paragons," 25.

17. Bald, *Michigan in Four Centuries*, 218.

18. Ibid.

19. Quoted in Catlin, *Story of Detroit*, 341.

20. Address to the legislature, January 7, 1839, folder 24, Stevens T. Mason Papers, Bentley Historical Library, Ann Arbor, MI.

21. Letter of March 18, 1839, box 151, Patriot War folder, Stevens T. Mason Papers, Michigan State Archives.

22. Quoted in Rosentreter, "Brigands or Paragons," 30.

23. Ibid.

24. Waggoner, *History of the City of Toledo*, 76.

25. Robert Bothwell, *The Penguin History of Canada* (Toronto: Penguin Canada, 2007), 182.

26. Catlin, *Story of Detroit*, 342.

Chapter Eight

1. Kent Sagendorph, *Stevens Thomson Mason: Misunderstood Patriot* (New York: E. P. Dutton, 1947), 261.

2. William L. Jenks, "Michigan's Five Million Dollar Loan," *Michigan History* 15 (Autumn 1931): 577, Ann Arbor District Library, Ann Arbor, MI.

3. Ibid., 578.

4. F. Clever Bald, *Michigan in Four Centuries* (New York: Harper and Row, 1954), 214.

5. Inaugural address of January 2, 1838, folder 21, Stevens T. Mason Papers, Bentley Historical Library, University of Michigan, Ann Arbor.

6. Ibid.

7. Message to the Senate, March 22, 1838, folder 23, Stevens T. Mason Papers, Bentley Historical Library.

8. George N. Fuller, ed., *Centennial History of Michigan* (Chicago: Lewis, 1939), 286.

9. Jenks, "Michigan's Five Million Dollar Loan," 580.

10. Bald, *Michigan in Four Centuries*, 215.

11. Lawton T. Hemans, *Life and Times of Stevens Thomson Mason* (Lansing: Michigan Historical Commission, 1920), 436.

12. Ibid.

13. George B. Catlin, *The Story of Detroit* (Detroit: Detroit News, 1926), 356.

14. Quoted in Hemans, *Life and Times of Stevens Thomson Mason*, 438.

15. Box 195, Secretary of State series, "The $5 million loan (1835–1853)," series 74, letter of June 18, 1838, Michigan State Archives, Lansing.

16. Hemans, *Life and Times of Stevens Thomson Mason*, 439.

17. Box 195, "The $5 million loan (1835–1853)," series 74, letter of November 18, 1838, Michigan State Archives, Lansing.

18. Box 195, "The $5 million loan (1835–1853)," series 74, letter of November 16, 1839, Michigan State Archives, Lansing.

19. Fuller, *Centennial History of Michigan*, 287.

20. Jenks, "Michigan's Five Million Dollar Loan," 591.

21. Address to the legislature, January 7, 1839, folder 24, Stevens T. Mason Papers, Bentley Historical Library.

22. Ibid.

23. Ibid.

24. Quoted in Sagendorph, *Stevens Thomson Mason: Misunderstood Patriot*, 293–94.

25. Ibid.

26. Ibid., 327.

27. Ibid., 339.

Chapter Nine

1. Quoted in Susan Crissman Gower, "Canal Dreams," *Michigan History* 81, no. 4 (July–August 1997): 41.

2. Leo Van Meer, "Clinton-Kalamazoo Canal," *Michigan History* 16 (Spring 1932): 229.

3. Message to the legislature, January 4, 1838, Stevens T. Mason Papers, Bentley Historical Library, University of Michigan, Ann Arbor.

4. Ibid.

5. William G. Shade, "Banks and Politics in Michigan, 1835–1845: A Reconsideration," *Michigan History* 57, no. 1 (Spring 1973): 29. Shade draws from and quotes Floyd B. Streeter, a leading student of Michigan politics in this period.

6. F. Clever Bald, *Michigan in Four Centuries* (New York: Harper and Row, 1954), 210.

7. Harry L. Watson, *Liberty and Power: The Politics of Jacksonian America* (New York: Hill and Wang, 1990), 161.

8. Quoted in ibid., 157.

9. Ibid.

10. Ibid.

11. Ibid., 40.

12. Ibid., 35.

13. George B. Catlin, *The Story of Detroit* (Detroit: Detroit News, 1926), 359.

14. Ibid., 360.

15. R. Carlyle Buley, *The Old Northwest Pioneer Period, 1815–1840*, vol. 2 (Bloomington: Indiana University Press, 1950), 303.

16. Ibid.

17. Dunbar, *Michigan through the Centuries*, vol. 1 (New York: Lewis Historical Publishing, 1955), 203.

18. Quoted in ibid., 204.

19. Bald, *Michigan in Four Centuries*, 211.

20. Willis Dunbar, *Michigan: A History of the Wolverine State* (Grand Rapids: Eerdmans, 1965), 263.

21. Bald, *Michigan in Four Centuries*, 211.

22. Lawton T. Hemans, *Life and Times of Stevens Thomson Mason* (Lansing: Michigan Historical Commission, 1920), 387.

23. Shade, "Banks and Politics in Michigan," 34.

24. Ibid., 44.

25. Box 190, Railroads, Secretary of State series, Stevens T. Mason Papers, Michigan State Archives, Lansing.

26. Dunbar, *Michigan: A History*, 267.

27. Dunbar, *Michigan through the Centuries*, 205.

28. Message to both houses of the legislature, January 2, 1837, in *Reports*, Stevens T. Mason Papers, Bentley Historical Library.

29. Report on internal improvements by the House Committee on Internal Improvements, in *Reports*, Stevens T. Mason Papers, Bentley Historical Library.

30. Ibid.

31. Ibid.

32. Frank N. Elliott, "When the Railroad Was King," *Michigan History* 49, no. 4 (December 1965): 294.

33. Ibid.

34. Message to the legislature, January 4, 1838, Stevens T. Mason Papers, Bentley Historical Library.

35. Ibid.

36. Address to the legislature, January 7, 1839, folder 24, Stevens T. Mason Papers, Bentley Historical Library.

37. Message to the legislature, January 6, 1840, in *Reports*, Stevens T. Mason Papers, Bentley Historical Library.

38. Elliott, "When Railroad Was King," 294.

39. James F. Joy, *Railroad History of Michigan* (Lansing: Robert Smith, 1894), in Michigan Pioneer and Historical Collections, vol. 22, 1893, 298.

40. Joseph Kellard, review of *The Empire Builder*, by Burton W. Folsom, *Capitalism Magazine*, April 8, 1998.

41. Buley, *Old Northwest Pioneer Period*, 301.

42. Dunbar, *Michigan: A History*, 208.

43. Quoted in Elliott, "When Railroad Was King," 293.

44. Ronald E. Seavoy, "Borrowed Laws to Speed Development: Michigan, 1835–1863," *Michigan History* 59, nos. 1–2 (Spring–Summer 1975): 56.

45. Quoted in Elliott, "When Railroad Was King," 296.

46. Ibid., 297.

47. Quoted in ibid., 292.

48. Quoted in Hemans, *Life and Times of Stevens Thomson Mason*, 422.

49. Dunbar, *Michigan: A History*, 204.

50. Message to both houses of the legislature, January 2, 1837, in *Reports*, Stevens T. Mason Papers, Bentley Historical Library.

51. Quoted in Gower, "Canal Dreams," 41.

52. Van Meer, "Clinton-Kalamazoo Canal," 226.

53. Message to the legislature, January 6, 1840, in *Reports*, Stevens T. Mason Papers, Bentley Historical Library.

54. Ibid.

55. Ibid.

56. Hemans, *Life and Times of Stevens Thomson Mason*, 405–6.

57. Buley, *Old Northwest Pioneer Period*, 301.

58. Ibid.

59. Ibid., 301–2.

60. Quoted in George Weeks, *Stewards of the State* (Detroit: Detroit News; Ann Arbor: Historical Society of Michigan, 1987), 25.

Chapter Ten

1. Quoted in George Weeks, *Stewards of the State* (Detroit: Detroit News; Ann Arbor: Historical Society of Michigan, 1987), 19.

2. Lawton T. Hemans, *Life and Times of Stevens Thomson Mason* (Lansing: Michigan Historical Commission, 1920), 453.

3. Willis Dunbar, *Michigan: A History of the Wolverine State* (Grand Rapids: William B. Eerdmans, 1965), 276–77.

4. Address to the legislature of January 7, 1839, folder 24, Stevens T. Mason Papers, Bentley Historical Library, University of Michigan, Ann Arbor.

5. Hemans, *Life and Times of Stevens Thomson Mason*, 469.

6. Letter of August 1, 1839, Correspondence, 1839, Stevens T. Mason Papers, Burton Historical Collection, Detroit Public Library, Detroit.

7. Letter of August 2, 1839, Correspondence, 1839, Stevens T. Mason Papers, Burton Historical Collection, Detroit Public Library.

8. Hemans, *Life and Times of Stevens Thomson Mason*, 470.

9. Ibid., 469.

10. Inaugural address of January 2, 1838, folder 21, Stevens T. Mason Papers, Bentley Historical Library.

11. Hemans, *Life and Times of Stevens Thomson Mason*, 476.

12. Details from the Senate journal for January 6–7, 1840, found in the William Woodbridge Papers, Burton Historical Collection, Detroit Public Library.

13. Quoted in Kent Sagendorph, *Stevens Thomson Mason: Misunderstood Patriot* (New York: E. P. Dutton, 1947), 371.

14. Letter of January 7, 1840, William Woodbridge Papers, Burton Historical Collection, Detroit Public Library.

15. Quoted in Sagendorph, *Stevens Thomson Mason: Misunderstood Patriot*, 372.

16. Letter of February 1, 1840, William Woodbridge Papers, Burton Historical Collection, Detroit Public Library.

17. Sagendorph, *Stevens Thomson Mason: Misunderstood Patriot*, 373.

18. Message to the legislature, January 6, 1840, Stevens T. Mason Papers, Bentley Historical Library.

19. Hemans, *Life and Times of Stevens Thomson Mason*, 476.

20. Letter of March 8, 1840, John Thomson Mason Papers, 1787–1850, Burton Historical Collection, Detroit Public Library.

21. Quoted in Harlan L. Hagman, *Bright Michigan Morning* (Brighton, MI: Green Oak Press, 1981), 124.

22. Sagendorph, *Stevens Thomson Mason: Misunderstood Patriot*, 374.

23. Hemans, *Life and Times of Stevens Thomson Mason*, 481.

24. Quoted in Sagendorph, *Stevens Thomson Mason: Misunderstood Patriot*, 375.

25. Quoted in Hemans, *Life and Times of Stevens Thomson Mason*, 480.

26. Ibid.

27. Quoted in ibid., 482.

28. Quoted in ibid., 482–83.

29. Ibid., 487.

30. Sagendorph, *Stevens Thomson Mason: Misunderstood Patriot,* 390.

31. Quoted in Hemans, *Life and Times of Stevens Thomson Mason,* 499.

32. Ibid.

33. Hagman, *Bright Michigan Morning,* 126.

34. Quoted in Hemans, *Life and Times of Stevens Thomson Mason,* 499.

35. Letter of April 20, 1841, Correspondence, 1841, Stevens T. Mason Papers, Burton Historical Collection, Detroit Public Library.

36. Quoted in Sagendorph, *Stevens Thomson Mason: Misunderstood Patriot,* 394.

37. Quoted in ibid., 394–95.

38. Ibid., 396.

39. Letter of August 17, 1841, to Charles E. Anderson, Correspondence, 1841, Stevens T. Mason Papers, Burton Historical Collection, Detroit Public Library.

40. Letter of September 28, 1841, to Charles E. Anderson, Correspondence, 1841, Stevens T. Mason Papers, Burton Historical Collection, Detroit Public Library.

41. Letter of April 4, 1841, John Thomson Mason Papers, 1787–1850, Burton Historical Collection, Detroit Public Library.

42. Letter of May 30, 1841, from Lucy Maria Woodbridge Henderson Abbott, William Woodbridge Papers, Burton Historical Collection, Detroit Public Library.

43. Letter of November 5, 1841, John Thomson Mason Papers, 1787–1850, Burton Historical Collection, Detroit Public Library.

44. Martin J. Hershock, *The Paradox of Progress: Economic Change, Individual Enterprise, and Political Culture in Michigan, 1838–1878* (Athens: Ohio University Press, 2003), 2.

45. Sagendorph, *Stevens Thomson Mason: Misunderstood Patriot,* 400.

46. *Report of the Joint Committee of the House of Representatives and the Senate, on the subject of the Five Million Loan Bonds,* (February 13, 1843), in *Reports,* Stevens T. Mason Papers, Bentley Historical Library, University of Michigan, Ann Arbor.

47. Ibid., 7–8.

48. Ibid., 10.

49. Sagendorph, *Stevens Thomson Mason: Misunderstood Patriot,* 276.

50. Hemans, *Life and Times of Stevens Thomson Mason,* 501.

51. Letter of January 31, 1842, Correspondence, 1842, Stevens T. Mason Papers, Burton Historical Collection, Detroit Public Library.

52. Letter of March 7, 1842, Correspondence, 1842, Stevens T. Mason Papers, Burton Historical Collection, Detroit Public Library.

53. Letter of August 17, 1841, Correspondence, 1841, Stevens T. Mason Papers, Burton Historical Collection, Detroit Public Library.

54. Letter of March 11, 1842, to Mason's father John Thomson Mason, Correspondence, 1842, Stevens T. Mason Papers, Burton Historical Collection, Detroit Public Library.

55. Letter of March 11, 1842, to Mason's sister Catherine (Kate) Rowland,

Correspondence, 1842, Stevens T. Mason Papers, Burton Historical Collection, Detroit Public Library.

56. Letter of July 16, 1842, Correspondence, 1842, Stevens T. Mason Papers, Burton Historical Collection, Detroit Public Library.

57. Ibid.

Chapter Eleven

1. Jean Frazier, "Who Is That Man? The Portrait of Michigan's First Governor," *Michigan History* 64, no. 1 (January–February 1980): 29.

2. Speech to the Richmond Lyceum on Staten Island, folder 26, Stevens T. Mason Papers, Bentley Historical Library, University of Michigan, Ann Arbor.

3. Kent Sagendorph, *Stevens Thomson Mason: Misunderstood Patriot* (New York: E. P. Dutton, 1947), 409.

4. Quoted in Lawton T. Hemans, *Life and Times of Stevens Thomson Mason* (Lansing: Michigan Historical Commission, 1920), 508–9.

5. Hemans, *Life and Times of Stevens Thomson Mason*, 510.

6. *Detroit Free Press*, January 13, 1843, Stevens T. Mason Papers, Burton Historical Collection, Detroit Public Library, Detroit.

7. Quoted in Hemans, *Life and Times of Stevens Thomson Mason*, 511.

8. Quoted in ibid., 511–12.

9. Letter of November 19, 1846, John Thomson Mason Papers, 1787–1850, Burton Historical Collection, Detroit Public Library.

10. Emily Virginia Mason, "Autobiography of an Octogenarian, 1830–1850," in Michigan Pioneer and Historical Collections, vol. 35, 1907, 248–52.

11. Ibid.

12. Hemans, *Life and Times of Stevens Thomson Mason*, 514.

13. Burton, "Removal of Governor Mason's Remains," in Michigan Pioneer and Historical Collections, vol. 35, 1905–6, 36–39.

14. *Detroit Tribune*, June 5, 1905, Burton Historical Collection, Detroit Public Library.

15. Ibid.

16. *Detroit Journal*, June 3, 1905, Burton Historical Collection, Detroit Public Library.

17. Ibid.

18. Ibid.

19. *Detroit Journal*, 1908 (no month and day available), Burton Historical Collection, Detroit Public Library.

20. The Hon. Thomas W. Palmer, quoted in *Unveiling Ceremonies of the Mason Monument, May 30, 1908*, 6 (Michigan F 566, M 43 P76, 1908, Michigan State Library, Lansing).

21. Ibid.

22. Ibid.

23. Ibid.

24. *Detroit Journal*, Burton Historical Collection, Detroit Public Library.

25. *Detroit Free Press*, box E & M, M 3566 "John Marshall," Stevens T. Mason Papers, Burton Historical Collection, Detroit Public Library.

26. Harlan L. Hagman, *Bright Michigan Morning* (Brighton, MI: Green Oak Press, 1981), 134.

27. *Detroit News*, June 30, 2010, A-3.

28. *Detroit News*, October 28, 2010, 4-A.

29. *Detroit Free Press*, October 28, 2010, 7-A.

30. Jean Frazier,"Who Is That Man?," 29.

31. Quoted in *Unveiling Ceremonies of the Mason Monument, May 30, 1908*, 13.

32. Rev. Walter Elliott, quoted in ibid., 8.

33. Message to the legislature of January 2, 1837, Stevens T. Mason Papers, Bentley Historical Library.

34. Message to the legislature, February 1, 1836, box 2, folder 20, Stevens T. Mason Papers, Bentley Historical Library.

35. Inaugural address of January 2, 1838, folder 21, Stevens T. Mason Papers, Bentley Historical Library.

36. Ibid.

37. Letter of June 30, 1833, Stevens Thomson, 1811–1843, Mason Papers, Burton Historical Collection, Detroit Public Library.

38. Letter of November 20, 1836, MS/Mason, Stevens Thomson, 1831–1842, Mason Papers, Burton Historical Collection, Detroit Public Library.

39. Letter of September 23, 1834, MS/Mason, Stevens Thomson, 1831–1842, Mason Papers, Burton Historical Collection, Detroit Public Library.

40. Letter of January 15, 1837, Correspondence, 1837, Mason Papers, Burton Historical Collection, Detroit Public Library.

41. Letter of September 22, 1834, Correspondence, 1834, Mason Papers, Burton Historical Collection, Detroit Public Library.

42. Inaugural address of January 2, 1838, folder 21, Stevens T. Mason Papers, Bentley Historical Library.

Epilogue

1. Jean Frazier, "Who Is That Man? The Portrait of Michigan's First Governor," *Michigan History* 64, no. 1 (January–February 1980): 30–31.

Index